CHASING LANCE

ALSO BY MARTIN DUGARD

The Last Voyage of Columbus

Into Africa

Farther Than Any Man

Knockdown

Surviving the Toughest
Race on Earth

CHASING LANCE

The 2005 Tour de France and Lance Armstrong's Ride of a Lifetime

MARTIN DUGARD

TIME WARNER
BOOKS

TIME WARNER BOOKS

First published in the USA in December 2005 by Little, Brown and
Company. First published in Great Britain in December 2005 by
Time Warner Books

Copyright © Martin Dugard 2005

The moral right of the author has been asserted.

A CIP catalogue record for this book
is available from the British Library.

Hardback ISBN 0 316 73326 1
C Format ISBN 0 316 73281 8

Map by G. W. Ward

Printed and bound in Great Britain by Clays Ltd, St Ives plc

Time Warner Books
An imprint of
Time Warner Book Group UK
Brettenham House
Lancaster Place
London WC2E 7EN

www.twbg.co.uk

For Murph

Contents

Part II: Mountains

92nd *Tour de France*

July 2–24, 2005

1 **Saturday, July 2 (Time Trial)**
Fromentine → Noirmoutier-en-l'Île   19 km

2 **Sunday, July 3**
Challans → Les Essarts   181.5 km

3 **Monday, July 4**
La Châtaigneraie → Tours   212.5 km

4 **Tuesday, July 5 (Team/Time Trial)**
Tours → Blois   67.5 km

5 **Wednesday, July 6**
Chambord → Montargis   183 km

6 **Thursday, July 7**
Troyes → Nancy   199 km

7 **Friday, July 8**
Lunéville → Karlsruhe   228.5 km

8 **Saturday, July 9**
Pforzheim → Gérardmer   231.5 km

9 **Sunday, July 10**
Gérardmer → Mulhouse   171 km

R **Monday, July 11**
Rest Day - Grenoble

10 **Tuesday, July 12**
Grenoble → Courchevel   192.5 km

11 **Wednesday, July 13**
Courchevel → Briançon   173 km

12 **Thursday, July 14**
Briançon → Digne-les-Bains   187 km

13 **Friday, July 15**
Miramas → Montpellier   173.5 km

14 **Saturday, July 16**
Agde → Ax-3 Domaines   220.5 km

15 **Sunday, July 17**
Lézat-sur-Lèze →   205.5 km
Saint-Lary-Soulan (Pla-d'Adet)

R **Monday, July 18**
Rest Day - Pau

16 **Tuesday, July 19**
Mourenx → Pau   180.5 km

17 **Wednesday, July 20**
Pau → Revel   239.5 km

18 **Thursday, July 21**
Albi → Mende   189 km

19 **Friday, July 22**
Issoire → Le Puy-en-Velay   153.5 km

20 **Saturday, July 23 (Time Trial)**
Saint-Étienne → Saint-Étienne   55 km

21 **Sunday, July 24**
Corbeil-Essonnes → Paris   144 km

G. W. Ward

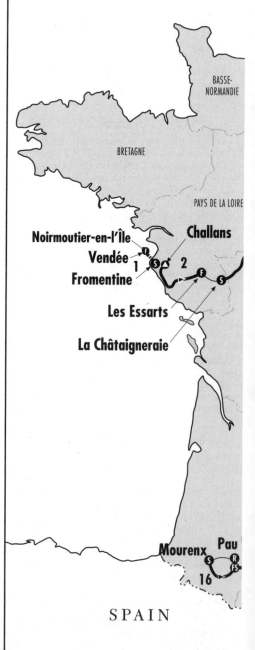

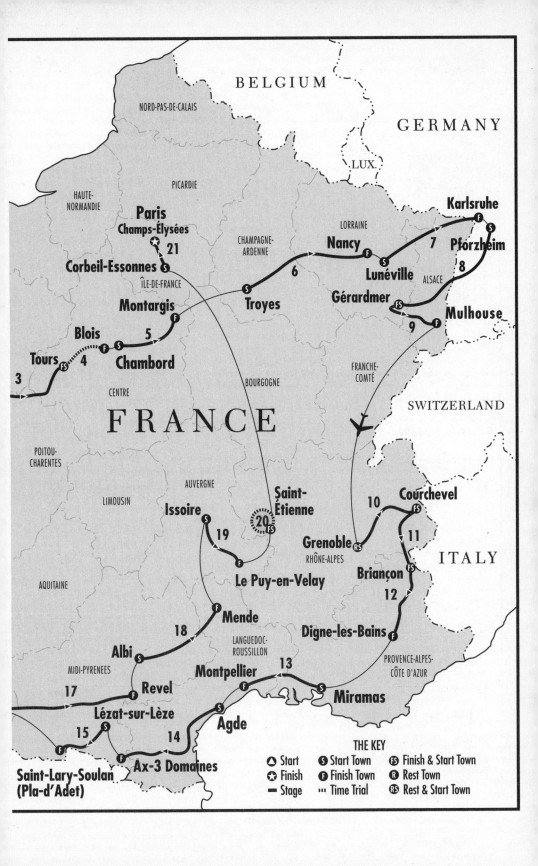

BELGIUM

GERMANY

NORD-PAS-DE-CALAIS

LUX.

PICARDIE

HAUTE-
NORMANDIE

LORRAINE

Paris
Champs-Élysées   21

CHAMPAGNE-
ARDENNE

Karlsruhe

Nancy

7   Pforzheim

Corbeil-Essonnes   S

6

Lunéville   8

ÎLE-DE-FRANCE

Montargis   F

Troyes   S

Gérardmer   FS

ALSACE

Mulhouse

Blois   F S   5

9   F

Tours   FS   4

Chambord

FRANCHE-
COMTÉ

CENTRE

BOURGOGNE

SWITZERLAND

FRANCE

POITOU-
CHARENTES

AUVERGNE

LIMOUSIN

Saint-
Étienne

Courchevel

Issoire   S

10   FS

19

20   FS

11

Grenoble   RS

Le Puy-en-Velay

Briançon   FS

AQUITAINE

RHÔNE-ALPES

ITALY

12

Mende   F

Digne-les-Bains   F

18

Albi   S

LANGUEDOC-
ROUSSILLON

MIDI-PYRENEES

Montpellier

13

PROVENCE-ALPES-
CÔTE D'AZUR

Revel   F

17

Miramas   S

Lézat-sur-Lèze   S

Agde   S

15

14

F

Saint-Lary-Soulan
(Pla-d'Adet)

Ax-3 Domaines   F

THE KEY

△ Start   S Start Town   FS Finish & Start Town
✪ Finish   F Finish Town   R Rest Town
━ Stage   ┅ Time Trial   RS Rest & Start Town

CHASING LANCE

Introduction

Welcome to France

I DROVE WEST out of Paris in a gunmetal gray Citroën that didn't so much as shimmy at a hundred miles per hour. It was a relief to be away. I had three hundred miles to drive, and a list of imperative tasks to accomplish when I got there. Foremost was finding the Tour de France. All I knew was that it started in Fromentine, a little fishing village famous for oysters and sea salt, located somewhere on the Bay of Biscay.

Fulfilling any stereotype one might have about the French being difficult, the Tour's starting point is rarely easy to find. One reason is that the start location varies annually. Localities pay the Tour upwards of a million francs to host one of the daily starts and finishes, and a king's ransom to host the beginning of the entire Tour. Sometimes, as an outreach to its traditional European fan base, the start is not even in France. The most dramatic example might be 1998, when the Tour began an overnight ferry ride away in Dublin.

But no matter where it starts, the Tour always ends in Paris, in the shadow of the Arc de Triomphe. Crowds line the Champs-Élysées on the last Sunday in July, cheering lustily from behind metal barricades as the riders fly past. The winner is the rider completing his tour of France in the lowest cumulative time. For his efforts, this man receives more than $400,000 in prize money, which he is expected to donate to the teammates who worked so selflessly to help him win.

But that finish line was still three weeks off. Paris could wait. It was time to find Fromentine. The fishing village was not in most guidebooks or even on many maps. So immediately upon driving away from the rental counter at de Gaulle, I had pulled into a roadside coffeehouse for a map study. The room was wreathed in cigarette smoke and the coffee was served in demi-tasse portions. I took a seat in the corner, directly behind a woman in a drab business skirt and white blouse. Her haircut was severe to the point of being frightening, and she angled her chin upward as she smoked, giving her an imperious air. Now and again the woman leaned toward her companion. When she did, her shirt rode up, exposing the small of her back and the lacy waistband of what appeared to be an expensive thong.

I studied my map — not just any map, but the *Michelin France Tourist and Motoring Atlas*, a 420-page, spiral-bound, 3.1-pound cartographic behemoth that listed every single highway, road, lane, and trail in the entire nation. The cover, coincidentally, was yellow, appropriate for charting a course through the Tour.

It is amazing to me that a nation that has existed for hundreds of years — if not more than a thousand if you start counting at Charlemagne, when France was a nation in concept and attitude only — has been unable to design a logical series of roads providing easy access to and from their most fabled and hallowed city. Democracy — yes. Champagne — yes. Catherine Deneuve — definitely yes. A simple way in and out of the City of Light — impossible.

Charles de Gaulle Airport is located northeast of Paris. The road to Fromentine is the A11, which begins southeast of the city. My atlas showed no easy path from one to the other. The last thing I wanted to do was cut through the city and get stuck in a Parisian traffic snarl. What I hoped to find was a perimeter expressway.

What I found, instead, was a confusing array of two-lane high-ways and autoroutes interweaving around and through Paris like so many strands of cooked spaghetti hurled onto a plate. They changed direction and numeric designation without warning, their design a vestige of the city's medieval origins. The roads were once paths connecting villages, grooved into the earth by cattle meandering from pasture to pasture — and it shows.

Far be it from me to suggest that France ignore its pastoral roots, but as I became more and more lost over the next three hours, lurching along in first gear surrounded by commuters who were also going nowhere fast, the rationale for allowing bovine wanderings to dictate the driving habits of thousands upon thousands of modern motorists seemed increasingly unclear. Not only was there the fear of getting lost, but with all the stop and go and road sign confusion, the chance of a fender bender (or worse) seemed awfully high. All I could do was inch forward and pray for the best.

But adventure, as Amelia Earhart once said so famously, is where you find it. So as the hours ticked past and the chance of making Fromentine before nightfall began to feel remote, I took deep calming breaths (Inhale peace. Exhale conflict. Repeat.) and reminded myself that even Parisian traffic could be considered a sort of fantastic voyage. Sooner or later I would find where I was going.

What was the worst possible thing that could happen? I would be unable to find the A11. In that case, I would be forced to drive into the heart of Paris to recharge my batteries for a night before trying again. I would rent a fabulously expensive hotel room with a king-size bed and one of those rain nozzles in the shower, eat an insanely overpriced meal, sleep off my jet lag, go for a 5:00 a.m. run along the Seine, then climb back into the Citroën and set forth.

Seen in that light, things weren't so bad.

I pushed on. Several times I almost ended up at Euro Disney.

I kept expecting to round a bend and see the Eiffel Tower, meaning that my stellar sense of direction had led me into, rather than out of, Paris. But I followed the signs to Versailles, which my Michelin map told me was very close to the A11. Then I saw another sign, this one pointing toward Le Mans, which reminded me of a Steve McQueen movie I'd seen as a kid about auto racing. That made me think of Yves Montand and his sad eyes in *Grand Prix* (a different car-racing movie, but more French, and thus more applicable to my situation). "Do you ever get tired of the driving?" Montand's character had asked another racer, then answered his own question. "I sometimes get tired of the driving."

Me, too.

In a way, those movies had inspired my current quest. They had provided some of my first impressions of France, and the nature of competition, instilling a desire to know what it was like firsthand. The great French writer and thinker Albert Camus once wrote, "You cannot create experience. You must undergo it."

That's why I had come to France: to undergo the entire Tour experience. I had been there many times before, but just for a week or several days at a time. That was just a tease. I wanted more. As I discovered at my first Tour, millions of others felt the same way. In the clog of traffic it was easy to momentarily forget the magic. But suddenly, thanks to Steve McQueen, my waning sense of adventure was replaced by a buoyant sensation. *You are in France,* I thought, *and over the next few weeks, you are going to witness one of the greatest athletic contests in the world. Forget about the traffic. Forget about the roads behind you. Forget about the road beneath you. Think only of the road in front of you.* As the man who has won the last six Tours might say, just do it.

Then, as if I had slipped through some magical portal, I was on the A11. There was no warning. It simply happened. The traffic jams vanished. I temporarily severed my emotional attachment to the Michelin book. There is nothing more comforting in a foreign land than knowing where you are. For the first time all day, I did.

I eased the Citroën into the fast lane and shifted into sixth gear. The view was of rolled bales of hay and pale yellow pastures, divided one from the other by towering green pine trees. A stout wind was tipping them sideways. Herds of white cows lay on the grass, as still as rocks. The sky was the color of ashes. It was Nebraska, with castles.

When getting lost had seemed inevitable, the rationalizations about Paris hotel rooms had seemed acceptable. But now that I was on my way, my head cleared. I needed to find Fromentine. Then I needed to find the Tour, to pick up my press pass (or risk standing in a long line the following morning, and perhaps missing the start). Then I needed to find a hotel. Assuming that the accreditation center closed at five, I had about four hours to make it.

A Tour press credential is the grown-up equivalent of Willy Wonka's golden ticket. It cannot be bought, only granted. It provides almost total access to any aspect of the Tour de France. A single flash of the credential means I can climb over the metal barricades onto the course to interview the riders before and after a stage. The credential procures access to the exquisite Tour buffet in each town along the way, with sideboards that groan with regional delicacies. It gets the stern, white-holstered Republican Guard gendarmes not only to wave my rental car through Tour roadblocks but also to snap off a quick nod of greeting as they do so, as if we are both part of some greater Tour brotherhood.

Most fun of all, the credential gets me that face time with Lance Armstrong and other top riders, a privilege not accorded the average Tour spectator. The credential is the difference between being woven into the Tour's daily fabric and being an observer, standing back to admire it all.

Traffic jammed again at Nîmes, an hour from the Atlantic coast. It was three o'clock in the afternoon. Everywhere on the road, I saw motor homes. Not those obnoxious behemoths clogging the roads in America, decorated with maps of the states the owner has visited and Good Sam Club stickers and towing a Honda and never easing to the side of the road to let anyone pass. These motor homes were small and low. Almost all of them had bikes racked to the bumper. More than one passed me.

That's when it hit me: It was Friday afternoon. The Tour de France started in less than twenty-four hours. Those motor homes were on their way to Fromentine. Some, I knew from past Tours, were just going for a weekend. But many would spend the next twenty-three days like me, following each and every stage as the Tour wound about France. The motor homes again reminded me why I'd flown six thousand miles to find Fromentine.

I was Chasing Lance. Just like them.

A game is played at the Tour each day. I call it Chasing Lance. The players are Lance Armstrong, the roughly twenty-five hundred members of the international press, and the hundreds of thousands of spectators. For some the goal is an interview, for others an autograph. But the pinnacle of Chasing Lance — the ultimate coup, to be kept entirely to oneself until the proceedings have been written up and published — is the one-on-one discussion. These are as uncommon as Easter breakfast with the pope.

The game can seem somewhat silly to the uninitiated. Lance, on the surface, is just a bike rider and the Tour de France is just a bike race. But just as the Tour's twenty-three grueling days are a symbol of endurance and suffering, so Lance's six Tour victories and famous triumph over cancer have made him a metaphor for perseverance. He is not a saint, and he has been known to carry a grudge to extreme lengths, but at the end of the day, what Armstrong has to say about life at the Tour — and, sometimes, life itself — carries a certain heft. Thus, Chasing Lance.

I was relieved to make Fromentine by four-thirty. Traffic was backed up for ten miles on the lone two-lane road leading into town. The land was flat and open near the coast, with the pines replaced by grassy estuary. Giant stone crucifixes towered over the roadside, the suffering Christ a subtle reminder of the religious wars that once divided France. And, always, the white cows, not a single one of them standing.

Fromentine bustled with preparation. A billboard with a picture of baby-faced French cyclist Thomas Voeckler proudly announced that the Vendée region, in which Fromentine perches on the far western edge, would be the site of the Tour's 2005 departure. Shiny metal barricades lined the roads. Bars and cafés overflowed with tourists. The houses were painted in cheery pastels, and the air smelled of the ocean.

But there was no sign of Tour headquarters. I parked and wandered the streets until I found a construction crew erecting metal fencing for the prerace village. In the morning it would be the site of a gala send-off. Now it was just a fence.

A Tour official approached. He had flinty eyes. A black soul patch sprouted like a burr from beneath his lower lip. A Tour credential hung around his neck. I could see that his last name was Hinault. The headquarters, he told me between long pulls on his cigarette, was twenty miles back up the road in Challans. "But the start is here," I insisted.

"Yes."

"And the accreditation center is supposed to be at the start?"

"Yes." His gaze was distracted by something over my right shoulder. He studied it at length and took another long drag on the Gitane. When he looked back at me, surprise passed over his face, as if he'd forgotten I was there.

"So there must be some sort of media center or other place where I can pick up my credential."

"There is. In Challans."

"That makes no sense."

He merely shrugged, lifting his shoulders toward his ears and turning his palms upward before exhaling forcefully and letting it all drop. There is a saying that I have reluctantly come to embrace: It is what it is. Don't get worked up about things you can't control, just accept them and move on. The Gallic shrug epitomizes that sentiment. It was what it was.

"Your last name is Hinault," I said, hoping my tone sounded warmer.

He smiled. "Yes."

"Is your father Bernard Hinault?" The Badger, as Bernard Hinault was known in his 1980s glory days, was a five-time Tour de France champion, famed for his aggressive riding tactics and brusque demeanor. Now Bernard Hinault made his living as a spokesman for the Tour. He was still brusque.

"Yes." His pride was obvious and quite touching. I think every son likes to feel that way about his father.

"That's pretty cool."

He just nodded as he took one last drag. "The accreditation does not close until ten o'clock," he told me. "I think you will make it."

Challans was famous throughout the Vendée region for its fairs and markets. Thus it was uniquely qualified to host the Tour de France. I parked on the outer limits of a street carnival, in the shadow of a giant video screen showing Tour highlights. A live band played something that sounded like a French version of "Eye of the Tiger." Local farmers and food vendors hawked their wares in open-air stalls. And a line of brightly decorated Tour team cars and team buses were parked close to a grand hall known as the Palais des Expositions. A great white tent stood nearby, as long and wide as half a football field. Inside was Matthieu, the bearded young Frenchman in charge of accreditation. I had worried all day that there would be no credential waiting; that all those forms, photos, and letters of assignment I had mailed to Paris months ago had never arrived. That, in fact, I would be forced to follow the Tour without the access that so enhanced the daily sense of joie de vivre. But they had.

Matthieu and I have spoken at length on several occasions, but he always pretends he has never met me before. Whether this says more about him or me, I don't know. When asked for my credentials, he did not hand them to me personally. Nor did his assistant, an icy young woman with gimlet eyes named Virginie. Those two merely oversaw the proceedings from a distance. Actual physical contact with the media was reserved for flunkies and interns. In my case, it was a guy with a ponytail who was passing the time juggling a trio of hacky sacks as I approached the desk.

He could have been juggling chainsaws for all I cared. It was all about the credential. The three-by-five bit of plastic was attached to a green lanyard. I slipped it over my head as if I were donning Harry Potter's cloak of invisibility. Both conferred special powers. I navigated back to the Citroën and affixed bright orange credential stickers to the front and rear windshields. Then I set out to find a room for the night.

I stopped first at a small inn. It was on a country lane, halfway back to Fromentine. A restaurant was in front. Guest rooms were in a separate building out back. The dining room was almost full as I stepped inside. The air smelled of garlic and seared steak. The proprietress ran the hotel and restaurant as her two teenaged daughters served the food. I assumed that the gentleman in chef's whites who emerged from the kitchen to pour a draft beer down his throat in a single gulp was her husband. "Vouz avez une réserve?" she responded to my inquiry.

"I'm sorry. No reservation. I was just hoping you had a room."

"No, monsieur," she replied in halting English. "We are *complet — full,* as you say." I couldn't tell who felt more successful: me, for understanding her original statement in French, or Madame, for translating my English.

L'Aubergine, as the establishment was known, was unassuming, and even a little tacky in a Thomas Kinkade sort of way. The room was decorated in French provincial fashion: wood plank floors, dark wooden chairs and tables. But the flowers on the tables were plastic and the artwork on the plaster walls had an offbeat cycling theme, such as the painting labeled *Tour 2005* that featured a group of cyclists pedaling along the ocean and was framed by, of all things, a life preserver.

But the food smelled delicious. I hadn't eaten since the curried chicken burrito at a rest stop in Le Mans, eight hours earlier. (In addition to forgoing hotel reservations, just for the sake of adventure, I had also made a pre-Tour vow that I would try any regional delicacy or house specialty — no matter how strange — placed before me. The curried chicken burrito had been very good.)

I asked for a table and ordered from the prix fixe menu: oysters first, followed by steak au poivre, then chocolate mousse for dessert. I would wash it all down with a glass of red table wine. The oysters were different from the ones I'd eaten before — smaller and slimier and served with a dark salty substance that looked and tasted a little like soy sauce. But they were interesting. I felt myself relaxing after the long day of pre-Tour meandering, and I passed the time between courses gazing at a particularly odd mural. It showed a white-haired gentleman sitting on a cloud, looking down upon the smiling faces of Lance Armstrong, Bernard Hinault, Eddy Merckx, Laurent Fignon, and a handful of other Tour champions. The mural covered an entire wall and was just weird enough to be cool.

A fabulous meal and one hour and a half dozen hotels later, I found a room in the charming little village of Notre-Dame-de-Monts. The mattress was lumpy and thin, a roll-up metal security curtain covered the window, and the "shower" was a metal tube poking out of the bathroom wall. But it was a place to lay my head. And after a long day of travel, that simple room looked as inviting as the Presidential Suite.

The bar was still open and I didn't quite feel like sleeping, so I sat outside with a tall dark glass of Leffe, searching the sky for Orion's belt but not finding it. The night air was warm. It felt good to be in that little coastal town, drinking cold beer under a sky shot through with stars. I opened my notebook and began writing.

The Tour de France, I realized, is an actual tour of France. Officially, there is no such thing as a starting line. The place where the riders begin their travel each day is known by the French word for start: *Départ*. I had traveled across a continent across an ocean across a nation to find charming little Notre-Dame-de-Monts. But for all the miles I had traveled, I had not yet departed on *my* tour of France. Nor, for that matter, had the man we would all be chasing. That departure would happen the next day.

The race begins where it begins.

Part I

Trials

Stage One

July 2, 2005
Fromentine–Noirmoutier-en-l'Île
11.8 Miles

THE TOUR DE FRANCE travels around France in a clock-wise direction in odd-numbered years and counterclockwise in even. As the race unfolds, the three-week duration entwines the Tour with the three-part structure vital to all great dramas. Week One is the setup, contested in the flat (and usually rainy) northern regions and known for sprint finishes and hard crashes. Week Two sees the agony of the long mountain climbs and descents. This is when a true leader emerges. Week Three is the final dash to Paris, where the winner is crowned. By then the riders are exhausted and have lost almost all their body fat. The third week is one of attrition. The rider who most desires victory must find it within himself to rise above his pain and fatigue.

As Charles de Gaulle once noted, "France is not France without grandeur." The Tour is a daily confirmation of those words. Pageantry on the grandest scale attends its progress. A miles-long advertisement caravan of absurdly decorated cars, buses, and motorcycles precedes the peloton (as the main pack of cyclists is known) each day. An entourage of mechanics, masseurs, managers, doctors, cooks, journalists, race officials, the Tour's private police force, and the mobile Tour bank (the only financial institution in France allowed to remain open on Bastille Day) accompanies the riders from town to town. Helicopters fill the skies. TV cameras document every moment of the action, broadcasting live to dozens of countries. Twenty million spectators stand alongside France's narrow country roads to witness the race in person. Many will have camped there for days, eating picnic-style from hampers of food, waiting for that blink of an eye when the riders whiz past. The spectators spread banners exhorting their personal favorites and paint their sentiments on the roadway in great brushstrokes. It is as if a giant force blows through France each July, unencumbered by traditional standards of scale, perspective, and passion — a metaphor for France itself.

The Tour typically comprises an opening prologue followed by twenty stages. Two rest days are held along the way, making the Tour twenty-three days soup to nuts.

If the Tour were a symphony, the prologue would be the overture. Starting alone, one minute apart, cyclists race against the clock. The distance varies from year to year, but Tour rules stipulate that a prologue can be no more than five miles long. Over such a short course, the gap between the first-place finisher and the last is rarely more than seconds. But competition isn't really the point. It's all about the great drama soon to unfold. Sending cyclists off one at a time is their introduction. Each man enjoys his sliver of glory before relegation to peloton anonymity, which happens to all but the elite in the three weeks of riding that follow.

Which is not to say that competition is absent. The yellow jersey denoting the overall Tour de France leader is awarded to the prologue winner, and wearing the *maillot jaune* is a dream of every professional cyclist. The chance to snatch it, if only for those mere twenty-four hours until the end of the next stage, when their talent catches up with them, compels many a middling rider to race out of his mind, turning in a performance far beyond any reasonable expectation.

Lance Armstrong appeared to do just that when he won the prologue in 1999. It was Armstrong's first year back after his battle with cancer. At the time, most people thought the prologue victory was a fluke or a gift. It was only later, when he punished the competition in the mountains and went on to win his first Tour, that it became clear there had been no gifts.

But Tour director Jean-Marie Leblanc had announced a break from tradition for 2005. There would be twenty-one stages instead of twenty. The first day of riding would still be an overture. The riders would make their entrance one at a time, allowing spectators and fellow racers to get a glimpse of who was fit and who was not, who was confident and who was not, who was hungry to wear the yellow jersey into Paris three weeks and a day later — and who was not.

This would be accomplished through a brutish contest known as the individual time trial. Cyclists call it "the race of truth." There are two at the Tour each year. A rider cannot possibly hope to become champion until he masters this event.

The individual time trial differs from a prologue only in its greater length. But therein lies the truth serum. With each additional mile in the saddle, a cyclist's relative strengths and weaknesses are revealed. It is possible to bluff one's way through a three-mile prologue, willing the legs to turn the pedals at a superhuman tempo for a scant seven or so minutes. But an individual time trial may last more than an hour longer. The gap between first place and last is not measured in seconds anymore but in multiples of minutes.

I feel a vulture's fascination watching lesser riders contest an individual time trial. They decompensate over the final miles, stop pedaling hard through turns, raise from their aerodynamic tuck more often, and sometimes just plain crash. Hubris and bravado vanish, done in by the brutal public display of mediocrity. Nothing in cycling, with the exception of a mountaintop finish, is as dramatic.

Leblanc was a professional cyclist in his youth. He had ridden the Tour twice and excelled at the race of truth. At sixty-one, the shrewd and gregarious director with the jaunty Franklin Delano Roosevelt chin and Roman nose was too old and heavy to dream of racing a bicycle. But he could be a competitive force in another way. The director used his power to ensure that the Tour's course would be a living adversary, not just the landscape but the order and layout of individual stages, right down to whether a finish was atop an Alpine crag or in the valley below. Throughout Armstrong's six-year run as champion, Leblanc had repeatedly been accused of jiggering the course to make it "Lance-proof." That is, he was said to design courses that played down Armstrong's strength and accentuated his minor weaknesses.

Tour directors have long enjoyed a reputation for petty tyranny. Race founder Henri Desgrange so frequently enraged Henri Pelissier in the 1920s that the great rider often quit the Tour in disgust long before the finish. But Leblanc's thinly veiled disdain for Armstrong set a new benchmark. They had jousted in the press and in person. I stood a few feet away as Armstrong chewed out Leblanc after a mountain stage in 2004, stabbing his finger and speaking angrily. Leblanc had taken a swipe at Armstrong just days before the start of the 2005 Tour, questioning his morale and professionalism. At the same time, Leblanc let slip a fondness for "old-fashioned" riders — those who raced hard from March to October rather than focusing only on the Tour, as Armstrong did.

After he had spent seventeen years at the helm, 2005 would be the last Tour for Leblanc — and for Armstrong. If the charges had merit, this was the final chance to Lance-proof a course. A long opening time trial might have allowed Armstrong to bust the race wide open, providing he was fit enough to outrace his opponents. Leblanc announced a time trial of absurd length to open their final Tour: too long to be a prologue but far too short for a respectable race of truth. The last time Leblanc had replaced the prologue with such a short time trial had been 2000. Armstrong was runner-up that day in Futuroscope, losing by just two seconds.

The route that would open the 2005 Tour was just under twelve miles long, from Fromentine to Noirmoutier-en-l'Île. The route would be entirely flat, with the exception of a tall, windblown causeway connecting the mainland and the island. That portion of the Atlantic coast was also an area of great history, dating back to Napoleon and the later civil wars of the French Revolution. The Nazi U-boat fleets had sheltered at nearby Lorient. The Vendée coast was the scene of intense fighting between German and Allied forces in August 1944. At low tide the hulls of sunken ships could still be seen.

Stage One was due to start at three-forty in the afternoon. Frenchman Ludovic Turpin would roll out of the starting house first. One hundred eighty-eight riders would follow in one-minute intervals (the number of riders varies by year, but in 2005 the Tour would be composed of twenty-one teams, each having nine riders). Defending champion Armstrong, the last racer onto the course, would roll out three hours and eight minutes after Turpin.

By day's end, the top tier of competitors would be separated from the also-rans like wheat being separated from chaff. The stage would be set for those elites to battle it out all the way to Paris.

I was up at seven-thirty and stumbling out the front door of the hotel for a run five minutes later. My hamstrings were stiff from too many hours sitting on planes and in cars, and my first steps were a glorified hobble. Lavender was growing by the road. I plucked a sprig and crushed it between my thumb and fore-finger, then lifted it to my nose and inhaled deeply. The aroma was shocking and sweet, as I'd hoped it would be.

I passed an old stone church with bright red wooden doors

and aimed toward a meadow marking the border between town and country. The rising sun was pale, and the flat farmland smelled of dew-covered grass. I was reminded that the area was once so known for cereal crops that *froment,* French for wheat, is how Fromentine got its name. An old woman cried, "Bonjour!" as I trotted past her whitewashed cottage. I yelled the same in reply, desperately hoping to sound French but knowing by her surprised look that I did not.

But it was a start. I travel best when I give in to my surroundings, letting their sights and smells wash over me until I forget when I arrived and when I will fly home.

I had no problem giving in to France.

Breakfast in the hotel's small mauve nook was croissants baked that morning and unrepentantly strong coffee. The room had six tables with frail wicker chairs but was empty. I read a two-day-old *Wall Street Journal,* focusing on an article stating that a bee had stung Lance Armstrong during a final pre-Tour training ride. Details were fuzzy, but it seemed the bee had flown up under his sunglasses. In the chaos that followed (visions of Oakleys being ripped from the cropped head, sputtered profanity, a surprised French bumblebee flying off to die, unaware that he had given his life for a six-time Tour champion), Armstrong crashed and got a black eye. Whether or not this would hurt his chances of winning a seventh consecutive Tour was anyone's guess.

Crash or no, his fitness was the matter of some debate. Armstrong's pre-Tour buildup had been anything but smooth. He had failed to finish the Paris–Nice stage race in March — and looked less than slender doing so. There had been a lackluster performance at the Tour de Georgia in April, his final race on American soil. Add in a jet-set lifestyle that saw his picture in *People* on a somewhat regular basis and it was difficult to be optimistic about Armstrong's possibilities.

The top threats were riders who had dogged his heels at the

2004 Tour: Italian Ivan Basso, who rode for Team CSC; Germany's Jan Ullrich, who rode for T-Mobile; and Alexandre Vinokourov — "Vino" — the national champion of Kazakhstan. Wily and unpredictable, Vino also rode for T-Mobile. There was no doubt that those three men were capable of humbling Armstrong. Some other threat would arise as the Tour unfolded. One always did.

That threat could be an American. Levi Leipheimer of Team Gerolsteiner and Floyd Landis of Team Phonak were said to be stronger. Leipheimer was a bold Montanan with an introvert's penchant for brooding. Landis, with his quick wit and air of defiance, had become a cyclist against his father's wishes. Both men had ridden on Armstrong's U.S. Postal Team in previous Tours (title sponsorship shifted to the Discovery Channel one day before the end of the 2004 Tour). When Landis and Leipheimer took their considerable talent to other squads for more money and the chance to be team leader, Armstrong considered it an act of disloyalty. There was no love lost between the three men.

The lead piece in the French papers was about Ullrich. I couldn't read the caption, but a full-color shot of a car's shattered rear window told the story: The German had also crashed. And, apparently, right through a panel of tempered glass on one of his team's assistance vehicles.

I downed the last of my coffee. It was time to watch the Tour de France in person.

The village square where I'd parked the Citroën reminded me of the opening scene from Disney's *Beauty and the Beast*. On the far side was the old stone church. The good people of Notre-Dame-de-Monts were using the structure as an elaborate bike rack, leaning their three-speeds against its weathered walls while they wandered through the Saturday market or across to the *boulangerie* for a fresh baguette.

My previous visits to the Tour had taken place during its second and third weeks. The air then sizzled with Tour fever — flags affixed to cars, homemade banners lining the roadway, amateur cyclists pedaling in the uniforms of their favorite teams. And, of course, the drunks. The Raider fans of Europe, the hooligans of cycling; Spanish, Dutch, German, and American, they lined the mountain stages as if it were their own personal party, taunting and spitting on riders they didn't like. Just as often they simply painted slogans on the road to get their point across.

I saw none of that in Notre-Dame-de-Monts. The bikes against the church were the only sign that the world's greatest cycling event was getting under way one town over. I had heard that there was a different vibe to the Tour's first week — more laid-back; more small-town French; less jingoistic. Perhaps, I thought, there would be just a handful of spectators on hand to witness the prologue.

I was wrong.

There is a reason the Tour is the world's biggest sporting event. That reason, in a word, is fanaticism.

Easing the Citroën onto the course, I plunged into a gauntlet of spectators. Thousands upon thousands lined the road. Cyclists wearing the colors of their favorite teams clogged the blustery two-lane. The motor homes were there, too, parked off the course with such neat precision that it was as if the parking-lot fairy had striped the roadside in the middle of the night. Banners supporting a favorite rider hung from individual vehicles. Teenagers painted slogans and riders' names on the pavement in three-foot block letters. Nothing like in 2004, when Lance Armstrong was greeted by "I Fucked Sheryl" as he climbed L'Alpe d'Huez. German fans had used white paint and toilet brushes to create that insult to Lance and his girlfriend, singer Sheryl Crow. Undeniably crude but stunning in its audacity, it had set a new standard for drunken Tour behavior. The American comeback ("Rip Their Balls Off, Lance") was corporate and vaguely impotent by comparison.

Portable tables were arranged on the shoulder. Whole chickens, hard sausages, bowls of fruit, long baguettes the shape of a flattened cylinder, and bottles of wine and water were laid out next to paper plates and plastic glasses. In hard-vinyl lawn chairs set facing the road, spectators claimed their spot. It would be at least six hours before the first rider came through, but they showed no signs of impatience.

The crowd corridor was like that all the way to the finish line, ten miles away. Oyster farms and low salt marshes defined the topography. The air smelled like low tide. It was as if the Tour were being held in Cape Cod on Fourth of July weekend.

Arriving at the finish area of the Tour is like driving into an extraordinary carnival with an equally extraordinary security fetish. Fences are everywhere. Security badges are checked constantly. But soon all that is just part of the scenery. There is a feeling that an exciting new world, one with an extremely focused sense of purpose, has been entered. There are impromptu television studios for beaming the Tour around the world, in dozens of languages. There is an inflatable amphitheater with a special awards podium where the yellow jersey is awarded each afternoon. A great blue-and-white banner signifies the finish line. Special VIP areas serve cocktails and appetizers. There is a press tent capable of holding a thousand media at the same time. The Tour finish area has its own telecommunications, sanitation, showers, drug-testing lab, kitchen, and massive video screen that broadcasts the race live for the spectator throngs lining the homestretch three-deep. A French television show named *Vélo-Club* is shot entirely on location at the conclusion of each stage.

This entire mass is broken down each and every night, then moved to the next day's finish and reconstructed. Hundreds of semitrucks are parked in neat rows near the finish, specifically for that purpose. The broadcast booths, amphitheater, VIP risers, and *Vélo-Club* set are all situated atop flatbed trailers. In an act of automotive origami, they fold in on themselves at the end of the day and get hitched to a cab for their overnight drive. It is the equivalent of setting up and breaking down a Super Bowl each and every night for twenty-three consecutive days, and easily the most amazing feat of logistics I have ever witnessed.

But most of all, the finish area is defined by a sense of expectation. It is the place, after all, where each stage's actions conclude. Two big questions are answered there each day: Who won the stage? And, who's wearing the yellow jersey? Excitement hangs in the air at all times — the awareness that sometime late in the afternoon, there will be pandemonium and exultation and despair and great wondrous confusion. Each and every person in attendance will scramble to make sense of it all. The sense of expectation is contagious and verily hums through your body. The air smells sweeter, food tastes better, the senses grow sharper, and fatigue has no place. It's not like being in love. And it's not like having sex. But it's very, very close.

Next to the victory podium, Bob Babbitt was having a discussion with Armstrong's coach, a somewhat bedraggled former racer named Chris Carmichael. Carmichael was laying out Armstrong's strategy for the entire Tour. A lot of "Lance wants it bad" and "Landis is too immature to win" and stuff like that. What struck me most were the comments that Armstrong had struggled to get himself in shape, that the daily motivation to get out of bed and push his body to a new level had been a chore. I liked that. It made him sound human, rather than like some guy who just snapped his fingers and won.

It was nice seeing Babbitt and Carmichael together; they had both played pivotal roles in Lance's career. Carmichael is best known as the coach who first tutored a young Armstrong in cycling tactics and later talked him into a comeback after cancer. His coaching career would end with Lance's final Tour.

Babbitt was on the scene even before Carmichael. An influential figure in the sport of triathlon, Babbitt first perceived Armstrong as the next big thing in endurance sports. This was back in 1986, when the brash Texan almost beat a world-class field in a Dallas-area triathlon (Armstrong had the lead but faded badly to finish ninetieth). Armstrong was just fifteen at the time.

The intense, wisecracking Babbitt became Lance's champion. Later, Babbitt was one of the first to learn of Armstrong's cancer and an ardent supporter throughout that battle. It was Babbitt who predicted to me (somewhat ludicrously, I thought at the time) that Lance would win the Tour back in 1999. Babbitt didn't make the statement after Armstrong won the prologue, but one week before that Tour began, when the rest of the world thought Lance was washed up. "I really only came here for Lance," Babbitt confided to me at the 2005 Tour. He'd never been to the Tour before. "I just want to see him race one last time."

Conversations like Babbitt and Carmichael's, in one language or another, were everywhere. The Tour thrives on rumor and speculation. For months, there had been gossip about whether Lance Armstrong could win, distilled to single-sentence sound bites: too old; too complacent; too distracted; and so on. Now the arguments focused on whether he could win *today*. No longer was the Tour being viewed in the abstract but on a stage-by-stage, here-and-now basis.

It was five hours later when Armstrong prepared to confront those rumors. He rolled his special time-trial bike with its low-slung handlebars into the start house. A small yellow line on the floor marked the departure point. As with all time trials, the start would see him ride out the front opening of the small hut, then down a short ramp onto the course. It was 6:47 and 45 seconds in the evening. He would start at 6:48 exactly. Ivan Basso had started two minutes before. Jan Ullrich was Armstrong's one-minute man.

Armstrong was wearing a skintight blue-and-white aerodynamic one-piece. He was unshaven. A yellow ring of fabric was sewn into one wrist to resemble a LiveStrong bracelet. An official stepped behind Armstrong's bicycle and straddled the rear wheel. Armstrong clipped his cycling shoes into his pedals so that he was completely attached to the bike, rendering it an extension of his hopes, dreams, desires, and upcoming moments of suffering. The official's thighs closed around the rear wheel and his hands were directly beneath Armstrong's seat, clenched tightly about the vertical tubing connecting it to the bike. This intimate act was performed wordlessly, unacknowledged. If the official were to remove his hands and legs, Armstrong would topple over. His job was to make sure that didn't happen. Thus the official was indispensable to Armstrong's ensuing performance, marking the only time all day he would need or be allowed physical assistance.

The same official had clutched Jan Ullrich's seat post a minute earlier, giving it the gentlest of shoves to send the German on his way. Like Armstrong, Ullrich was a formidable time trialist, having won two world championships and an Olympic silver medal at the discipline. If Armstrong could take a few seconds out of that one-minute head start it would prove to the world that he was fit. Ullrich was already far down the course. His location was easily spotted by the television helicopter directly overhead, stalking his every move.

At five seconds before it was time for Armstrong to begin, an electronic tone beeped in the start house, counting down the seconds to the start. An official standing to one side held up his right hand, fingers outstretched and splayed, manually mimicking the electronic beeps by curling in a finger for each second that passed. Five . . . four . . . three . . . two . . . and then there were no more outstretched fingers, just a fist. It was time to go.

Armstrong stood in the pedals and cranked down the ramp, straining to gain speed and momentum.

It is a curiosity of cycling that the optimal pedaling motion involves not just mashing down on the pedal with the forward foot, but also pulling upward with the rear foot. Less than two seconds into his pivotal time trial, Armstrong exerted so much torque while pulling up that he wrenched his right foot completely out of the pedal. Until he could get it back in, Armstrong wasn't going anywhere.

I stood in the pressroom, watching one of the two dozen flat-screen monitors showing the race. The gasp that arose sucked the air out of the room. Then came the buzz. Was Armstrong so inept? Hadn't he done the same thing at the Dauphiné Libéré? This was the Tour de France, not some backwater warm-up race. How could he have let this happen?

And then I was grabbing my notebook and running out to the finish line, to be there when he was done, for better or worse. The announcer's voice grew louder as I got closer. The crowd was banging their palms on the metal signage affixed to the barricades, creating a thunderous din for the rider then coming in. I took a spot thirty yards past the line, in a crowd of photographers. A dun-colored salt marsh lay to one side of the road. Its serenity was a stark contrast to the finish-line bedlam.

A no-name who'd started three hours before Armstrong was in first place. His name was David Zabriskie, and he was from Salt Lake City. Landis was slower. Leipheimer, too. Santiago Botero of Team Phonak, the current world time-trial champion, had also failed to beat the mystery man. The only riders remaining on the course were Ivan Basso of Team CSC, Ullrich, and Armstrong. The doe-eyed Basso was just as much a threat to Armstrong's championship hopes as Ullrich — if not more so. I alternately watched their performances on yet another bank of flat screens and monitored their progress by the location of the helicopters. They were still far in the distance, but, little by little, the helicopters neared the finish line.

Yet a strange thing was taking place. The helicopters above Ullrich and Armstrong appeared to be on a collision course. A crowd surged to the flat screens. I was blocked and couldn't see. I forced my way through and was stunned by the image: Armstrong was about to pass Ullrich. He hadn't just taken a few seconds out of his one-minute man, he had taken the *entire minute*. And Ullrich wasn't just any rider. He was Armstrong's foil, the man whose career had been marked by clashes with the American. If not for Armstrong, Ullrich would be the foremost cyclist in the world.

Armstrong showed no mercy. He blew past Ullrich fast and hard so the German wouldn't even have a chance to think about feeding off his momentum. He wanted to break Ullrich's will with an act of total public humiliation. He succeeded.

And then the helicopters began drifting apart. Only this time, Armstrong's was in front.

There was madness at the finish line. Ivan Basso shot down the homestretch. His time was fast, but still slower than Zabriskie's. By then I was in the center of the road, looking directly back down the final straightaway. So it was that I saw the familiar silhouette of Armstrong powering around the final turn and hauling ass for home. I was trying to be impartial about the whole thing — professional, journalistic, oblivious to all but the essence of what I was seeing. But there is something primal and raw about watching a human being performing at their mental, physical, and emotional best. A lump rose in my throat. Armstrong's supremacy was beyond question. The moment was utterly spectacular.

Then he was past me, an aerodynamic, 30 mph blur. The Lance-proof course had been mocked. The questions of fitness and mental focus had been answered. Armstrong was not there just to race the Tour de France. He was there to win.

Stage Two

July 3, 2005 — Challans–Les Essarts
112.53 Miles

Overall Standings

1. David Zabriskie (USA), CSC, 20:51
2. Lance Armstrong (USA), Discovery Channel, 00:02
3. Alexandre Vinokourov (Kaz), T-Mobile, 00:53
4. George Hincapie (USA), Discovery Channel, 00:57
5. Laszlo Bodrogi (Hun), Crédit Agricole, 00:59
6. Floyd Landis (USA), Phonak, 1:02
7. Fabian Cancellara (Swi), Fassa Bortolo, 1:02
8. Jens Voigt (G), CSC, 1:04
9. Vladimir Karpets (Rus), Illes Balears, 1:05
10. Igor Gonzalez Galdeano (Sp), Liberty Seguros, 1:06

AN AMERICAN was wearing the yellow jersey as the second stage prepared to get under way on a scorching sunny Sunday morning. That American, however, was David Zabriskie. When the dust had cleared and the excitement had calmed, Lance Armstrong had finished the time trial two seconds behind the preternaturally calm Zabriskie, a man with such an abundance of talent and desperate shyness that he came across as a cycling savant. "I'm just Dave Zabriskie. I do what I do and that's all I can do," was how he put it. His voice was flat and without affect.

Those who knew him well said Zabriskie had a bone-dry sense of humor. But to the unenlightened, he came off a little like Forrest Gump.

Zabriskie's Achilles' heel was his habit of crashing — badly. In 2003, a sport-utility vehicle had pulled out in front of him during the downhill portion of a training ride in Utah. The results were horrific, to say the least. A year later, metal pins from the Suburban collision still in his legs, Zabriskie had been involved in a high-speed collision with several other cyclists during the Redlands Classic in Southern California, smacking his head so hard he almost suffered brain damage. His body slid so far on the pavement that his clothing and chunks of his flesh had been ripped from his upper torso. Zabriskie had lain in his hospital bed and sobbed that he could never face that sort of pain again. He almost quit cycling.

Yet there he was, in first. Zabriskie had come back, and in a most brilliant fashion.

In most other sports, the plainspoken American's triumph would have been praised as a superlative act of bravery. But the peloton is a callous place. The corps of other riders wasn't impressed. You were supposed to be tough to ride a bike. Even the word "peloton" implied a military-style toughness and courage. In French it means "platoon."

Those in the dark considered sports like football or rugby more violent. Those folks viewed cycling as a skinny man's hobby, implying that the riders were weak, or lesser men. But football players wore so many pads they couldn't walk right, and rugby players landed on grass when they got tackled. When a cyclist slammed into the pavement, he was wearing a skintight uniform and traveling more than 30 mph — sometimes twice that. Very often an entire group would tangle and crash, meaning that when a rider fell down, there were often multiple bikes and riders falling with him, on top of him, impaling elbows and teeth and brake levers and pedal cranks into all that bone and flesh. Yet a crash wasn't an excuse to quit. A cyclist was expected to get right back on his bike and keep riding, because there was still a race to finish. If the bike was disabled, a new one would be provided from the nearby team assistance vehicle. If the rider was bleeding, a team assistant would lean out the window and slap on a bandage while the rider pedaled alongside the car. There was nothing weak about cycling.

Each and every cyclist in the peloton had crashed hard at one time or another. They had the chipped teeth, road-rash scars, and peculiar X-rays to prove it. Some, like Armstrong and Vino, had friends who had died. So there was little sympathy in the peloton for a guy with a crashing problem. The peloton whispered that Zabriskie was a head case, now so terrified of kissing the pavement that he was dangerous to ride alongside — the ultimate signal of distrust among a pack of men who pedaled so close that they literally rubbed elbows. There was no evidence of that and Zabriskie the savant was wearing the yellow jersey on the first Sunday in July. Teammate Ivan Basso was 86 seconds back, Jan Ullrich was 68 behind, and Vino Vinokourov was 53 seconds off the lead.

Armstrong, those two slim seconds back, had once handpicked the stoic young Zabriskie to be a member of the U.S Postal Service Team. But team director Johan Bruyneel had never really understood Zabriskie's quirky, offbeat style. The crashes only sealed Zabriskie's fate. After the end of the 2004 season, Bruyneel offered the Utah native such an absurdly low contract that accepting would have been a form of disgrace. CSC's team director, a dour former Tour champion named Bjarne Riis, was only too happy when Zabriskie came on the market. Riis liked the twenty-five-year-old's youth and time-trialing ability. In Zabriskie, Bjarne Riis saw potential.

The irony was that Zabriskie's departure to CSC after his spate of crashes vaguely mirrored Lance Armstrong's firing after he was diagnosed with testicular cancer. Just before being diagnosed in 1996, Armstrong had signed a two-year, two-million-dollar contract to ride for the French team Cofidis. It appeared Armstrong might never race again, so Cofidis terminated his contract. Gone was the lucrative contract. Gone, too, was Armstrong from Cofidis. It was an act they would come to regret each and every time he won the Tour.

Zabriskie's crashes and Armstrong's cancer were tragedies of wildly different proportion. But the fact remained that Zabriskie, like Armstrong, had been shown the door. Left unsaid was whether Zabriskie would find as much redemption as Armstrong over the course of his career.

Fromentine was a good start. Still, there were questions. The gap between him and Armstrong was so close that many wondered if Armstrong had let Zabriskie win. That way CSC would have to expend valuable energy early in the Tour defending the yellow jersey. It was a great honor for a team to have one of its riders wearing the *maillot jaune* (or "mellow Johnny," as Armstrong liked to call it). CSC would marshal their collective resources to make sure he stayed out in front.

The defense would require that CSC ride in a tight pack at the front of the peloton. Riis would follow at the rear in the team car. If a rider from another team sprinted away in an attempt to win the stage, Riis would make the decision either to have his riders chase the cyclist down immediately or to let him go, gambling that the rider wasn't strong enough to last. Riis would relay his conclusion to the team via radio (each rider wore an earbud). In this way, CSC would ride herd on the peloton. A strong team such as Discovery defended masterfully. They'd had years of experience. A weaker team, such as Italy's Lampre-Caffita, could barely manage — which didn't matter much, because it would be an epic fluke if one of their riders stumbled into yellow.

Yes, it was an honor, but defending yellow was also exhausting. The force of the peloton was so great that riders traveling within that massive pack were simply pulled along in the collective slipstream. It was a form of sanctuary. The riders in its midst took it easy, feathering their pedal stroke. They used a third less energy by sheltering in the group's draft. Meanwhile, the riders at the tip of the spear did the hard work of pedaling into the wind and setting a powerful tempo.

Defending yellow meant being the tip of the spear. And though it wasn't in CSC's best interests to exhaust their legs so early in the Tour defending a *maillot jaune* that Dave Zabriskie would never wear into Paris (even Riis thought that Zabriskie was six pounds too heavy to be a factor in the mountains), Riis was a proud man, with a reputation as a Tour traditionalist. The smart move would have been to simply let the jersey go. But Zabriskie was the first rider in the history of CSC to wear yellow. The team had celebrated with a champagne toast. There was no way Riis was letting go without a fight.

Discovery, meanwhile, would be resting their legs directly behind CSC. Armstrong would hover just off Zabriskie's shoulder like an eagle watching over his prey, ready to attack when the mood suited him.

But Lance wasn't going to challenge Zabriskie during the second stage. Its 112.5-mile course ran eastward up the Loire Valley from Challans to Les Essarts. The route was so flat that the course profile showed no elevation of any sort until the last forty miles. (The profile was a simple graphic, distributed each day in the pressroom, that condensed the entire stage into a single six-inch-wide drawing, thus making it possible to know a stage's difficulty at a glance. The start was at one side, the finish at the other. In between, all elevation gains, feed zones, towns, and other points of interest were drawn from left to right, according to their exact proportional location on the course. The profile of a flat stage looked like what it was, a flat line. A mountain stage profile looked jagged, like the blade of a lumberjack's saw.)

It was a day of recovery, Jean-Marie Leblanc's way of letting the peloton recoup their legs after the time trial. Smart riders like Armstrong and the other elites took advantage of days like that. There was plenty of time before Paris, plenty of time to make a go at yellow.

Time, time, time: The Tour is all about time. Lowest cumulative minutes when crossing that finish line in Paris wins. It's that simple. A cyclist gains time on his rivals through four methods: a faster time trial, predetermined time bonuses, some sort of grand failure by an opponent, or a breakaway. The first two are self-explanatory. The third signals weakness, exhaustion, or a crash. But the fourth involves a sprint away from the peloton. It is an act of supreme courage.

The breakaway rarely results in a stage victory. The rider (or riders, when other willing souls take the leap) usually burns out and is caught before the finish. But when it works, the break-away is glorious. A rider might race alone for more than a hundred miles. When the breakaway is a group, the riders work together, riding single file, taking turns at the front, allowing the others to rest in the draft while one man does the hard labor up front — anything to keep the peloton at bay. Then they sprint it out among themselves for the stage victory.

Armstrong, Ullrich, Basso, Landis, and anyone else who hoped to win the Tour saved their breakaways for the mountain stages. Those were the most transcendent breakaways of all, the sort that guaranteed a spot among the Tour's legends. The riders winning those stages were genetically blessed with a preponder-ance of the slow-twitch muscle fibers that denote a man of great endurance. Those fibers gave their legs a long and lean look.

Flat breakaways are for lesser mortals, but demanding in their own way. The breakaway rider knows, from the instant he stands up in the pedals and bolts, that the sprinters in the peloton will soon hunt him down. Sprinters make for poor mountain climbers, what with their bulky musculature, caused by a high percentage of fast-twitch muscle fibers. To watch a sprinter climb the mountains is like watching a one-hundred-meter runner attempt the Olympic steeplechase. Cycling, even in the sprints, is as much about moderation and conservation as it is about explosive spurts. Still, sprinters own the course on days without geographical obstacles.

Sprinters win stages by forming an alliance with the team defending yellow. If all goes well, they will combine to ratchet the peloton's pace upward and reel in the breakaway, and then each team's sprinters (most teams have one man designated solely for that task; Discovery was a notable exception) duke it out for the stage win.

Meanwhile, the yellow jersey avoids the bedlam of the sprint. He rides a few hundred yards back, safe from a crash. Since all riders finishing within two kilometers of one another during a sprint stage receive exactly the same time, the jersey will be successfully defended. And everyone is happy, with the exception of the poor breakaway rider whose dreams of winning a Tour stage have just been crushed.

Lazy courses along the Atlantic coast are ideal for sprint finishes and breakaways. The road from Challans to Les Essarts was just such a stage.

On paper, the journey from my hotel to the starting line appeared confusing, so when I checked out, I asked for directions. The front desk doubled as the bar, and a dedicated crew of locals were holding court. They were gruff men with large calloused hands, smoking unfiltered cigarettes and drinking milky glasses of pastis, unrepentantly observing the occasional French custom of morning fortification. Their conversation was animated but not loud, punctuated by shrugs and hand gestures.

They argued among themselves as they looked at my map, using French verbiage I could not understand. They had been comrades when I walked in, but now they treated one another like adversaries. This went on for several minutes. I was no longer a part of the discussion, just a lost foreigner who had thrust himself, unbeckoned, into their midst.

An older man put a meaty palm on my shoulder. He had a bald head and gray handlebar mustache. His breath smelled of black licorice. He pointed out the front door with the other hand, aiming toward the road in front of the church. "À droit," he said, flicking his entire forearm right to indicate a turn in that direction. "À droit, à droit, à droit." He paused and stubbed a finger into my Michelin map as if killing a bug, pinpointing a vital turn in the road. "Ici" — and here he wagged the finger in my face — "à gauche."

He removed his palm from my shoulder and hefted his pastis off the bar with the greatest delicacy. His look was serene, as if he'd just explained the meaning of the universe.

The route was unlikely, avoiding any semblance of a main road. The narrow lanes were lined with canals of green water and the occasional whitewashed farmhouse. It was a leap of faith, but I turned right every time I was supposed to, and didn't miss the left. Not only did I arrive in Challans without getting lost, but I also enjoyed the quiet drive and empty roads immensely.

There was nothing quiet about Challans. It was 10:00 a.m. The temperature was already eighty-five degrees. I parked on a residential street not far from the center of town, one wheel up on the sidewalk. I could hear the music and hoopla of the starting area, but it was too far away to see. The Cofidis team bus almost ran me over when I looked the wrong way before crossing the street.

If I had been feeling ambitious I might have followed the Cofidis group. The buses all park together in a designated area, and I could have located Discovery Team's bus and perhaps gotten a few words with Lance Armstrong. The day before, I had been in the crush of journalists interviewing him after the time trial. And when I say a crush, I mean a crush: bodies pressed against me on all sides, more a scrum than a casual collective. A pair of rather large gendarmes protected Armstrong. He was bathed in sweat. The whites of his eyes were clear instead of having that bloodshot look they get after a long mountain stage. There was no sign of a black eye. A fan was banging on the Discovery Team bus, screaming, "Hook 'em Horns, Lance. Hook 'em Horns." It was all I could do to take notes in all the jostling, but Armstrong was composed and hardly out of breath. "I was hungry today," he said. "I'm excited to be here. I wanted to show the world my commitment to this race, that I didn't come to run a retirement race, but to win this race."

His most trusted teammate, affable and lanky George Hincapie, could be seen lounging in a chair just inside the team bus. Hincapie, who had just finished a surprising fourth in the time trial, had seen dozens of such scenes in his years riding with Armstrong. His lack of interest in the chaos outside the door suggested it was business as usual.

But there were plenty of days to get quotes from Lance — or even Hincapie, whom I considered one of the Tour's great unsung talents. No, my goal was the prerace village.

Just as the finish line represents the culmination of the racer's daily journey, so the village epitomizes the hope that accompanies a fresh start. The village is not the starting line itself, or even an actual permanent settlement, but an open-air extravaganza situated very close by. It is roughly the size of a football field. Those with the proper credentials — sponsors, media, team functionaries, the Tour organization, and local guests with the pull to wangle a one-day pass — are invited inside to begin their day properly. There is local cuisine, telephones, free Internet, newspapers, a hair salon, and, of course, a centrally located wine bar. In Challans, the prerace village featured heaping platters of oysters on ice; the requisite copies of the French newspapers *Le Monde* and *L'Équipe* (the latter is owned, coincidentally, by Amaury Sports Organization, the same company that owns the

Tour); three red-clad female models in the Grand-Mère coffee booth pouring complimentary paper cups of free java; and, at a round booth in the center of it all, soft, odiferous Normandy Camembert served with chunks of sourdough bread.

Each town provides its own entertainment. One city, during a previous Tour, featured a local jazz-fusion band — electric violin, bass, and drum machine. There was a musician dressed as a chicken, another as a medieval wizard, and the third as Rumpelstiltskin — and on stilts. Nearby was a life-size model of a brown cow shooting milk out its rear (not its udders).

There were stilt-people in Challans, too, only here it was two voluptuous women dressed as ballerinas. There was also an accordion band wearing identical black suits. They looked like musical Mennonites.

Bob Babbitt was there, too. He would be flying home after the fourth stage and was dedicated to getting the most from his Tour experience. Because they were pretty, and because it is uncommon to see women wandering about on stilts near his home in San Diego, he asked the ballerinas to pose for a photo. But Babbitt forgot that the stilts made them several inches higher off the ground than the average woman. When Babbitt wrapped a friendly arm around their waists, what he got was two handfuls of upper thigh.

"Monsieur!" the ballerinas cried. Babbitt quickly repositioned his hands and I took the picture.

Babbitt was still aglow from a very subtle connection he'd made with Armstrong the day before. The cyclist had picked him out of the throngs at the finish. "What are you doing here?" he'd yelled, grinning as he pointed at Babbitt.

There hadn't been much chance for conversation, but that acknowledgment was huge. Before the 2004 Tour, Armstrong had changed his e-mail address; too many people knew it. He needed to focus on training, not emotions. Only a tight inner circle was told the new address. Babbitt, the man who had been Armstrong's cheerleader for almost twenty years and who'd seen Armstrong's potential when others did not (a month before the 1999 Tour he'd pitched the idea of a book about Armstrong and his battle with cancer. "It'll never sell," he was told. Babbitt let the idea drop. Just months later *It's Not About the Bike* became a runaway bestseller for Armstrong and Sally Jenkins), wasn't on that list. Babbitt didn't feel slighted, but he'd missed being a part of the inner circle. For Armstrong to pick him out of the crowd had been a salve to that year-old wound.

"Here's what I don't get," I said to Babbitt as we walked around the village. "Armstrong's just a guy on a bike. What is it about him that makes you, me, and just about every spectator come all the way to France to watch him in action?"

"He's Lance Armstrong."

"I know. But why are we chasing him around France? We wouldn't do that for any other rider. We wouldn't do that for any other *athlete*."

Babbitt was a diplomatic man. He'd been following endurance sports for decades. He knew as much, if not more, about them than anyone I knew. So when he answered once again, and in a tone of mild impatience, I listened. "Think what 'Lance Armstrong' means nowadays. It's a universal symbol of hope. He's not just a bike rider."

The stage got under way shortly after one, the riders gathering en masse and pedaling a casual parade mile for the fans. Then on a signal (Jean-Marie Leblanc poking his head out the sunroof of a bright red car and waving a flag) the racing began.

By that time I was long gone from Challans, hoping to make the finish with plenty of time to spare.

Les Essarts was a quaint town, built around what had once been an eleventh-century fortress. It had been plundered, burned, and rebuilt several times over the centuries. A marching band played along the homestretch as the crowd awaited the riders. The band members were all of an advanced age and wore red wool uniforms that must have been unbearable on such a hot day. Yet they marched with great vigor. It was as if they'd been rehearsing months just to be out there in the sun, playing their failing hearts out — which they probably had.

The peloton, meanwhile, was dealing with the first breakaway of the Tour. Just six miles into the stage, Frenchman Thomas Voeckler was off the front with a fourteen-man group. CSC let them go. The peloton kept track of the development via radio. Each team director strategized while following in his team car. The layout inside the Subaru driven by Discovery's Bruyneel was fairly standard: a video monitor on the dash (connected to a satellite receiver on top of the car, next to the racks of spare bikes); a two-way radio; a profile of the day's stage taped to the dashboard; and a roster listing every cyclist's race number in order to quickly identify who was involved in breakaways.

Typically, the peloton gives the breakaway a little rope, letting them gain a slight time advantage before stepping up the pace to reel them in. Often "the catch" happens in sight of the finish line. Then the sprinters race one another for the victory, dashing past the hapless but now exhausted members of the breakaway, who had worked so hard, for so long.

At the 2004 Tour, Voeckler had successfully sprinted from the pack and won by such a large margin that he moved into first place overall. He eventually wore the yellow jersey for eleven days. All of France fell in love with the heroic rookie. He was eager to repeat history.

But the baby-faced national hero was unsuccessful on that blistering Sunday afternoon. With just forty-five miles left in the stage, his breakaway group was caught. Team Quick Step's Tom Boonen, a hulking Belgian with an easy smile, got the win in a sprint breakaway.

Voeckler's day, however, wasn't a total washout. Thanks to a time bonus awarded the first cyclist to pass the stage's 150-kilometer mark, he now wore the polka-dotted jersey. This is awarded daily to the best mountain rider. The day's "mountain" was the renowned 230-foot summit, Château Guibert. Still, the polka dots belonged to Voeckler.

The team time trial would be Tuesday, still a couple days away as the squads departed forgettable Les Essarts after Stage Two and headed for their hotels, spread out in a fifty-mile radius from the finish. There they would shower, get a massage, eat, have a team meeting, and sleep. It was a fairly predictable routine. The focus was helping the riders' bodies recover as quickly as possible.

That recovery began the instant the rider crossed the finish line. He pedaled immediately to the team bus, which was usually located a half mile down the road from the finish. He would weave through the crowd of fans and journalists on the way. If the rider was famous or had done something significant like lead a breakaway, he might be stopped for an autograph or a question. If he was not, the rider would pedal unmolested. Either way, the goal was getting to the bus as quickly as possible to rest his legs.

If the rider won the stage, however, or wore the yellow jersey, there were other responsibilities that precluded going straight to the bus: drug testing, formal media interviews, and the podium ceremony for presentation of the jersey. The podium girls who do the presenting are selected for their beauty and poise. An urban legend circulating at the Tour stated that the girls were known to give the rider a little manual help backstage. That way he could go out and look his manliest as he stood atop the podium in his skintight shorts. This may or may not be true, but cyclists have been known to look impressively priapic on the podium. That extra hour or two cut into recovery time and was a primary reason that Lance Armstrong actually preferred not to wear the yellow jersey for significant chunks of the Tour.

I pushed on for the city of Tours, where Stage Three would end. I was skipping the morning's start in the hopes of basking in a full dose of finish-line atmosphere. It was almost eight and I'd missed dinner. Suddenly I felt ravenous and concerned. It was Sunday, and the restaurants had all closed early. There was a McDonald's just outside town, but the lines were so long at the drive-thru and walk-up windows that I would have had to wait an hour. The lines were just as atrocious in the next town, too. The French, it seemed, couldn't get enough of their Big Macs.

The drive from Les Essarts to Tours was longer than I expected, though the journey along the N160 was wondrous. I had the window rolled down and could smell fresh-cut alfalfa as I passed through the farmland and small towns, with their cobbled streets and brown exteriors (a sudden contrast to the whitewashed colors along the coast).

The road grew progressively hillier as I approached the Loire River. I passed fields of sunflowers and wheat and saw my first vineyards of the trip.

What I wasn't seeing was restaurants, let alone someplace open for an impromptu feast. Then I spied a solitary roadside stand. It was just a shack in a gravel parking lot, and why the proprietor stayed open so late on a Sunday night, I had no clue. Nor could I tell what he was selling, although by his hunched and methodical appearance it seemed to involve preparing some sort of food product. Without thinking twice I jammed on the brakes and yanked the Citroën into the lot. The gravel scattered and tinged up against the bottom of the car as I braked to a stop. I stepped out, sauntered over, and poked my head inside the stand.

A crowd of Tour gendarmes were standing nearby, waiting for the meal. One of them had shaved legs, which marked him as a cyclist, though it looked as odd as lipstick on a member of the ultramacho gendarmerie.

The food turned out to be small pizzas, prepared and baked fresh. But I was so hungry I would have eaten cardboard. I ordered by pointing at the menu — not that I understood what it said. I just pointed and hoped for the best. The smell of garlic and baking dough wafted from the oven. I walked in small circles as I waited for my pizza pie to cook, trying not to look impatient. The pièce de résistance came out fifteen minutes later. Hot to the touch and dripping a most wonderfully greasy tomato and pimento sauce, it was topped with anchovies, sausage, and unpitted olives. I blistered the roof of my mouth with the first eager bite. I burned it even more with the next two mouthfuls, but by then the surprise gourmet dinner was done. I guzzled an ice-cold Orangina and then raced the setting sun for Tours.

Stage Three

July 4, 2005 — La Châtaigneraie–Tours
131.75 Miles

Overall Standings

1. David Zabriskie (USA), CSC, 4:12:27
2. Lance Armstrong (USA), Discovery Channel, 00:02
3. Laszlo Bodrogi (Hun), Crédit Agricole, 00:47
4. Alexandre Vinokourov (Kaz), T-Mobile, 00:53
5. George Hincapie (USA), Discovery Channel, 00:57
6. Floyd Landis (USA), Phonak, 01:02
7. Fabian Cancellara (Swi), Fassa Bortolo, 01:02
8. Jan Ullrich (G), T-Mobile, 01:03
9. Jens Voigt (G), CSC, 01:04
10. Vladimir Karpets (Rus), Illes Balears, 01:05

HERE'S EVERYTHING YOU NEED to know about Tours: It's very old, and its name has absolutely nothing to do with taking a trip.

Emperor Augustus founded Tours all the way back in the first century. He saw the need for a new city along the Loire River so that travelers might rest in safety between what is now Bourges and Le Mans. At first it was known as Caesarodunum ("hill of Caesar"), then inexplicably changed to Civitas Turonorum three centuries later. Turonorum soon became just Tours.

At just about the same time, a Roman legionnaire was patrolling in the snow outside Amiens one winter night. This soldier, known as Martin, came upon a shivering beggar. Martin took pity on the man and gave him his cloak. Legend has it that the following night Christ appeared to Martin in a dream. Only Christ was now wearing the cloak, which led Martin to believe that the beggar had actually been Jesus, and that he must now dedicate his life to Christianity — which he did. In fact, Martin took to his new calling with such fervor that he was soon converting the entire region around Tours. It became the religious capital of the Gallic people, and by 371 he was the city's bishop. In the years that followed, Tours assumed renown as a haven for Christian pilgrims, thanks to the pious Martin. It was said that on the day of Martin's funeral in November 397 the fields around Tours awoke from their autumn slumber and turned green again. Ever after, the locals have referred to such a day as "the autumn of St. Martin."

I like stories like that. Not too many guys with my name have made history. Sadly, however, Martin's life was something of a high-water mark for Tours. In the centuries that followed, the city seemed to be cursed. Norman barbarians burned the place down in 853, destroying the churches Martin had built and forcing his relics to be spirited out of town for safekeeping. A few centuries after that the Black Death killed off most of Tours' inhabitants, and then the Hundred Years War saw the town pillaged and burned once again. A seventeen-year-old Joan of Arc ordered her battle armor there in 1429, launching her quest to thwart the English invaders and restoring Tours' luster somewhat. But there was more destruction to come, particularly in the religious wars following the Reformation. The millennia of decline that began with the Normans continued through World War II, when the Germans bombed the city in 1940 and the Allies did it again in 1944.

Tours was the first big city of the race, a place with a sense of bustle and purpose. I had arrived near midnight and taken a walk down the Boulevard Heurteloup after checking into my hotel. It was broad enough for a parade and lined with sycamore trees. I was looking for a small corner café where I could sip a beer and write up my notes. The best I could do was the Brussels Café. It had the standardized look of a chain: slick menus, computer terminals for punching in orders, and a manager jiggling a thick ring of keys while she made laps from the restaurant into the bar into the kitchen. But the Brussels Café wasn't fussy or loud, and it had a certain welcoming ambience. I took a seat outside.

Legendary cycling commentators Phil Liggett and Paul Sherwen were just finishing a bottle of wine at the next table. Liggett was British, a former top amateur rider whose mellifluous voice was synonymous with cycling commentary in the United States and Britain. He was in the process of covering his thirty-third Tour and had just been presented with the Order of the British Empire by Queen Elizabeth for his contributions to cycling.

Sherwen was more of a maverick. He had raced the Tour seven times between 1978 and 1985, won the British National Road Racing Championship shortly before his competitive retirement in 1987, and then transitioned into broadcasting. When not on the air, Sherwen lived in Uganda, where he owned a gold mine.

Liggett was wry and understated, while Sherwen had a more arch sense of humor. Their encyclopedic knowledge of cycling, easy on-air banter, and wide vocabularies had made them something of a cult phenomenon among Tour junkies. There was even a drinking game played by hard-core Tour fans, which involved chugging a beer whenever Liggett used an idiosyncratic expression like "once more into the breech" or Sherwen intoned, "The speed of the peloton is fantastic." The truly dedicated partiers took it one step further, knocking back spirits every time Liggett and Sherwen said "Lance Armstrong" (the whole name, not just "Lance" or "Armstrong"), a phrase, quite obviously, that was invoked with alarming regularity.

Liggett and Sherwen were even more famous than most Tour racers. American and British cycling fans walking by the Brussels Café were stopping to stare, titillated by their late-night Tour celebrity sighting.

At another table, an American couple were holding hands. The air was warm and there was no wind and I basked in the sense of achievement that accompanies arrival after a long drive. Tours was far enough inland (the Michelin atlas showed I was now fully one-fourth the distance from the Atlantic to Germany) to give me a palpable sense that my tour of France was fully in motion. I wasn't in any hurry to call it a night, so I made conversation with Liggett and Sherwen, and with the lovey-dovey Americans, and with Babbitt, who was at the Brussels, too, sipping a Leffe. The conversations were all about the same thing: the Tour. Would Discovery beat CSC in the team time trial? Was Zabriskie a real threat to have a go at Armstrong? Why did Landis and Armstrong dislike each other so much? There was so much chatter about alliances and teams and villains and heroes that it sometimes felt like we were talking about *Survivor*.

It was almost two when I walked back up the boulevard to L'Hôtel de l'Univers. Rooms were tight, so Babbitt and I had arranged to share. L'Hôtel de l'Univers in Tours was one of those hotels that bring the phrase "once upon a time" to mind. Hemingway and Hepburn and Churchill and Edith Piaf had all stayed at L'Univers in its heyday. It had fallen, but it still possessed a certain shabby beauty, and what it lacked in opulence it made up in character. Our fifth-floor room was small but inspiring, with old-fashioned wood-pane windows that swung open to reveal slanted black rooftops below. I looked out directly toward the city's eight-story clock tower, with its bronze cupola and bell.

The face of the clock was illuminated. Ornate stone carvings of Greek gods and lion-headed gargoyles lined the block-wide tower, and a tolling bell marked the passing of each hour.

The thunder and lightning began right after the bells announced 3:00 a.m. As the windows banged open, an aroma of summer rain wafted in.

At four bells, Babbitt was up to host his radio call-in show via telephone. It was airing live back in San Diego, nine hours behind us. I'd been warned, so when Bob went on the air I packed a pillow and blanket to sleep in the bathtub. The porcelain dug into my hips, but I was too tired to care. When I finally woke up, it was eleven o'clock in the morning. Stage Three was about to get under way.

The stage would be deceptively grueling. The riders would see their first real climbs during their 131.75-mile journey from La Châtaigneraie, the hamlet that was once home to Lord François de Vivonne, the tragic hero of the last duel authorized by a king of France. In 1543, Henri II gave Vivonne permission to defend his honor against the very cruel Baron de Jarnac. Not only did de Jarnac win, but he severed Vivonne's hamstrings with his sword as His Lordship lay dying.

A climb is rated based on its length and its gradient. Fourth-category is the easiest. The somewhat whimsically named *hors catégorie* ("beyond categorization") is by far the most fearsome and occurs in the Alps and Pyrenees. In the hundred miles of Stage Three there would be only three fourth-category climbs.

But perhaps the biggest obstacle would be the nature of the rural towns along the route. Houses and buildings pressed right up to the roadway, spilling spectators onto the streets. There were many abrupt turns, and an abundance of roundabouts and medians ("road furniture" in Tour parlance). The finish was a two-mile-long straightaway direct into the vibrant center of Tours that ran the length of the Avenue de Grammont and finished at the spot where the street "T"-ed into the Boulevard Heurteloup. The riders would charge past sidewalk cafés, patisseries, and the front doors to apartments, hotels, and clothing shops. The avenue was wide enough to accommodate no more than a dozen cyclists abreast. On a day with narrow roads, sudden turns, and spectators jumping out onto the roads for a better view, the potential for a crash was very high.

Like the day before, Stage Three was for sprinters and breakaway artists. It was the Fourth of July and I wondered if an American would try to win the stage, in much the same patriotic manner that a Frenchman craves the win on Bastille Day. No matter who won, Dave Zabriskie's two-second lead over the yellow jersey was probably safe — unless, of course, he found a way to do something crazy and blow it. You know, like crash.

When I stepped outside, the tree-lined Boulevard Heurteloup had been transformed. The Tour had rolled into town while I slept. The finish area had been constructed in its entirety right outside the front door of L'Univers: the rabbit warren of fencing (I wondered which poor guy got the job of handling those giant chunks of steel during the lightning); the TV trucks and their miles of snaking black cable; the giant video screen; the VIP section; the drug-testing laboratory; the *Vélo-Club* set; and all the rest.

I wandered through the forest of TV trucks. They were parked close together and blotted out the horizon. Thick black power cables covered the gravel earth, on their way from the trucks to some great generator that powered them all. I had never seen this generator, or even heard its mighty thrum, but I could only imagine the juice it must emanate to power all those broadcasters. Perhaps it was nuclear.

Triumphal music swelled from the inflatable amphitheater. A woman wearing a headset knelt down in front, directly before the podium. An unshaven young man stepped ceremoniously from a wall behind the podium, then climbed its three steps. He raised his arms in victory. As he did so, two stunning models dressed in matching blue skirts, blue shoes, and yellow blouses walked out from behind the wall and stood on either side of him. The woman down front held up hand paddles. The first had a picture of the yellow jersey, and the two models dutifully slipped a yellow jersey onto the young man.

Then the woman down front held up a hand paddle showing a cartoon lion. One model presented the guy with a stuffed lion.

Finally, the woman down front held up a picture of flowers. The other model presented a bouquet to the young man. He then thrust his arms to the heavens, lion in one hand and flowers in the other.

Then, abruptly, the music stopped. The woman down front said something into her headset, then walked to the podium to have a word with all involved. After a few words of direction and understanding nods, everyone separated. Then, after speaking urgently into her headset, she knelt down front again with her hand paddles. Then the canned triumphal music swelled one more time from a speaker near my head, and they did the whole thing all over.

The Tour, it was clear, left nothing but the weather and the winner to chance. Every last detail was taken into account. Even something so simple as the yellow jersey ceremony was rehearsed until it was perfect.

At the press center Suzanne Halliburton was sitting alone at a large round table. I walked over and joined her.

Suzanne was with the *Austin American-Statesman*. She had a sweet Texas drawl and a smart-ass comeback for just about any comment. She cared deeply about many things but pretended she cared about nothing at all. Most famously, Suzanne was the only member of the media who didn't play Chasing Lance. She didn't need to. Suzanne not only had Lance's cell number, but very often Lance called her. Indeed, this wisecracking woman, who dedicated herself to covering University of Texas football when she wasn't on the Tour beat, may have been the most well-connected journalist in the cycling world. Armstrong was devastatingly candid with Suzanne, talking off the record about Landis, Leipheimer, Tyler Hamilton, Bjarne Riis, and anyone else with whom he had a bone to pick. Just the night before, she'd interviewed him in his room. Suzanne didn't share all of their bedroom conversation with me. Some of it was gossip; pissy stuff about Landis, for instance. Some of it was insightful: Lance had been watching a video of the Stage Two finish. He marveled at the daredevil nature of the sprinters and told her he was glad not to be among them. It was a rare admission of fear. Discovery Team was one of the few squads not to use a dedicated sprinter at the Tour. They were unwilling to risk losing a rider to a finish-line crash.

"And you know what else?" she said, sipping her wine, then continued before I could reply. "Lance threw his CrackBerry in Lake Austin a couple months ago. That's how he got himself to focus on the race."

Armstrong didn't have a personal assistant. He preferred to personally manage the details of his life and was notoriously addicted to his BlackBerry. Like changing his e-mail address the year before, sinking the handheld was a symbolic act of self-discipline. Chris Carmichael had told me that Armstrong was much more committed to the Tour after his retirement announcement in March. And then there had been a now-notorious moment at the Tour de Georgia when he'd taunted Floyd Landis at the finish line, jabbing his finger at the time clock to indicate that Landis had been beaten.

All of those acts were methods of sharpening the mind, total commitment actions that forced Armstrong to either perform or fail. I was reminded of a conversation I'd had the night before. Thirty-year-old Jordan Redner and his wife, Mary, had been the hand-holding Americans at the Brussels Café. Redner told me of the changes he'd made in his life since beating Hodgkin's disease seven years before, and about how he'd been inspired by Armstrong while undergoing treatment at Stanford University's medical center. Since Redner's disease went into remission, his passion had become living every day to the fullest — like Lance. He had flown to Tours to see Lance race one last time.

What struck me most about the conversation wasn't just Redner's eagerness to share his story but the direct method in which he told it. The tone lacked any self-pity or bullshit. It reminded me of Armstrong. It seemed there was a correlation between cancer and that inability to endure b.s.

My little sister, Monique, had been like that. Before she got sick she had lived in Paris, and she spoke fluent French. She read Armstrong's book as she lay dying, furious that he had survived cancer and she would not. But she had challenged each day, and lived five years longer than she was supposed to. I would like to think she'd still be doing the same thing if she had lived, just like Armstrong and Redner.

"This pig is good," I told Suzanne, waving toward the media buffet. "Tastes like carnitas."

"Pig is pig. It is what it is."

When the yellow jersey was first introduced in 1919, it was because Henri Desgrange thought the race leader should wear something unique. That way, spectators could distinguish him from the rest of the peloton. Desgrange chose yellow because his newspaper, *L'Auto,* was printed on yellow paper. Not only is yellow distinctive, but it makes the man wearing it an easy target. At the end of the third stage, Zabriskie was still the man with that target on his back, despite failing to win. (He did not, however, crash.) The victor was again Tom Boonen, by half a wheel in a sprint finish. Armstrong was credited with the same time.

Which meant that he was still two seconds back and well within striking distance on the eve of the Tour's fourth stage. And, of course, everyone knew it. Still, the stages thus far painted a somewhat ominous picture for the Texan. Boonen's second consecutive victory meant that every stage thus far had been won by a former teammate of Lance Armstrong's. This was significant because he had personally chosen those riders and allowed them to observe his training and racing philosophies. It was as if Lance had personally shaped the current state of cycling.

But I had a sneaking suspicion that might backfire on Armstrong. I was thinking in particular about Landis. Maybe he had learned so well from the master that he would beat him. I'd spent the better part of the afternoon talking to his coach, who assured me that Floyd Landis would win the 2005 Tour de France. Allen Lim was a slight man with a scientist's eye for detail and data. He was easily Landis's biggest cheerleader. The Discovery Team had privately scoffed at Landis's chances in the coming mountain stages, but Lim assured me that would be Landis's forte.

"Over the past two months he has climbed more than three hundred fifty thousand vertical feet in training, an average of seven thousand to fifteen thousand feet up the Pyrenees each day," Lim told me. He was pointing to a laptop that showed all sorts of squiggles and charts. I stared at it very hard, as if I understood any of it. "He trains anywhere from eighty to one hundred fifty miles per day, an average of thirty hours per week. Here, look at his wattage expenditures from yesterday . . ."

The technical mumbo jumbo put me to sleep. I've known guys who can talk for days about their resting heart and VO2 max and anaerobic threshold, but when it comes right down to it, they don't have the mental toughness to win — they don't have the guts. The best part about a race is two guys going head-to-head to beat each other. It's primal and raw. Sooner or later one of them is going to crack. Who's it going to be? It's a cliché, but in a situation like that, it all comes down to who wants it more. I knew Lance wanted it; that's all he talked about. I could tell by the look on his face that Zabriskie was scared of it. But I just didn't know about Landis. Like a great poker player's, his face was so impassive as to be indifferent. People were already talking about an all-American podium. I found it interesting that Zabriskie and Landis were roommates, and they shared an apartment in Girona, Spain. Armstrong had a home there, too. This would make for an all-Girona podium. I thought that had a rather nice ring. But nobody knew. A crash could change anything. An injury, the same. You could measure wattages and talk about the materials used to manufacture a bicycle until the cows came home, but the crucial variable remained unmeasurable except at the finish line.

Later, over dinner with Babbitt, I told him about the conversation with Lim. We were eating lamb shank and foie gras at a place called La Chope. Hot dogs and apple pie were in short supply, so it was our way of celebrating the Fourth of July. The food was ridiculously magnificent. I wouldn't mind making the Fourth in Tours a new tradition. "You really think Floyd can win?" Babbitt asked me. Everyone called the riders by their first names.

"Lim says that he's never coached a rider with more guts and intensity."

"That doesn't mean squat if his team sucks. Landis could lose a boatload of time tomorrow during that team time trial if his boys can't keep up with him." Babbitt sipped his wine. "My money's still on Lance. How about you?"

"I'm not sure. What I want to see is an exciting race. I want something unpredictable to happen."

"This is the Tour," Babbitt concluded. "You never know."

Stage Four

July 5, 2005 — Tours–Blois
41.85 Miles

Overall Standings

1. David Zabriskie (USA), CSC, 8:48:31
2. Lance Armstrong (USA), Discovery Channel, 00:02
3. Laszlo Bodrogi (Hun), Crédit Agricole, 00:47
4. Alexandre Vinokourov (Kaz), T-Mobile, 00:53
5. George Hincapie (USA), Discovery Channel, 00:57
6. Floyd Landis (USA), Phonak, 01:02
7. Fabian Cancellara (Swi), Fassa Bortolo, 01:02
8. Jens Voigt (G), CSC, 01:04
9. Vladimir Karpets (Rus), Illes Balears, 01:05
10. Igor Gonzalez Galdeano (Sp), Liberty Seguros, 01:06

BIG TUESDAY dawned cold and blustery. The team time-trial course from Tours to Blois followed the Loire's meandering path on its southern shore. The way was green and lush, passing through Amboise, the town where Leonardo da Vinci is buried.

Charles VIII, king of Amboise, had visited Italy in 1496 and was so impressed by the arts, gardens, and new philosophy of humanism he encountered there that he began importing Italian thinkers and artists to his palace. This marked the beginning of the Italian influence on French art and the start of the French

Renaissance. Ironic (or fitting) for one with such lofty aspirations, Charles died after hitting his forehead on a low door, but the tradition of patronage continued long after, leading to da Vinci's arrival in 1516. White-haired, bearded, and paralyzed on the right side of his body, the great genius died there three years later.

Blois, ten miles farther west down the Loire, was also a city of some history. Pronounced without the *s* or even the *oi* sound, it sounded more like "bleu-wah" (or, in more graphic terms, like someone hurling). Taking its name from the wolves — in Celtic, *bleiz* — who used to howl at the city's gates, the city was at the epicenter of the brutal religious wars that split France after the Reformation.

None of that mattered to the riders. Those cities, and the other eleven towns of great historical significance between Tours and Blois (cities that had seen centuries of warfare, beheadings and hangings and burnings in the name of faith, and the first post-Revolution stirrings of French democracy), would be just a blur as they pedaled past.

Dave Zabriskie of CSC was still in yellow, those two slim seconds ahead of Lance Armstrong. At the end of the day, either that situation would be reversed or Zabriskie's choke hold would be tighter. It was that simple. Until the serious mountain stages began exactly one week hence, the stages would be predominantly flat, offering few opportunities for Armstrong to gain time. On paper, CSC looked like a much stronger time-trialing squad than Disco, as Discovery was sometimes called. A decisive CSC victory could keep Zabriskie in yellow for at least those next seven days.

Barring calamity, no other teams were going to win. It would be a battle between CSC and Discovery. The best the other contenders could hope for was not to lose too much time. During a team time trial, all team members get the exact same time as the first member to cross the line. But Jan Ullrich was more than a minute back, and there was no way his T-Mobile Team could make up that much time on CSC or Discovery. (The clock would stop when a team's top five riders crossed the finish line. A special jury would watch from a reviewing stand along President Wilson Avenue in Blois, which lay at the end of a twelve-hundred-meter finish straight.)

Stable team leadership was one secret to a successful team time trial. But T-Mobile was a fractured unit, divided by the rivalry among Ullrich, fellow German Andréas Klöden, and Kazakhstan's Alexandre Vinokourov. Ullrich was the official team leader, and wore the "1" suffix on his number to show it, but Klöden and Vinokourov pretended the job was up for grabs. (Every rider in the peloton is given a sequential race number. But there are two Tour eccentricities that bear noting: First, each team is grouped together, with their leader numbered first — Armstrong was 1, Ullrich was 11, Basso was 21, and so on. The other teammates are generally listed alphabetically. Second, there is no number ending in zero. So instead of the peloton being numbered 1 through 189, the highest number is 209. That, of course, belonged to Ludovic Turpin of France, whose high number, thanks to his alphabetical listing on the AG2R Team, made him the first man to roll out of the starting house during the opening stage.)

As for the others, Levi Leipheimer's Gerolsteiner squad was too weak, and though Floyd Landis was telling anyone who would listen that his Phonak team was a budding powerhouse, the truth was that they, like T-Mobile, were a house divided. Landis liked to pretend that he was the team leader, as did teammate and world time-trialing champion Santiago Botero. Both were conveniently forgetting that the real team leader was a guy named Tyler Hamilton, the Olympic gold medalist who had just begun serving a two-year suspension for transfusing someone else's blood into his body. Hamilton had waged a lengthy defense before the suspension was handed down, claiming that the foreign blood found in his system was the result of a "phantom twin" with whom he had once shared his mother's womb.

So, no, Phonak did not have stable team leadership, either.

The rules to a team time trial are simple: All nine team members start side by side, atop a Tour-yellow starting ramp. They wear the same skintight aerodynamic suits and teardrop helmets as during the individual time trial. At the bottom of the ramp they immediately form a single-file pace line. Ideally, they stay in the pace line for the rest of the course, taking turns "pulling" up front while the rest of the team drafts behind.

The science of drafting is complex, and its aerodynamics seem more appropriate to a *Top Gun* preflight briefing than the Tour de France. A lone cyclist, even on a calm day, encounters resistance from the air in front of him as he moves forward. The act of parting the air creates a turbulent wake. This air swirls about, creating a low-pressure wind system that moves along with the cyclist. The current of that swirling wind then doubles back on itself to form an eddy behind the rider. If another cyclist moves into that eddy, it actually pushes him along, while the swirling wind system simultaneously pulls him forward. This allows the trailing cyclist to expend a third less energy while maintaining the same speed as the rider in front of him. Curiously, the rider in front benefits, too. By having a second rider filling in the vortices and eddies, there is less turbulent air pulling him backward. Two cyclists working together work far more efficiently than just one. Nine cyclists drafting off one another prove the *Top Gun* comparison apt, for those nine fairly fly.

The key is sticking together. Front wheels are mere inches from rear wheels in the team time trial, one cyclist right behind the other. It is a delicate art. Too close and they clip tires and crash. An inch too far apart and the towing and shoving power of the draft is minimized.

A good team leader keeps his troops in line and encourages them to work in synch during the time trial's early moments, when too much adrenaline can scuttle organization. A good leader also shows by example, motivating his teammates by taking extended pulls up front late in the stage, when everyone is getting tired. Who will win and who will lose is just as much a matter of team leadership as athletic potential. A good leader rallies his men, exhorting them to push on when their legs are unwilling. Lance Armstrong of Discovery was such a leader. So was Ivan Basso of Team CSC.

The first showdown between CSC and Discovery of the 2005 Tour had been the opening time trial. CSC had prevailed. During their two stages protecting the yellow jersey thus far, CSC had been shadowed very closely by Discovery. The TV feed showed a telling moment as Armstrong pedaled up real close to Zabriskie and stared him down. Lance may well have learned how to smile for the television cameras, but he was a fierce competitor with a heart that sometimes seemed to pump as much Freon as blood. The stare was Lance's way of getting inside Zabriskie's psyche, reminding him that the yellow jersey was on loan. A similar look had probably been witnessed on the faces of gunfighters before a Main Street killing.

The former teammates weren't the only ones growling. At the center of the duel were the two team directors. Johan Bruyneel of Discovery was the forthright tactician, a former rider fluent in several languages who would break down the Tour months before it began. It was Bruyneel who made the decision not to chase down Voeckler's 2004 breakaway. "Boys," he told his team over the radio as Voeckler built his lead, "we're going to make this guy a national hero." Bruyneel knew the Frenchman's glory would be momentary. A rider needs several tools to win the Tour. He must be able to time-trial, lead the way up the mountains, and have a strong team. In Bruyneel's opinion, Voeckler lacked each and every one of those tools. He was no threat to Armstrong.

Voeckler rode for the Brioche-Boulangerie squad, whose sponsor was a French bakery. Bruyneel knew that they would be under great pressure to defend if he was in yellow. That pressure would not come so much from the team itself but from above: In addition to being a classic Tour tactic, defending the yellow jersey offered a team's sponsor an outrageous amount of free advertising. This was especially the case if the sponsor was, as in Voeckler's case, a French company. Knowing this allowed Armstrong's squad to rest within the draft of the peloton until the crucial mountain stages, whereupon Team Brioche-Boulangerie collapsed like a bad soufflé and Lance snatched the jersey.

Not only did Bruyneel recognize those nuances as Voeckler's 2004 attack took place, but he'd planned for them. Months before, while laying out strategy, he'd hoped that a nonthreat — preferably a Frenchman, sure to be driven by patriotism — would attack early in the Tour and defend yellow until the mountains.

Bruyneel was also the guy who believed that the way to win the Tour de France was having a single rider be the center of a team. The other eight riders sacrificed themselves to help that team leader win. They were the Pips, so to speak, to the team leader's Gladys Knight. It was a strategy Bruyneel had used most effectively. He had never lost a Tour de France in his six years as a team director.

Of course, some said it was all luck. Anyone could win if Lance Armstrong was their team leader.

CSC team director Bjarne Riis thought he had his Lance Armstrong in Ivan Basso. Like Bruyneel, Riis was a former rider. But unlike Bruyneel, with his journeyman career, the balding and fiercely competitive Dane had won a Tour de France on the bike. This came in 1996, competing for Germany's Deutsche Telekom squad. Riis had not, however, won a single Tour as a team director.

Not for lack of trying. Riis owned a reputation for getting the very best out of his riders. His motivational tactics were legendary, such as the wilderness survival course he put his team through in the off-season. Dave Zabriskie had joked that the time in the wild "made a man" out of him. And while the humor was appreciated, the fact remained that it had a ring of truth. Professional cyclists are free agents, no different from baseball or football players. Their allegiance is primarily to themselves. By forcing his team to work together in the Scandinavian wilderness, Riis ensured that they knew one another better and were emotionally tougher, which would make for a stronger team at the Tour.

Two thousand five seemed like the year Riis might finally win his Tour. Armstrong had shown great mettle in the time trial, but CSC was the deep favorite (intellectually, and among the anti-Armstrong crowd) to win the dash from Tours to Blois. Riis felt that the Tour could be won or lost with a strong team time trial. He was determined to win the event — so much so that he'd made an extraordinary tactical decision.

Luke Roberts was part of the Australian gold medal victory in the four-thousand-meter team pursuit at last year's Olympics. Team pursuit is a shorter sort of team time trial. Roberts was signed to CSC solely for his time-trialing expertise. It was an innovative gamble on Riis's part. The young Aussie had little skill as a climber, which might hurt the team in the mountains. And if Roberts had a bad day during the team time trial, Riis would look foolish for placing him on the roster. But the CSC team director saw the team time trial as vital to thwarting Discovery, which was vital to helping Ivan Basso win the Tour. Roberts was worth the risk.

How badly did Riis want to beat Lance Armstrong and Discovery? Very badly indeed.

Yet Lance Armstrong had a deep and abiding passion for the team time trial. He often said that winning it meant far more than winning individual time trials. It was a reflection on him not just as a body but as a mind, on his management as well as muscle. A victory showed strength and character. It sent a signal, too: You take on one of us, and you will take on all of us. And we *will* destroy you.

Tours to Blois would be the last team time trial of Armstrong's career. That was the underlying theme of the Tour: Everything was Armstrong's "last." Last team time trial, last first stage, last second stage, and so on. People in the cafés of Tours and along the course could already be heard talking about the upcoming mountain stages, breaking them down by range: Lance's last stage in the Alps; Lance's last stage in the Pyrenees.

But most of all, it was his last Tour. And people from around the world were coming out to see him. The crowds had grown stronger and more vocal with each stage. Every day I would survey the sea of people and think there was no way that the crowd could get bigger. But it always did. The crowds along the road grew from one- and two-deep to four- and five-deep. At Fromentine the crowd had been almost entirely French. But by Tours we were just a few hours south of Paris, and there were more Americans than before. As I walked around the starting area, some guy was handing out Texas flags to a group of French schoolkids. Another man was wearing a T-shirt with the Stars and Stripes superimposed on the Discovery Team logo. The jingoism seemed to have less to do with patriotism than some sort of imaginary Jedi alliance between themselves and Lance Armstrong.

Most of the Americans were men, traveling in small wolf

packs. They were all of a certain age (early forties) and financial status (somewhere past struggling and not yet filthy rich). I got the feeling these guys were the sort who traveled to Augusta or the Final Four each year, just to be part of the scenery. Now that Lance had become so huge, they'd added the Tour to that list. It would have been disconcerting if they weren't so sincerely glad to be in France.

There was a very specific look to the Yanks. Not so much their boisterousness, but in the way they dressed. Baseball caps, running shoes with ankle socks made of synthetic fibers, T-shirts or golf shirts with some sort of logo (preferably something about Lance or the flag), Oakley sunglasses, and baggy shorts. You could pick them out of the crowd before they said a word. And as much as I wanted to insinuate myself into the Tour and France, all I had to do was look at my reflection in the store windows to know that my own nationality was apparent. It was what it was. I consoled myself by noting that I wasn't wearing a baseball cap. But every nation had its look. Frenchmen, for instance, wore capri pants. The women often wore sheer white pants with a thong. I was glad it wasn't the other way around.

Cyclists are the exception to the nation-driven dress code. The amateur riders pedaling the roads before, during, and after stages often wear their favorite team's uniform. Cycling teams are international in the makeup of their rosters, and the growth of multinational corporations means that a team's sponsor could be based in Britain, for instance, but the team's fan base could be anyplace on earth.

I got to chatting with a pair of Australians that morning in Tours. Brad Tuohy and his fiancée, Bianca Mauch, were from Canberra but were proudly wearing the orange colors of Spain's Euskaltel-Euskadi team. Tuohy, a bike shop owner, had just come from the team bus area and had gotten Euskaltel-Euskadi's riders to autograph his bike frame in black Sharpie.

"So you're an Euskaltel fan?" I asked. The thought was odd to me. They were a good-natured team, a collection of dark-haired Spaniards (and one Venezuelan) with pipe cleaner arms and dark olive farmer tans. But the once great Euskaltel-Euskadi had fallen on hard times. An Aussie swearing allegiance to Euskaltel-Euskadi was like a Cambodian with a passion for the Arizona Cardinals.

"Nah, mate. I'm going to hang this frame in my bike shop back home."

"So, do you have a favorite team?"

"No team, mate. Just Lance. He's the reason we're here."

Up until a few years before, Tuohy went on to tell me, he didn't know anything about cycling. He made his living as a professional motocross racer. But Tuohy's motorcycle stalled during a race shortly before he and Mauch were to be married. As he struggled to get it restarted, a rider blindsided him from behind at top speed. He somehow got back on his bike and won the race, but he could no longer feel the left side of his body. At first, Tuohy was diagnosed with a broken leg. When the numbness persisted, doctors told Tuohy that he was merely depressed.

Finally, six weeks later, an MRI revealed that Tuohy had three broken vertebrae and three ruptured discs, and that a chemical leaking out of the discs was having a negative effect on his spinal cord. When doctors told Tuohy he would soon lose the use of his legs, he got another opinion. And another. And another. In all, twenty-one doctors confirmed Tuohy's impending paralysis.

But the twenty-second doctor said he could fix Tuohy's back.

After a series of operations, Tuohy was well enough to begin riding a stationary bike. At first he could barely turn the pedals. Then he was up to a few miles a day. Then a few more. And a few more after that, until he could ride thirty miles. As his fondness for cycling grew, he began reading up on Lance Armstrong. The unemployed Tuohy then used his savings to open the bike shop. As we talked that blustery morning in Tours, he still needed another costly back operation. But he was fine with that — whatever it took to be fully recovered. "I figure there's two types of people: people who give up and people who don't," he told me. Mauch was at his side, obviously very proud of Tuohy's perseverance.

From near and from far the pilgrims had come. Not the millions of fans there to glimpse a passing celebrity, but the men and women who had climbed the mountains of their own lives. Lance was their man, truly, madly, deeply. I'd be rich if I had a dollar for every time I heard a fan say that Lance was his inspiration. He has touched so many lives that I felt like a hagiographer as I listened to, or overheard, their stories. The crowd was especially dense at the Discovery bus. Crowds carrying camcorders, cameras, placards, flags, Sharpie pens, and a hopeful look waited for Lance and his teammates to emerge. (What no one was telling them was that Discovery wasn't on the bus. They weren't planning to leave their hotel in Nantes until one-thirty, and wouldn't arrive until almost three.)

All the team buses were in place five hours before the stage would begin, parked in a long row along the Avenue de Grammont. A crowd filled the sidewalk on the other side of the barricades, disrupting business at a café. The buses were not just a mode of transportation. The area surrounding them was a workstation for the mechanics. Discovery's area was precisely arranged. The bus and bike truck were parked end to end. The inside of the bus could not be seen, but the open rear door of the bike truck revealed every piece of equipment a Tour de France team would ever need: bikes, hubs, spokes, disc covers, tools, helmets, and wheels that swayed slightly as they hung from the ceiling.

Nine Tacx spin trainers were arranged with geometric precision outside the bus, ready when Lance and the Disco Boys decided it was time to warm up. Each of the nine time-trial bikes was being removed, one at a time and with great care, from the open rear door of the bike truck. Every aspect of the bikes — from the width of the front fork to the position of the handlebars — had been tested in a wind tunnel prior to the Tour so as to achieve maximum aerodynamic efficiency. They were placed on a stand, then wiped down thoroughly to remove all grit. When the carbon fiber frames and disc wheels had attained a high sheen, the bikes were attached to the spin trainers. The discs had a swirly color scheme. If you looked too long at a bike while the wheels were spinning, it would give you a headache.

Meanwhile, over at the Euskaltel-Euskadi bus, where the spin trainers were arranged as if someone had simply hurled them out the door, a rider was duct-taping a wristwatch to his handlebars.

The official race feed predicted that a "slight breeze" would blow at the riders' backs, but that's because the starting chute in Tours was protected by tall buildings and the spectator throng. The wind along the Loire was anything but slight; it was a weather system unto itself, a swirling, gusting force that was sure to play havoc with the riders.

Rain beat a tattoo on the press tent in Blois as I watched Euskaltel-Euskadi on the video monitor. They looked like boys, wide-eyed and a little scared. I doubted all nine of them would finish together.

The passing of the afternoon was marked not by hours or even minutes but by the procession of teams racing their time trial. The precision of it all was glorious, nine riders lined up tip to tail, playing follow the leader across the French countryside. The riders were slung low in their aero position, arms straight out in front to cut the wind. When the gusts heaved from the side, they shifted the shape of their single-file line and rode *en filade*. When a professional cyclist is off the bicycle, all you notice is his skinniness. But on the bike, all you see are those enormous shaved quadriceps, churning without ceasing. There was a poetry to it, all sinew and brawn and ego and speed, seemingly immune to fatigue.

But even the best riders get tired. You could tell who was and who wasn't by their team's final times. The performance of Levi Leipheimer's Gerolsteiner team was only so-so. Floyd Landis's Phonak squad imploded so completely on their way to a fifth-place finish that it would have been comical if it hadn't been so sad. Landis lost so much time that he dropped from sixth to twentieth overall. And Jan Ullrich's T-Mobile Team rode power-fully on their way to a third-place finish, but without the preda-tory ruthlessness of a team bent on winning at all costs. It was as if they had already ceded the podium's top two spots to CSC and Discovery. "We did all we could," Jan Ullrich sighed afterward.

CSC and Discovery, however, seemed impervious to exhaus-tion. Their performances showcased the difference between those teams that wanted to do well and those teams that would be satisfied with nothing less than victory.

They were the last two competitors of the day. The rain had stopped and a slight tailwind skipped along the river, as pre-dicted. Discovery started five minutes before CSC.

Discovery set a torrid pace. They went through the twenty-five-kilometer checkpoint in 25:51 and forty-six kilometers in 47:14. But CSC was faster at every checkpoint, Zabriskie's yel-low jersey popping vividly against the threatening gray sky. The gap was fifteen seconds at the first time check and six at the second. Riis's addition of Luke Roberts to the squad was paying huge dividends as the Aussie took long pulls at the front of the pace line. When both teams entered the old section of Blois and began the final miles to the finish, CSC's poise and relentless tempo made them a lock to beat Discovery.

The crowd at the finish was rabid to the point of hysteria. There was no separation between the media area and the spectators, so when teams finished, they were immediately engulfed in an enormous mob. Fans clutching pens and camcorders clamored to touch the riders, to actually feel their sweat in a handshake or by casually bumping up against them. It was hard to watch as young children battled with grown adults for access. And it was only going to be worse for the Disco Boys. Actual bona fide paparazzi were in attendance to snap Sheryl and Lance. The crowds that mashed in for lesser-knowns hardly compared with the crush that would accompany Armstrong's crossing the line. It would have been easy for someone to be trampled underneath the swarm, and it was amazing that someone hadn't yet been.

Not surprisingly, the crowd exploded when Discovery Team came across the line. Their time was 1:10:39. It was the fastest of the day, but a simple glance at the video screens showed that CSC hadn't slowed a whit. The instant they crossed the finish, Riis would have his win.

And then Dave Zabriskie crashed.

Funny how some guys always find a way to crash and some guys always find a way to win.

Some said a gendarme got in Zabriskie's way. Television replays were inconclusive. But however it happened, Zabriskie went down hard. CSC paused for a second, but only that, and then they were sprinting to the line. With just over a mile remaining, losing focus would have been disastrous.

CSC's final time was 1:10:41. Zabriskie, his skin suit in tatters and flesh burned and bleeding from sliding on the pavement, limped in ninety seconds later. His face was drawn and pale as he rolled through the finish crowd. It was as if he had lost a loved one. And, in a way, he had.

Zabriskie had started the day two seconds up on Armstrong. He well knew that during the team time trial, the whole team shared the time attained by the first member to cross the line. Since the gap between Discovery and CSC was two seconds, logically Zabriskie and Armstrong should have been tied for yellow. But the unlucky Zabriskie had crashed into the barricades just before crossing under the *flame rouge*, that triangular red banner denoting just one kilometer remaining. Tour rules state that a rider gets the same time as his teammates only if they drop him after he has passed under the *flame rouge*. He finished a minute and a half behind his team and slipped to ninth overall.

When all was said and done, Lance Armstrong was wearing the yellow jersey.

It was like old times. The Disco Boys watched CSC's debacle on television from inside their bus. The reception was bad, but it came through well enough for them to know they had won the team time trial. They jumped up and down for joy, then Lance went out for his first yellow jersey ceremony of 2005. Sheryl Crow was by his side as he signed souvenir yellow jerseys. He spoke to Spanish television in Spanish and to French television in French. At the postrace news conference, held in a room that was the size of a small kitchen, Lance was asked about his strategy going forward — namely, would he try to stay in yellow for the rest of the race? It was an absurd notion, slightly selfish, something only a superhuman team could manage. Lance passed the question over to his podium-mate Bruyneel, who hemmed and hawed about the difficulty of protecting the yellow jersey for the next seventeen stages. Something like that just wasn't done. It would weaken the team horribly.

Bruyneel was right, of course. Wearing the yellow now was good, but wearing it come Paris was what mattered. In avoiding the question and letting Bruyneel respond, Armstrong had been momentarily out of character. Lance was known as a straight shooter, direct and blunt. It was oddly diplomatic of him to shrug and stay silent.

And his silence was not long lasting. Before reporters could move on to the next question, the old, audacious Lance returned. "I'm gonna put a little pressure on him to let me keep it," he announced. The comment harkened back to what he had said after the very first stage, that he had come to race the Tour, not retire. And it appeared that he planned on doing so in glorious fashion. But at what cost?

Later, a furious Bjarne Riis brazenly suggested that Armstrong didn't belong in the *maillot jaune*. "The man in the yellow jersey," he said, pointedly not mentioning Armstrong's name, "is there because of luck." The quote infuriated Armstrong so much that he posted it as wallpaper on his computer screen as yet another source of motivation.

Come to race indeed.

Stage Five

July 6, 2005 — Chambord–Montargis
113.46 Miles

Overall Standings

1. Lance Armstrong (USA), Discovery Channel, 9:59:12
2. George Hincapie (USA), Discovery Channel, 00:55
3. Jens Voigt (G), CSC, 01:04
4. Bobby Julich (USA), CSC, 01:07
5. José Luis Rubiera (Sp), Discovery Channel, 01:14
6. Yaroslav Popovych (Ukr), Discovery Channel, 01:16
7. Alexandre Vinokourov (Kaz), T-Mobile, 01:21
8. Benjamin Noval Gonzalez (Sp), Discovery Channel, 01:26
9. David Zabriskie (USA), CSC, 01:26
10. Ivan Basso (I), CSC, 01:26

BY THE FIFTH DAY of the Tour I had become chemically dependent on Camembert. I took it for granted that the one true way to eat breakfast was to slather butter and jam on a warm croissant. And I had developed an attachment to my press credential that could only be described as infantile. That pass took me inside the Tour, back to the team buses and into the press conferences and behind the barricades. It was a backstage pass to the biggest sporting event on earth. I was terrified of losing it, only taking it off when I showered — and even then I'd feel a stab of worry.

But on the morning of the fifth stage I prepared to remove the credential from around my neck for an entire day, at least in a manner of speaking. I had urgent business in Paris that morning. My wife and I were refinancing our home back in California. As luck would have it, the time-sensitive loan documents hadn't shown up until I was walking out the door to fly to the Tour. There was no time for me to sign them then. My only option was to carry the documents with me and find a notary in France — an American notary, I was reminded by the loan officer. Such a person existed in Paris, or so I hoped. Since the fifth stage wouldn't begin until early afternoon, it seemed like the best day to leave behind rural France for a short spell, and return to a world where bicycles were uncommon on the streets. The fifth was a minor stage, one whose purpose felt more like functional travel from one point to another than bike racing. It began in Chambord, a village famous for its enormous and legendary château, built by Francis I in 1519 as a hunting lodge. It was a city proud of its past and resistant to growth. To live in Chambord an individual had to be born, marry, or work there — thus a population of just 215.

Montargis, the finish, had been founded at the crossroads of former medieval trade routes, and it was still a city known for commerce. In between the two communities were rural villages like Lamotte-Beuvron, Vailly-sur-Sauldre, and sleepy Aubigny-sur-Nère, where ten thousand Scottish soldiers allied themselves with the French to defeat the British army in 1419, during the Hundred Years War. The Salereine and Sauldre rivers flowed through the countryside, and boar ran wild in the local forests. Given the flat nature of the 183-kilometer stage, the tired legs in the peloton after the team time trial, and the likelihood that Lance Armstrong, with a leadership gap that allowed him to go a bit easy, probably didn't plan on defending the yellow jersey anyway, I figured nothing dramatic would happen. My plan was to dash into the city, then right back to the French countryside in time for the start.

There was another reason for my jaunt into Paris: Babbitt needed a ride from Blois to Charles de Gaulle Airport. He'd been in France for five days, which would be a very long time to cover a more normal sporting event. Yet the Tour is so epic and Herculean that his five days merely marked the beginning of a great adventure. I felt like he was missing out on many things to come, but he had made his peace with Armstrong and was eager to be home.

In the few minutes it took me to drive away from the airport I witnessed the arrival of a whole new wave of American Tour spectators. I saw bike boxes from Miami, watched over protectively by two elderly men who'd come as part of a cycling tour group; college students with shaved legs wearing Discovery Channel Team baseball caps; entire families wearing T-shirts and sweatshirts and caps emblazoned with something about Lance and the Tour de Lance and the Stars and Stripes and Texas; and, on almost every wrist I could see, yellow LiveStrong bracelets. The mind boggled at the impact that lone man was having on the French economy and the U.S. airline industry.

Traffic was backed up on the A1, the main road leading into Paris, and my frustration rose as the minutes ticked past. (Inhale peace. Exhale conflict. Repeat.) Things would have to get better in a hurry to make the start.

But the traffic got even worse, and then became gridlock when I entered the city. It could have been my imagination, but there seemed to be construction taking place on each and every street in Paris. I realized it was time for desperate measures. Taking a sharp left turn near Gare du Nord, I parked the Citroën and prepared to take the Métro.

The Métro ride was jammed and humid, the train smelling of body odor and stale sweat, but the real throngs were aboveground. The Place de la Concorde was awash in the hustle-bustle of

Paris — Vespas, honking horns, cigarette smoke, tourists of a hundred nations.

The Place de la Concorde is the spiritual heart of Paris — and the Tour. The Louvre is off to one side, the Arc de Triomphe and Champs-Élysées to another, and the Seine is a short jog away. It is here that the Tour de France concludes. Though that day was still more than two weeks off, bleachers and a reviewing stand had already been partially erected.

The year before, on the morning after the Tour ended, I had gone for a run through Paris. My route took me across the Place de la Concorde. It was well before sunrise and there was virtually no traffic. Precisely halfway across the Champs-Élysées, at the point where that grand boulevard and the Place converged, I spied a small chalk mark on the ground. I knew exactly what it was. On that spot, less than a dozen hours earlier, the victory podium had risen. I stopped in the darkness and stood there, facing the Arc de Triomphe. This was the exact spot where Lance Armstrong had heard "The Star-Spangled Banner" after his sixth consecutive victory. I imagined what it was like to have such a moment of pomp and fanfare, of reward and ovation for a job well done. Deciding it would be tremendous indeed, I continued on toward the Eiffel Tower.

Once upon a time the precise spot where Tour winners are crowned was marshy, hostile terrain. In 1748 architect Jacques-Ange Gabriel was hired to transform the area. He did, designing one of the most beautiful public squares in the world (although he was overruled on his insistence that it all be surrounded by a moat). Originally known as Place Louis XV, it was rechristened Place de la Révolution in 1792 after Louis's son was toppled from the throne. More than thirteen hundred persons had their heads lopped off by the guillotine very near that podium spot in 1793, including King Louis XVI and Marie Antoinette. The name was changed to the Place de la Concorde in 1836, as a means of effecting greater national unity. The Place is rectangular. An obelisk, originally from the Amon temple at Luxor, Egypt, rises in its center. I always thought the French had stolen it during Napoleon's occupation of Egypt, but it was actually a gift from that nation's viceroy in 1829, long after the French had been sent packing.

The American Embassy was on the far side of the Place, in the shade of some trees near the Champs-Élysées. I scurried across the Rue de Rivoli and made my way to the entrance. Anti–car bomb barricades lined the road leading to the guard shack. Gendarmes patrolled the streets around the building and controlled access to the gates. They were wary, watchful. And, it turned out, helpful. It wasn't the embassy I wanted, they told me, it was the consulate.

I know this sounds naive, but I always thought consulates were located in cities other than a nation's capital, which was where one found the embassy. In any case, it was just a little after ten o'clock. If things went very smoothly, I could still hustle back in time for the start.

It felt wrong to be in Paris. The City of Light was not an interim stopover. It was the place of the grand arrival and final departure. Paris was to be anticipated, longed for, then savored.

It had been that way since my first Tour, in 1999. I'd been following the Tour casually since I was a kid. Cycling was an endurance sport and I was a runner, an endurance sport athlete. Obviously the sports were different, but there was a brotherhood in that common embrace of suffering. My annual obsession began with Greg LeMond. He was the first American to win a Tour de France, and would go on to win three. During his 1986 victory, he dueled head-to-head with Bernard Hinault, a teammate. Even just reading about the back-and-forth was exciting. Three years later, things were even more dramatic. In 1989 LeMond successfully came back from a hunting accident that sprayed buckshot into his back, backside, those all-important legs, and even the lining around his heart. LeMond was in second place going into the final stage, an individual time trial that would finish on the Champs-Élysées. He was 50 seconds behind bespectacled Laurent Fignon, a Frenchman who went by the nickname The Professor in the peloton because he had once studied to become a dentist. College educations were rare in the peloton, and the moniker was an act of deflation.

LeMond charged into Paris at an average speed of 33.8 mph, a pace never before seen at the Tour. It was the first time aerodynamic handlebars and helmets were used in a time trial, and LeMond was ridiculed by cycling traditionalists, who scoffed at the idea that such contrivances would do anything to boost speed. But when LeMond beat Fignon's time by 58 seconds to win the Tour, the scoffing stopped.

LeMond was beloved by the French. His ancestors were French, and his surname was proof that he was merely a great French cyclist with the poor luck to have been born in another nation. Yet his victory was not entirely popular. No Frenchman had won the Tour since Hinault's 1985 win. It had been LeMond in 1986, Ireland's Stephen Roche in 1987, and then Spain's Pedro Delgado in 1988. Then it was LeMond again. Prior to that sudden foreign incursion, French riders had dominated the Tour. When, the people of France asked, would a Frenchman win the Tour again? It is a question they are still asking.

LeMond retired in 1992. He had been the Great American Cyclist, a man whose three Tour wins might never be matched by another American. For some fans, it seemed the future of American cycling had nowhere to go but downhill. And subsequent years proved them right. The next generation of American cyclists seemed OK, but certainly not of the LeMond caliber.

Except, perhaps, one. The top up-and-coming rider at the time of LeMond's retirement was a young guy from Texas named Lance Armstrong. He was brash and cocky, with big arms and shoulders from spending his teenaged years in the pool while training as a professional triathlete. Armstrong had made the transition to cycling after enlisting in a U.S. Olympic developmental cycling program for junior athletes. He flourished. By 1991 he was the U.S. junior national champion, and he made the decision to turn professional, signing a contract with the Subaru-Montgomery team.

By the mid-1990s Armstrong had won world road race championships and two stages of the Tour de France, had been ranked the number one cyclist in the world, and had competed as a member of the U.S. Olympic team. Yet America was still in search of LeMond's successor at the Tour de France. Armstrong's big upper body meant that he could never win a Tour, because he had just too much muscle mass to climb the mountains. Speed is a function of the strength-to-weight ratio. Even the best cyclists have to pare away all unnecessary bulk. Armstrong's years in the pool and weight room gave him a decidedly studly upper body, but those big biceps and pecs weren't much good for pedaling a bike up the Alps.

Yet Armstrong did have some astounding physiology in his favor. Years later, when Lance was already a record-setting champion, doctors studied his body, searching for what might have given him such remarkable superiority. They found that Lance Armstrong had been gifted by God — or, depending on your religious persuasion, was a mutant. His heart was physically bigger than a normal heart, allowing him to pump more blood — and thus more oxygen — per minute than almost anyone on earth. For an endurance athlete, it was an incredible advantage, though only a starting point. Winning the Tour required much more than a productive heart. It required brains and discipline and courage. Armstrong, it would turn out, had been blessed with these qualities, too.

But then, on October 2, 1996, Armstrong was diagnosed with testicular cancer. It had spread all the way up his body to his brain. This came just months after a disappointing sixth-place finish in the 1996 Atlanta Olympic Games and soon after signing that huge contract with Cofidis. Armstrong had never applied himself in school, but the diagnosis made him a student as never before. "Getting cancer turned his brain on," was how one friend put it. Armstrong threw himself into finding the smartest methods of treatment. He researched his disease with the same focus he had applied to competition, then chose to endure a radical new Platinol-based chemotherapy. The choice saved his life. In 1999, against all odds, he returned to cycling.

It had long been my dream to attend the Tour in person. In 1999 I got the chance, thanks to Greg LeMond. By then he was doing what many former professional riders do: taking amateur cyclists for a guided ride alongside the Tour. At the best companies, amateur cyclists pay a hefty fee to indulge their Tour jones. They stay in fine hotels, eat at the best restaurants, and ride sections of the actual Tour course each morning, several hours before the racers. I was asked to come along and write about LeMond's new venture. LeMond even loaned me one of his personal bicycles for our daily rides. It was a quiet thrill to pedal along each day, the name of a three-time Tour winner written in Sharpie on the tires, just in case some other cyclist was tempted to confuse his bike with one from LeMond's quiver.

Through a quirk of fate, the formation of LeMond's tour company coincided with Armstrong's return to the Tour after winning his battle with cancer.

LeMond's tour group took place during the glamorous middle week of the Tour, when the mountain stages are contested and the spectator frenzy is greatest. One morning our ride took us directly to the start, rather than to a random segment of the course.

It was in the town of Le Grand-Bornand that the riders had begun to converge for the rollout when LeMond and I arrived.

He eased his bike into the mix as if he were still a competitor, and urged me to do the same. I felt like an impostor, but in the most exhilarating sense of the word. LeMond immediately found U.S. Postal rider Frankie Andreu and asked where we could find Armstrong. Frankie, tall and cool, directed LeMond to a small trailer a hundred yards away. We pedaled quickly to the trailer. It was tiny, with barely enough room for more than a handful of people. Inside, Armstrong was conducting a last-minute strategy session with Tyler Hamilton, his top domestique. The cancer had reshaped Armstrong's body, stripping away all that upper body musculature. In its place was the stick-thin torso the world has come to know so well. His heart, by contrast, was bigger — not physically, but metaphysically. Lance Armstrong had faced death and miraculously returned to life. He knew what it was to race against time. And he knew what it was to fight. Now, on the verge of a crucial mountain stage, he was making plans to win it.

I lacked the competitive credentials to enter the trailer, so as LeMond slipped in the door I waited. I leaned my bike against the metal side, next to Armstrong's bike. His looked so small and so ordinary. For all its carbon fiber technology, it was just a bike, nothing more. Whether or not the bike went fast or slowly was all up to the rider.

It was just myself, Armstrong's bike mechanic, and the bikes outside the trailer. But LeMond's journey to the strategy session had not gone unnoticed. Word soon leaked out that the Past and possible Future of American Cycling were together. A swarm of photographers soon joined the mechanic and me, pushing and jostling. The mechanic positioned his body protectively in front of Armstrong's bike, like a Secret Service agent shielding the president.

Then Armstrong and LeMond stepped outside, arm in arm, and smiled for the cameras. The moment had a fine, historic feel — a torch being passed.

LeMond lingered at the top of the steps as Armstrong brushed past me and mounted his bike. Then Lance was gone. He would destroy the competition that day with a brutal attack on the final climb to Sestriere, Italy. Thereafter, Armstrong wore the yellow the rest of the Tour, all the way into Paris, winning his first Tour de France.

I was there again in 2001, when Armstrong destroyed Ullrich in the mountains, and when he did the same in 2004. I was also on hand when he was confronted about suspicions of drug use. I had the surreal experience of sitting in the media tent in 2001, interviewing LeMond over the phone from the States about his personal drug accusations against Lance, while just a few feet away, Armstrong gave a press conference defending himself against the accusations. I literally had LeMond talking in my left ear and Armstrong in my right.

LeMond later recanted his comments, no doubt told to toe the company line by Trek bicycles, with whom he and Armstrong were both under contract. But three years later, with Armstrong attempting to double his victory total, LeMond seemed once again incapable of stanching the bile. He publicly accused Armstrong of using performance-enhancing drugs on the eve of 2004's mountain stages. There was no proof and by the time the Tour reached Paris ten days later, the allegations had somewhat faded from discussion. But they would never totally go away — though perhaps not for the best of reasons.

Performance-enhancing drugs had long been part of the Tour's subculture, and were reaching their zenith when LeMond rode. The Tour is such a long and exhausting bicycle race that as early as the 1920s, cyclists carried a special personal suitcase containing pharmaceutical assistance. Cocaine was not uncommon. Nor were cigarettes, which jacked up adrenaline levels and increased the flow of blood sugar from the liver into the bloodstream. Caffeine and amphetamines were commonly used to boost a fatigued rider's performance. The cyclists were open about popping pills before World War II, talking to the press about the way their many stimulants kept them up all night, shaking. But drug use later became so prevalent that riders didn't even talk about it among themselves.

However, when Britain's Tom Simpson collapsed and died in 1967 while climbing Mont Ventoux, thanks to a combination of amphetamine usage and the blistering Provençal heat, the Tour drew up a list of banned substances and began urine testing stage winners and randomly chosen riders each day. The indignant cyclists, many of whom felt they could not complete the Tour without help, rebelled openly at first. The entire peloton stepped off their bikes during a stage and actually walked down the road for two hundred meters, chanting "Merde!" before remounting. The Tour's organizers responded by ramping up their anti-doping efforts. So the riders fought back in another way: they began looking for ways to beat the tests.

In the mid-1970s it became common for a rider to practice blood doping, which was the practice of draining pints of blood from his body, having it medically stored as he trained, then having it transfused back into his system shortly before a major competition. The extra blood would increase the number of red blood cells in the body, allowing more oxygen to be transported through the system. This made it possible to ride harder, longer. Best of all, simple urine tests that would catch amphetamines could not detect the increased hematocrit levels of blood doping. The introduction of erythropoietin (EPO) in 1983, and other blood-boosting products soon after, made blood doping somewhat old-fashioned by the late 1990s. This despite the deaths of several cyclists whose blood had thickened to the consistency of sludge from misuse of these products, and the constant risk of infection from dirty needles.

In 1998 Willie Voet, a masseur for Team Festina, was arrested when French officials found erythropoietin and anabolic steroids in his car just prior to the Tour's start. The scandal devastated the Tour. A number of teams were disqualified, and less than half the peloton finished. Voet went on to write a book about his years helping cyclists cheat: having them stuff a condom of clean urine into their anus for use during a drug test, or giving them intravenous saline solution drips to dilute their blood before a test.

Germane to Armstrong's situation was the medical use of EPO in treating anemia brought on by cancer. The fact remained that he had undergone years of urine and blood testing and had never shown evidence of drug use. Despite the frequency of the testing (some of it done on a surprise basis, at his home at all hours, even in the off-season), LeMond and other naysayers were intent on tarring Armstrong.

I didn't know if Armstrong was taking performance-enhancing drugs. But it seemed like a dumb thing to do for a guy who would lose everything if he got caught. Then again, he'd almost lost everything when he got cancer. I chose to trust in the tests and believe he was innocent until proven guilty. I thought then, and I still think now, that LeMond was out of line. His personal legacy deserved better.

The lines inside the consulate were endless and tinged with bureaucratic despair. With every tick of the clock it became obvious I wasn't going to make it to Chambord in time for the start. I'd looked forward to seeing the Château de Chambord, the largest castle in the Loire Valley, with its turrets and spires, so big that it required 365 chimneys for its 440 rooms. But I didn't leave the consulate until two-thirty. I was frustrated and mad, exhausted by lines and the alteration of my plans. I missed the Tour and wanted to get back.

For security reasons, laptops were not allowed in the consulate. I had been instructed to check mine at a café up the street. When I went to retrieve my pack, the TV in the café was tuned to the race. So it was that I ordered a salade niçoise and a glass of sauvignon blanc and settled in to watch. Australian Robbie McEwen, who raced for Davitamon-Lotto, edged Tom Boonen by half a wheel-length for the victory. The entire peloton was just behind — a massive squadron pedaling as one. When the peloton finishes together like this, everyone gets the same time. So even though Lance Armstrong finished well back in the pack, he remained in yellow.

In fact, in between stages Armstrong had relinquished the *maillot jaune* — by choice. That morning, he had shown up at the starting line wearing his Discovery Channel Team jersey instead of the racer's yellow. It was a salute to Dave Zabriskie, who would still have been wearing yellow if he hadn't crashed during the team time trial. Eddy Merckx had done the same thing at the 1971 Tour, when the Spaniard Luis Ocaña crashed out of yellow during a Pyrenean descent. Still, it was a curious gesture on Armstrong's part, either a media ploy or a subtle jab at Riis's comments that Armstrong was lucky to be in yellow — I couldn't quite tell which, and Armstrong wasn't saying. He knew Tour organizers would force him to change into yellow, but the symbolism was nonetheless powerful.

I spent the night in Paris. The hotel night clerk was a guy from California who'd moved to France to become a writer. It sounded like something from a short story, or a B movie. And while I enjoyed my time in the city, and had taken a long evening walk to take in the sights, all I wanted to do was get back to the Tour.

It was too early to be in Paris. The race was far from over.

Stage Six

July 7, 2005 — Troyes–Nancy
123.38 Miles

Overall Standings

1. Lance Armstrong (USA), Discovery Channel, 13:45:12
2. George Hincapie (USA), Discovery Channel, 00:55
3. Jens Voigt (G), CSC, 01:04
4. Bobby Julich (USA), CSC, 01:07
5. José Luis Rubiera (Sp), Discovery Channel, 01:14
6. Yaroslav Popovych (Ukr), Discovery Channel, 01:16
7. Alexandre Vinokourov (Kaz), T-Mobile, 01:21
8. Benjamin Noval Gonzalez (Sp), Discovery Channel, 01:26
9. David Zabriskie (USA), CSC, 01:26
10. Ivan Basso (I), CSC, 01:26

IT WAS DAWN when I left Paris, crossing the Seine on the broad span of the Pont de la Concorde, then angling left onto the Boulevard Saint-Germain. The only other vehicles on the road were delivery lorries and garbage trucks, but I got lost anyway. The streets of Paris change names without warning, sometimes every block. That's what happens in a nation with so much history — instead of their own streets, heroes get a span of concrete less than two hundred yards long to call their own, which must be very discouraging for their descendants and is very confusing for out-of-towners trying to read a map, eat a croissant, and drive at the same time.

The Tour had not missed me, but I raced toward it like I was late to see an old friend. Open prairie and vast wheat farms lined the route. From the air the farms must have looked like a quilt thrown across the land, symmetrical and right-angled. Silos jutted among that precision, and pockets of trees were all that remained of a forest primeval that once stretched from Germany clear down to Spain.

The day's stage would be 123 miles long, entering into the Alsace-Lorraine region, some of the most hotly contested landscape on earth. France and Germany have long staked a claim to this buffer zone. Beginning with the Franco-Prussian War in 1870–71, Germany has invaded France three times through this corridor. The famously failed Maginot Line is located there, as are battlefields like Verdun and Metz. Each town along the way has its own dramatic story to tell, and some of those stories go back much farther than just the past century.

Take Troyes, site of the start. The Mongol barbarian Attila the Hun was dissuaded from burning Troyes during his fifth-century invasion of Europe. What Attila failed to do, the Normans achieved quite handily four hundred years later. (Troyes would burn again in 1188 and 1524, the latter conflagration decimating its burgeoning hosiery industry.) The surprisingly well-traveled Joan of Arc made an appearance in Troyes, too, liberating it from the British during the Hundred Years War. Interestingly, Joan's successful siege of Troyes took place July 5–9, 1429 — exactly 576 years to the date that the sixth stage would get under way.

I don't know what the weather was like for Joan back then, but if it was anything like it was at the starting line in Troyes, it must have been mighty cold under that battle armor of hers. Thick black clouds scudded across the sky. It was a toss-up whether it was going to rain before the stage began or after. The prerace village served comfort food to ward off the chill: hot andouille sausage in a champagne sauce, a chunk of hard brown bread, and a slice of Camembert so soft it felt like they had submitted it to the heresy of microwaving.

For the riders, the day was again transitional. They would meander through the bucolic flatlands of central France before encountering their first bit of real climbing. The hills wouldn't be long, nor could they even be compared to an Alpine foothill. But those pseudoclimbs thrust themselves up from the prairie in a way that foreshadowed the next week's Alpine and Pyrenean stages. If it rained the roads would be slick, making for greater caution on the downhills. But all in all, it was another day for breakaways and sprinters.

Just in case a rider who could threaten the yellow jersey led one of those breakaways, Johan Bruyneel had selected George Hincapie to lead an immediate counterattack that would kill the break. It was an unenviable chore, but the sort of selfless act on which Hincapie had built his career. Thirty-two-year-old "Big George" was six three but weighed just a sinewy 165 pounds. He had pared down from 178, at which he'd ridden earlier in his career, in order to climb and time-trial faster for the 2005 Tour. The native New Yorker was circumspect and gregarious in his own quiet way, married to a former runway model and Tour podium girl. Hincapie's father, a Colombian, had introduced him to cycling as a child, and his first race was in Central Park. Hincapie had a reputation for being a classics rider, which meant that he conditioned himself for the summer season by racing grueling one-day events during the early spring. Often contested in rain and snow, in northern France and the Low Countries, through mud and over cobblestones, the classics favored riders with a predisposition to enduring punishment. Hincapie was such a man. After years of trying, he had finally made the podium at the infamous Paris–Roubaix race in April, perhaps the best known of all the classics.

Finishing second at the Hell of the North, as Paris–Roubaix

was known, summarized Hincapie's career nicely. He had won several events in a professional career that had begun when he was a teenager, but was more often in someone else's shadow. He was the only team member who had ridden with Armstrong in each of his Tour victories. Hincapie had quietly become excellent in the Tour's vital disciplines of time-trialing and climbing, and he was a logical candidate to take over as team leader of Discovery Channel when Armstrong retired. But no one really believed that would happen. Hincapie, if anything, was too selfless to make a good team leader. He'd been so busy sacrificing for Armstrong that he had never even won a stage at the Tour, although 2005 would mark the tenth time he'd raced it.

Hincapie was only 55 seconds behind Armstrong in the overall standings. There was talk he might launch a breakaway of his own. If he pulled it off, and won by more than those 55 seconds, he would be in yellow. Johan Bruyneel thought there was no better way to thank a quiet, loyal rider for his many years of service to Lance Armstrong. "Everyone on the team is hoping George might wear the jersey," Dan Osipow, the team's media director, told me. He said it with a tinge of emotion in his voice, as if the honor was long overdue.

A half hour before the start I strolled over and stood on the starting line. It was painted in yellow, from one side of the narrow Rue de la République to the other. A tobacco store was on one side of the street and a new bank in an old building on the other. Crowds pushed hard against the barricades on either side of the narrow road, filling the sidewalks completely. The riders were a hundred yards behind me, bounding up onto the sign-in stage to scribble their names in the Tour's official book of competitors. Tour tradition stipulates that each rider sign in before every stage (there is a small fine for not doing so). As they climbed the steps, each rider was introduced by a public address announcer fond of emphasizing the second syllable of surnames (Ivan Bas-SO! Lance Arm-STRONG!). The riders scrawled their names and waved to the crowd, then used the handrail to descend the stairs because their stiff-soled bike shoes lacked traction.

High up the bank wall next to the starting line, I noticed a plaque. It was tarnished and worn, with some of the lettering rubbed away by wind and rain. And though my French is limited, I could make out the details. The plaque pointed out that the bank building was once the deportation center for the more than three thousand citizens of Troyes who were then marched to the train center just a half mile down the Rue de la République and shipped to Nazi death camps.

Ironically, the Tour's roots had traces of anti-Semitism. When Alfred Dreyfus, a French army captain and Alsatian Jew, was put on trial and convicted for passing secrets to Germany in 1894, there was a great public outcry. To many, the case hinged as much on his religion as his alleged crimes. Dreyfus was retried in 1899 and offered clemency by France's president. A major industrialist named Comte Dion was so enraged by Dreyfus's newfound freedom that he was arrested during a public protest. At the time, Dion was advertising heavily in an all-sports newspaper called *Le Vélo,* owned by a man named Pierre Giffard. The two men disagreed violently over the Dreyfus Affair. As a result, Dion pulled all his advertising from *Le Vélo* and began an upstart newspaper to battle Giffard. Dion named this new publication *L'Auto Vélo* and hired a former world record–holding bike racer named Henri Desgrange to be editor. The rest was history.

Very few things are accidental at the Tour. But I wondered whether Jean-Marie Leblanc knew about the fact that the starting line of the seventh stage was the exact spot from which France's Jewry had been deported. Some of his course designs had shown a puckish quality, making a subtle point that went beyond cycling. For 2005, the sixtieth anniversary of World War II's end, the route was following a path very close to the Allies'

1944 liberation of France. A start at the D-day beaches would have been too obvious, but departing at an Allied beachhead on the Atlantic had made the point just as effectively for those paying attention. Routing the course near battlefields like Verdun and through cities like Nancy, where the French resistance had been instrumental in helping Patton's Third Army secure the city, was just as powerful. The fact that the eastward push ended with a symbolic crossing of the Rhine for a day of racing in Germany was just icing on the cake.

So what might be the symbolism here? I wasn't sure. A bad-taste joke about hellacious journeys and survival? A sober reminder? Perhaps just an idiosyncratic nod to the Tour's origins? Whatever the case, that moment at the starting line momentarily brought me low. Word had also just begun circulating about the terrorist bombings of London commuter trains that morning.

A bicycle race seemed almost absurd by comparison. But it's precisely at such times that races like the Tour become so vital. The attacks by those who had willingly disenfranchised themselves from the rest of the world, choosing to see themselves as self-righteous victims instead of murderers, stood in stark contrast to an event where men empowered themselves each day to be at their absolute mental, physical, and emotional best. I could see it when I drove the course each day, passing through literal throngs of people beaming with anticipation. They didn't come to watch a bike race. They came to watch humankind at its finest, and hope that maybe some of that excellence would rub off on them. Maybe that's why I was there, too.

A great mystery to us Americans — OK, to me — is how France remains so thoroughly undeveloped. Each day of the Tour, I was seeing one lush landscape after another. Indeed, it was hard to keep my eyes on the road because the scenery was so inspiring. That was certainly the case on the drive from Troyes to Nancy.

The villages along the way were small and surrounded by end-less miles of farmland, and forests as thick as jungles. The church in Pont-Sainte-Marie was built in the twelfth century, and Brienne was such a perfect little town that I understood why Napoleon Bonaparte, who went to military school there as a youth (his superiors thought him weak in charm and recom-mended he become a sailor), called it his homeland. This was truly a place to call home.

It had been raining since the exact moment that the stage began. The final yards before the finish line were a winding, treacherous corridor through Nancy. The barricades had been up all night, and snaked through the town in very random fash-ion. There was lightning in the air, the pavement was slick with rain, and the spectators were absolutely drenched. These wet fans spoke a mixture of German and French, and French with a German accent, because the border was so close. Even the houses had a dark, Teutonic look.

If the stage came down to a sprint finish, I had the feeling there could be a big crash. There were several blind corners near the line. One of them was so close to the finish that the riders wouldn't be able to see the finish arch until they were within a few hundred yards. The moist streets wouldn't make it any safer.

Early in the stage, CSC's Bobby Julich had attacked the pelo-ton, pulling dramatically ahead. Julich, an American, was a threat to the yellow jersey. George Hincapie dutifully chased him down, quickly killing the breakaway.

Just a few miles later, off went a journeyman rider named Chris-tophe Mengin. His daring breakaway at the 10-mile (out of 123) mark was a gutsy day at the office. At one point his lead over the field was a fat eight minutes and thirty seconds. But riding so long without a break weakens not just the legs, but the mind also. With only two miles left, his lead had dwindled to just ten seconds.

Still, it looked like Mengin just might win. The tight turns and short straights of the final mile favored a solo rider. The peloton is an unwieldy beast, more suited to broad, straight roads than snaking turns. It was easy to get bottled up on those sharp angles and to tangle bike parts in the hurry to get to the finish. But here, the one place where he had an advantage, the exhausted Mengin got sloppy. Dashing into the final turn too quickly, the Frenchman crashed hard on the slick new pavement. He fell sideways as his bike tires slipped out from under him, and then his unprotected torso slid all the way across the width of the street into a metal barricade.

Normally in a situation like that, a rider quickly picks himself up and keeps going. There is still a race to be won. But the peloton was so close behind that Mengin's crash and the slick pavement caused a chain-reaction pileup. Other riders failed to navigate the tight turn. They hit the road hard, then slid into Mengin. He was pinned against the cold wet steel of the barricades, unable to move. Someone or something slammed into his head, making one eye swell shut.

The peloton is a life force, ever adjusting to calamity. Even as the crashes were under way, other riders found a path around them. Those who had stayed on their bikes pedaled carefully to the finish. The fallen rose slowly, their uniforms in tatters, their shaved legs shiny from blood and sweat, and blemished with black from the new pavement. Each racer checked his bike to make sure the rims weren't bent and that the pedals still turned, then mounted and rode slowly to the finish line.

Christophe Mengin was the last to get up. Moments before, he had been in first place, on the verge of winning a stage in the Tour de France. Now he was dead last. But he was given credit for a finish and tomorrow would be there at the sign-in, ready to race again. "You must take risks to win," he explained. "Today I took the risk and lost. I will not be afraid to take the same risks tomorrow or the next day, no matter what the cost." Then he limped away.

Stage Seven

July 8, 2005 — Lunéville–Karlsruhe
141.67 Miles

Overall Standings

1. Lance Armstrong (USA), Discovery Channel, 17:58:11
2. George Hincapie (USA), Discovery Channel, 00:55
3. Alexandre Vinokourov (Kaz), T-Mobile, 01:02
4. Jens Voigt (G), CSC, 01:04
5. Bobby Julich (USA), CSC, 01:07
6. José Luis Rubiera (Sp), Discovery Channel, 01:14
7. Yaroslav Popovych (Ukr), Discovery Channel, 01:16
8. Benjamin Noval Gonzalez (Sp), Discovery Channel, 01:26
9. Ivan Basso (I), CSC, 01:26
10. Kurt-Asle Arvesen (Nor), CSC, 01:32

ONLY THREE MEN in the history of the Tour de France have worn the yellow jersey from start to finish. The most intriguing was Ottavio Bottechia, an introverted bricklayer and World War I veteran from northern Italy who accomplished that feat in 1924. Bottechia won the first stage then steadily built his lead with every passing day. He was one of the premier climbers in Tour history and so thoroughly dominated in the mountains that his lead became insurmountable. But just for good measure, Bottechia made sure to win the final stage, too.

Lance Armstrong would never duplicate that feat. But as the first week of the Tour came to an end, there was a growing suspicion that, having won the jersey on the fourth stage of his final Tour, he planned to wear it each and every stage until Paris, then retire with the *maillot jaune* swaddling his skinny, slightly stooped shoulders.

Armstrong had long felt proprietary toward the jersey. Over his six championships he had spent more time in yellow than wearing his own team colors. He was poised to pass Bernard Hinault to take second behind Eddy "The Cannibal" Merckx for the total number of days wearing yellow. There was a lot of mileage between Lunéville and Paris. Wearing yellow the entire way would not be easy — and was not entirely practical. Armstrong wasn't deterred in the least.

For the rest of the peloton, Armstrong's emotional vise grip on yellow was just an interesting sidelight to a very troubling first week: the astonishing opening time trial, the brutal division of the peloton into haves and have-nots during the team trial, the dramatic crashes by Dave Zabriskie and Christophe Mengin, and a record average peloton speed near thirty miles per hour — speed so fast it had drained the enthusiasm from the riders by the time they arrived in Lunéville for Stage Seven. The first week had flat out sucked. Surviving had been an achievement.

That was the problem: The first week was supposed to have been the *easy* one. So on a drizzly Friday morning, on the day that would see the Tour cross the Rhine River and finish in Germany, there was a grumpy vibe throughout the peloton. If the first week was so hard, went the thinking, there was no telling how difficult the next two weeks were going to be.

The lighthearted exception was Chris Horner of Team Saunier Duval. At thirty-four, he was a year older than Armstrong. But Armstrong's last Tour was Horner's first. Like a career minor-league baseball player who finally makes it to the majors, Horner was eager to make the most of the chance. "I want to win a stage," he told me. We were standing next to his team car. He had the hatchback open as he rummaged around for his gear bag, then doffed his wet-weather cycling shoe covers because the on-and-off rain had temporarily stopped. "That's what I do best: try to find a spot to attack so I can win a stage."

Horner had freckles and was going bald. He looked like an aging Huck Finn. Horner was cocky and likable in that way, too.

"But what if your team director tells you not to go?"

"They can't see everything from inside the car," Horner said with a wink. "You gotta go when you can go."

Time would tell if he would be bold enough to attack. A lot of riders talked a big race, but a whole lot of them didn't back it up.

A shining example of this timidity could be seen in the riders who were supposed to be Lance Armstrong's biggest challengers. The collective grouping of Ivan Basso, Jan Ullrich, Floyd Landis, and Levi Leipheimer seemed cowed. None of them were stepping up to make the bold, definitive move it would take to beat him.

Of course, laying back meant that Discovery was having to work defending, breaking the wind while others rode in their draft, chasing down breakaways. The top riders and their teams were playing possum, using the pre–mountain stages to rest. Discovery might become so exhausted from defending the jersey that they would be unable to retaliate against a properly timed mountain breakaway. As popular as Lance was, and despite his accomplishments, none of those teams were throwing him a retirement party, and none were even remotely close to conceding. Eventually there would be attacks and counter-attacks, and the forging of unlikely alliances with also-ran teams looking for the dose of glory that a stage win could provide.

Although the full-throttle attack could wait until the mountains, the contenders needed to at least show their presence more visibly at the front of the peloton by sending a teammate off onto a breakaway in an effort to make Discovery work extra hard. But they were passive and boring and playing right into Armstrong's strategy. Sometimes it's not strength that wins the battle, but the perception of strength, and Armstrong looked very strong indeed.

I found Bjarne Riis and asked him who was going to make the first move. "Bobby Julich," CSC's team director told me. Riis had the preternatural calm of a monk and a Danish lilt to his voice; I felt like Max von Sydow playing chess with Death.

Julich was in fifth place, 67 seconds behind Armstrong. But while he could slip into yellow with a good move, even I knew he wouldn't hold it long. Julich's time-trialing was very good but not great, and his climbing wasn't going to put the fear of God in anyone.

I found Julich. "Bjarne says you're going to make a breakaway today."

This was news to Julich. "If I did make a move like that, it wouldn't be today. It's too long. It would be tomorrow."

"Are you saying that because you really intend to attack today and don't want anyone to know it, or are you saying that because you're really going to attack tomorrow?" We were right in front of the sign-in stage. Bernard Hinault was poking me with an umbrella because I had unwittingly stepped in front of a rider on his way to the steps.

"Anything could happen."

Now we were getting somewhere. "Where on the course would you make your move?" The route was a dog's breakfast of terrain: farmland, forest, small hills, the Rhine crossing, small towns.

"I don't know the course. We can't preride every course in the world we race. It's impossible. You've got to take it as it comes. That way you get to see new things."

He was trying to sound lighthearted and profound, but I got the feeling he really wanted me to go away. Riders hate talking strategy with journalists. More often what they pass along as information is actually disinformation, just in case I run over to an opposing team and share what I've heard in hope of getting a good quote from the opposition.

Which is exactly what I did. "CSC says Julich is going to make a breakaway," I told Dan Osipow over at the Discovery bus.

"Nah. Today's a day for the sprinters," Osipow said, before pausing to think about it. "But if he does go, George'll take care of it."

As if on cue, Hincapie emerged from the bus and grabbed his bike from where it was leaning. He pedaled wordlessly off to the start, not acknowledging the cries of "George!" from the fans behind the barricades. Almost all of them were Americans, and knowledgeable about the Discovery Team roster. They yelled for Hincapie as if he were a rock star's roadie — buddylike, admiring, faintly jealous of his close proximity to The Man.

Lance Armstrong came out of the bus a minute later. He'd taken off his black cycling booties with the Nike swoosh, figuring that the rain wasn't going to come after all. The fans began screaming his name with a fervor reserved for messiahs and Beatles. Armstrong smiled and clipped into his pedals. He had a wary, slightly haunted look, as if girding for unexpected calamity. Then he was away.

"You can tell you're at the Tour," a journalist once remarked to me, "when you don't look twice at a sedan shaped like a hard sausage."

He was right: I barely gave such vehicles a second thought, even a giant phallus driving through the countryside, its driver hidden somewhere inside its girth, propelling itself with an eros so extraordinary as to be supernatural.

These vehicles were known collectively as the publicity caravan. Forty-two of the Tour's sponsors paid an additional fee for the privilege of advertising and distributing their brand-name products to the crowds lining the course via these oddly shaped cars — the more outrageous, the better. The caravan was more than twelve miles long and comprised some two hundred vehicles that put on a forty-five-minute "show" that would flaunt those products and distribute eleven million gifts over the course of the Tour.

The caravan, in effect, was the Tour's warm-up act.

Each morning, three hours before the start, the publicity caravan comes together and forms a single-file line. Two hours before the riders clip into their pedals and begin their afternoon-long battle, the caravan sets out on the exact same course. For the twenty-three days of the Tour, the employees of the caravan drive pell-mell from whichever sleepy burg they spent the night in, assume their predetermined position in line, and spend the day trapped inside a preposterous vehicle, traveling at an average speed of fifteen miles per hour, working for minimal wages at a three-week summer job that will never fail to raise an eyebrow from the prospective future employer who notes it on a résumé.

It is a sight to behold.

Many of the vehicles were just advertisements in and of themselves: the giant red wheel of Brie, for instance. Some were more like floats in a parade, with models clutching a handrail while lobbing candies or cheap product samples to spectators lining the course. There were cars shaped like coffeepots, Mickey Mouse ears, gnomes, and Aquarel water bottles. A drama was being acted out on a stage atop another Aquarel vehicle, in which an actor dressed as a priest blessed a marriage ceremony using Aquarel as holy water. PMU, a bank, featured a statue of three racehorses, complete with jockeys. The National Police threw out recruiting brochures, which didn't receive as much enthusiasm as the Buckler Beer truck, which was handing out free tallboys of ale. The South Australia Tourism Bureau featured a kangaroo atop its car, and so on.

Grown adults fought small children for the free Crédit Lyonnais hats, candy, and even the La Redoute lingerie thrown from the vehicles. Horns honked, music played, and every day the caravan rolled on. What did it have to do with cycling? Absolutely nothing. What did it have to do with the Tour de France? Everything.

Osipow was right: It was definitely a day for the sprinters. A weather system was powering in, bringing wet gusts of wind and rain that would slow a solo rider's breakaway. It wouldn't have been so bad if the roads wound through a forest, but much of the course was open farmland of such an incredibly horizontal nature that it brought to mind Kansas. Exposed, the riders would be subject to Mother Nature in the worst possible way.

After crossing the mighty Rhine near Beinheim, the course continued for several miles on a highway — unheard of when the race was in France. Such a wide expanse offered a rider even less chance of hiding from the wind. The finish line lay at the end of a long road outside Karlsruhe, through a large field near the town's convention center. The setting felt industrial and impersonal.

The Germans didn't wave at the Tour cars the way the French did, but they were animated in other ways. The spectators drank beer instead of wine. A man in cycling shorts, with a Charlie Chaplin mustache and bowler, stood at one crossroads; an entire spin class was conducting a workout on stationary bikes just three miles before the finish; a father and son wearing sombreros rode stationary bikes atop a van next to a field of wheat (I could only imagine what family life must have been like on that farm); a policeman in Karlsruhe took the time to answer my queries about the make and model of his sidearm (Heckler & Koch P2000VS); and, my personal favorite, one guy who rode his bike along the course until he found an empty spot, set out a folding chair, stripped off his shirt and cycling cleats, lit up a smoke, and lay back to get a tan while he waited for the race to pass by. They were all part of an estimated four hundred thousand Germans lining the twenty-five-mile section of course inside their country.

Appropriately, it was a German from a German team who

made a breakaway and led the peloton across the Rhine. Fabian Wegmann of Team Gerolsteiner sprinted away from the field after just twenty-five miles. Robbie McEwen went with him. But McEwen, a sprinter, decided after just six miles that he wasn't in the mood to push the next hundred-plus miles to the finish at top speed, so he let Wegmann continue on alone, then drifted back toward the peloton in a most unusual fashion.

Usually a rider just reduces his speed and lets the field catch up. But McEwen had a different idea. He quickly stopped and hid behind a bush, then waited until the peloton passed by before jumping back in. He wanted the other sprinters to think he was far ahead, hoping one of them might chase after him, thus tiring his legs long before the final sprint. It was a far-fetched dream, because someone would eventually see him and relay the word to a teammate. Still, it was possible he could pull it off. For that reason alone it was worth the try.

Nobody bit. Wegmann's breakaway was enthusiastically received by the German crowds, but the peloton didn't share their sentiment. Slowly, they reeled him in.

With about ten miles to go, Wegmann had company. His solitary hundred-mile breakaway had been heroic, and if not for those broad German highways that gave him little protection from a stiff wind, he might have gone on to win the stage. But he was caught, and then it was the sprinters' turn.

I've watched sprint finishes for years on television. And I've watched them in person, head-on, beyond the finish line, at the end of the straightaway. But until Karlsruhe, I'd never felt the sense of speed as the riders passed — that *whoosh*. So I posted myself along the barricades, thirty-five meters from the finish, squeezing into a spot along the rail, my body pressed into the unpainted metal. The sprinters seemed spread randomly across the road, but I knew the aerial shot would show them carefully aligned off one another as they prepared for the final charge. A sprinter would draft behind a teammate, known as his lead-out man, until he spotted an opening. Sprinters and lead-out men would be arrayed across the width of the road, waiting for their moment to pounce. Sprint past the lead-out man too soon, and a sprinter from another team would immediately swerve over and suck the first sprinter's wheel — in effect, using *him* as a lead-out man. But sprint too late, and another sprinter might already have made the pivotal move and be too far in front to catch.

The finish in Karlsruhe was very broad and very straight. Riders began making their move a quarter mile early, with sprinters finding their lead-out man, and even a secondary lead-out man, who would fall away like a spent rocket booster before giving way to the other. The sprinters muscled against one another as they jockeyed for position, using heads and shoulders to push other riders aside, all the while pedaling at top speed.

The crash came with 150 yards to go: Isaac Gálvez of Illes Balears-Caisse D'Epargne and Angelo Furlan of Domina Vacanze went caterwauling into the barricades. They lay there, dazed and bleeding, as the field left them behind.

And still the sprint continued. A sudden blast of speed and air and bright colors and bike frames and helmets passed me by, just inches away. It felt like standing along a flight line as a fighter jet takes off.

Sprinters look so large and muscular on television. And some are — Italy's Mario Cipollini, the recently retired "Lion King" of the peloton, was a formidable presence. Magnus Backstedt of Team Liquigas-Bianchi weighs in at a hulking 190 pounds. McEwen is small and borderline petite, however, with oversize quadriceps honed through years of sprinting. And it was McEwen, the man who had hidden in the bushes to fool his rivals, who followed lead-out man Freddie Rodriguez until just the right moment, then squirted past and lofted his arms in victory.

Of the two riders who went down hardest, Furlan got up first. His jersey hung from his body in rags, and his flesh was pink but not bleeding after sliding across the new pavement. He pounded his fist forlornly on the handlebars as he pedaled slowly to the finish line (every rider must finish or he cannot continue the Tour). His path was not straight. Rather, he wobbled down the final straightaway, knowing better than to ask for help.

Gálvez was the exact opposite. His front wheel was broken, so he walked the final 150 meters carrying his bike by the handlebars and holding it so that it rode on the back wheel while the useless front rim was up near his eyes. He strode close to the barricades, chest out and head held high. His eyes looked straight forward. The left side of his shorts was torn away. He ignored the sympathy applause and the fans reaching out, eager to pat him on the back. Looking very much like a rooster who has been badly wounded in a cockfight, the proud Gálvez finally crossed the line and thrust the bike to a handler.

McEwen's victory meant little in the overall standings. Lance Armstrong was in first. George Hincapie, his teammate and loyal enforcer, was 55 seconds back in second place. Alexandre Vinokourov was 1:02 behind, in third.

Typically the cramped interview trailer is overflowing with journalists. But no one expected Armstrong to make an appearance after the sprint stage, so I pretty much had the place to myself. "Nice crowd," Armstrong joked as he walked in. He looked calm and relaxed, so different from the way he'd looked before the stage.

I asked whether or not he would defend yellow for the rest of the race. "We might be defending it," he replied calmly, "but we're also getting a lot of help. Three or four other teams are finding it in their interest to chase down each breakaway so we have a field sprint.

"But we've been through the first week. Now the race is about to start."

As for Chris Horner, he finished sixty-eighth on the day, crossing the line two seconds behind Lance Armstrong but receiving the same time. His stage win would have to wait for another day.

Stage Eight

July 9, 2005 — Pforzheim–Gérardmer
143.53 Miles

Overall Standings

1. Lance Armstrong (USA), Discovery Channel, 23:01:56
2. George Hincapie (USA), Discovery Channel, 00:55
3. Alexandre Vinokourov (Kaz), T-Mobile, 01:02
4. Jens Voigt (G), CSC, 01:04
5. Bobby Julich (USA), CSC, 01:07
6. José Luis Rubiera (Sp), Discovery Channel, 01:14
7. Yaroslav Popovych (Ukr), Discovery Channel, 01:16
8. Benjamin Noval Gonzalez (Sp), Discovery Channel, 01:26
9. Ivan Basso (I), CSC, 01:26
10. Kurt-Asle Arvesen (Nor), CSC, 01:32

LANCE ARMSTRONG'S first mistake of the 2005 Tour came on a day that dawned clear and bright. No longer was the Tour traveling west to east; now we were all headed due south. The change of direction was invigorating. It meant that the rest day in Grenoble was just two days away, and that the first crucial mountain stages would follow soon after.

Pforzheim had the relaxed air of a midsummer carnival. The throngs of fans included an abundance of small children, holding their parents' hands as they made the long walk from wherever they had parked the car on the fringe of town. I found a spot for the Citroën at the confluence of the rivers Enz and Nagold, and walked over a bridge built in 1365 as I went off in search of the Tour village. The waters below were placid, dotted with wildflower-covered islands, and the banks were lined with weeping willows. The weather was hot, with wispy white clouds. Thunderstorms had been predicted, but for the moment the forecast appeared inaccurate.

The center of Pforzheim was relatively new, done up in that rectangular cellblock look defining postwar European architecture. The rest of the city had a Victorian quality, and the streets spoked out in random, confusing fashion. Pforzheim was known for its gold jewelry, and eleven gold-painted bicycles hung from the support cables of a bridge next to the village. Three gray-haired men in maroon jackets and ZZ Top beards appeared to be the town's official greeters, and welcomed me warmly into the heart of town.

The village, as always, was happening: Internet, newspapers, coffee, and the usual Tour faces. The Grand-Mère girls were there, still dressed all in red and still pouring coffee. Jean-Marie Leblanc sat in the shade, looking relaxed and wearing sunglasses. The fortification crowd was over at the bar, but being served Katskeller Pils instead of a French wine. A wacky French morning show was taping live in the midst of it all. It crossed my mind that there must be a universal constant: Morning shows are always wacky, no matter the language.

Due to the large weekend crowds, the buses were all placed within a circular ring of barricades. The fans are generally just ten or twenty feet from the buses, but in Pforzheim they were a good fifty yards back. Riders pedaled past me, on their way to sign in, as I wandered down the start corridor — Jan Ullrich, Floyd Landis, Ivan Basso, and dozens of domestiques, the up-and-coming riders whose job it was to ferry water, food, and carbohydrate beverages to their team's top riders during a race. I did not know the names of those young men, nor will I probably ever. I was like a salmon swimming upstream.

There were an abnormally large number of American flags in Pforzheim, and the number only increased outside the Discovery bus. Servicemen and their families stationed in Germany had driven over for the morning. They packed the barricades and draped their flags atop the steel-like bunting. The men's heads were shorn and the mothers held young children up so they might get a better view of Lance Armstrong.

For a change, he wasn't locked up inside the bus. Armstrong was standing out front, talking to reporters while wearing a Navy "SEAL Team Ten" hat, out of respect for two members of that squad he'd met in his hotel's bar the night before. He stayed out there as long as he could, lingering until the last possible minute before heading off for the start.

Traditionally, two Discovery Team assistants led Armstrong to the start each day to protect him from overeager mobs of fans. But after changing into his helmet, Armstrong slipped away from his de facto bodyguards. He veered toward the barricades and signed autographs for the large American crowd — the children in particular. When Armstrong finally clipped in and pedaled for the start, he made a point to take the long way, riding along the barricades before all his countrymen. There were still two weeks in this Tour. Much as he longed for victory to be decided, Armstrong seemed to be savoring every last stage of his career.

I'd never seen Lance so engaging at such an early point in the Tour. Normally Armstrong was reclusive until victory was assured. And even when he did appear in public, he was wary and tight-lipped. Now he looked perhaps too confident — not overconfident, as if he were taking things for granted, but just a little too loose.

My big plan for the day was to hang with the Germans. In partic-ular, the rabid Germans who come to the Tour to drink too much beer, blow their party horns, paint their bodies, and spit on Armstrong. Next to the Spaniards, no group of partiers at the Tour is as dedicated. A warm Saturday afternoon seemed like the best time to find them. The spot I had in mind, however, wasn't actually in Germany, but back across the border in France, where the stage would end and hordes of hardcore fans could be found. The final climb of the day was a 16.8-kilometer, second-category ascent called the Col de la Schlucht. Even the name sounded German.

The Tour always offers two different ways for media and Tour officials to drive from start to finish. The first way is the actual course. This can be tricky and time-consuming, because the roads are lined with fans, who tend to run out across the road on a whim. Driving the course is the best way to see the actual physical obstacles the riders will be encountering, but it's not the best way to go if speed is an issue. You also have to plan ahead, because if you're still driving the course once the race is catching up to you, serious trouble with the Tour authorities is likely. The course becomes closed to all vehicles. Those lingering on the route too long, as I discovered while entering Nancy on Stage Six, receive the dubious honor of having a motorcycle gendarme pull up alongside the driver's window and order them in extremely aggressive French to either pull over for the peloton or make all haste for the finish line. On days when the caravan is slowed by heavy crowds this often becomes an issue. A long line of media and official vehicles can be strung out behind, unable to pass the caravan but desperately needing to get to the finish.

The other option is something known as the *hors* course, which combines chunks of the course with the less scenic but far more speedy autoroute. A good average on the country roads the course follows is about 50 mph. On the autoroute, however, the posted speed limit is 130 kilometers per hour — a little over

80 mph. Strict observation of the law is rare, and the average speed is probably above the limit. Until I covered the Tour, I never knew that it was possible to drive a hundred miles an hour and read a map at the same time without being scared absolutely shitless. But when chasing Lance it became second nature.

So I was ready for a big, fast push down the A5 once I got out of Pforzheim. But Saturday in Germany, I quickly learned, is driving day. The entire country seemed to be indulging a passion for taking to the autobahn. The A5 was clogged with cars as far as I could see. It was as if all of Germany had made "Thunder Road" their mission statement. The roads were jammed, and I've never seen so many people taking the concept of a rest stop so literally — pulling off to the side of the road to picnic, kick the soccer ball, read a magazine in the sun. They were going nowhere in a hurry, and didn't seem to mind sharing their leisure space with a gas station, convenience store, and a thousand like-minded strangers.

Things got quicker when I crossed back over the Rhine at Sasbach. There I got off the autoroute and onto a small farm road. Someone had erected a half-size replica of the Statue of Liberty at a rotary. Lady Liberty looked surreal and strangely beautiful as she presided over the Alsatian countryside, and I took her presence as a good sign.

At the base of the Col de la Schlucht, I drove through the village of Saint-Dié-des-Vosges, which was small and charming and surrounded by forest, with flower boxes and shutters on the windows. But it was really no different from a dozen other remote villages I'd driven through that day. I had the faint awareness that it was somehow an important place, but couldn't figure out why. It took a minute before I remembered: Shortly after Christopher Columbus died, in 1506, a monk and mapmaker living in Saint-Dié decided that Amerigo Vespucci had discovered the Novus Mundo (New World) instead of Columbus. The monk named this land "America," feminizing Vespucci's name to keep with the practice of naming continents in that manner. That bit of knowledge fit nicely with the Statue of Liberty sighting, though it seemed astounding that such a small village had had such an enduring effect on Western civilization.

From bottom to top of the Col de la Schlucht, the crowds were five- and six-deep. I found myself scared for the small children along the course, who I feared would dart in front of a Tour car or rider. The crowd was very, very German, and the Discovery Channel Team car riding behind me (not Johan Bruyneel's car, but one of the technical vehicles) was booed constantly. That disdain, however, was not universal. When I spotted two women waving an American flag and wearing Discovery jerseys, I slowed down to ask them where they were from. The women didn't understand the question. They only spoke German.

The German flag flew from motor homes, T-Mobile flags and jerseys outnumbered all others, and quite a few men without their shirts (and a few bikini-clad women, too) were chugging large green bottles of beer. The Germans had a reputation for being some of the harshest spectators; few riders in the Tour had not been splattered with spit as they passed by German fans. But there was nothing unruly about this crowd. Children waved at me, spectators made polite gestures of apology for straying too far into the road, and even at the top of the climb, where the crowds were so thick that there was barely enough room through which to squeeze the Citroën, no one thumped a hand on the hood or gave me a hard time. The Germans, it seemed, were not so bad after all.

At least not from my perspective. As with so many past Tours, it was the Germans who were making Lance Armstrong's day hellish — and not just longtime rival Jan Ullrich, but also Andréas Klöden, who also rode for the T-Mobile Team. On a day when the T-Mobile juggernaut had an overabundance of crowd support, their plan was simple: Attack.

The stage was easily the hilliest of the Tour thus far, beginning with four third-category climbs (defined by the Tour as a climb lasting at least three miles, with an average grade of 5 percent) in the Black Forest, but T-Mobile waited for the Col de la Schlucht to make their move.

For his part, Armstrong had a group of teammates known as the Spanish Armada whose job was to protect him from such attacks. Benjamin Noval, Manuel Beltran, and José Luis Rubiera. They were all talented cyclists in their own right, and on a lesser team might even be the leaders, but here they were paid to provide a draft and to pace Lance Armstrong up the Tour de France's long climbs. Their actions helped him conserve his strength for that moment when he veered out of their draft and attacked the top of the mountain. When the peloton was riding together, all nine of the Discovery riders would clump as a small pack. Lance would be in the middle, his teammates surrounding and protecting him. One by one they would peel off, and Lance would generally be left with just his Spanish Armada to pace him up the mountain. They would be his infantry in the attempt to fight back the T-Mobile assault.

Kazakhstan's Alexandre Vinokourov (the lone non-German star on the T-Mobile squad) launched the first attack, midway up the Schlucht. At the time, a Dutch rider named Pieter Weening was far ahead in the lead, but no one was paying any attention because he was no threat to the yellow jersey. Vino's attack, however, was a different story. He was just 1:02 behind Armstrong in the overall rankings. A decisive stage victory would put the yellow jersey on his back.

And Team Discovery Channel was tired. The peloton's high average speed had deadened their legs. Chasing down breakaways to protect the yellow jersey had drained them even further. When Vino attacked, they had no strength to answer.

Yet one of them tried. Paolo Savoldelli, an affable young Italian who had won the *Giro d'Italia* (Tour of Italy) in June, was able to reel in Vinokourov's first two attacks. But soon Savoldelli dropped back, too. Armstrong, for the first time at the 2005 Tour, was forced to cover the attacks all by himself. "I've never seen a team implode like that before," Ullrich marveled later.

Armstrong was clearly exhausted, his face lined with strain as he struggled to keep track of all his top rivals. There was nobody else for him to rely on; if a rider passed him, he had to catch up and keep pace; had to match the threat until it receded. Making matters more difficult was the size of the group around Armstrong — some thirty-four riders. With a length of just more than ten miles, the Schlucht was a long climb, but it was not a steep one. The winding road was lined with a dense, damp pine forest that blocked out heat and wind. Conditions were ideal for those riders who'd been riding easily in the peloton's draft all week. Legs fresh, they were eager to make a go for the stage win.

But it was a stage T-Mobile wanted all to itself. Once again, team director Walter Godefroot ordered an attack. Next to go was Klöden, the 2004 Tour runner-up, with the tattoo of a devil's face on his right arm. Six miles below the top of the climb, he stood up in the pedals and sprinted away.

Only this time Armstrong let him go.

It was a tactical decision. There was only so much gas in the tank. Klöden was in twenty-fourth place overall at the start of the stage, some 2:29 behind Armstrong. If Armstrong chased down Klöden but blew up (cycling parlance for overextending oneself, to the point that the legs can barely turn the pedals) in the process, men like Basso, Ullrich, and Vino would sense Armstrong's condition. His face might assume a hangdog look. There might be a sudden pallor to his complexion. He would struggle to turn the pedals, his cadence dropping far below the 80–85 revolutions per minute he maintained on climbs. Then, seeing Armstrong's collapse, those rivals would seize the moment and quickly launch the attacks that might strip the yellow jersey from the American, perhaps for good.

Incredibly, Jan Ullrich found his way to Lance and stayed at Armstrong's side. On a day when the dangerous German might have gained significant time in the standings, Ullrich mysteriously marked Armstrong, pedaling steadily at his side while waiting for the American to make a move that would lead to his blowing up — but a move that Armstrong was clearly too exhausted to make. Ullrich's logic was that he could let everyone else attempting to break away from the pack exhaust themselves, and once he knew Armstrong was gone he would pull ahead, fresh and rested. But it was a huge tactical blunder on the German's part, a patience unrewarded. It also spoke to a greater lack of coordination among the T-Mobile squad. Neither Klöden, Vino, nor Ullrich seemed to be riding as part of a team. When they took Armstrong on, it was as three individuals seeking to further their own goals, not as a unit that was, in some planned and synchronized fashion, wearing him out so one of them — whichever best suited the team's purpose — could finally pull ahead. They could have put several minutes between themselves and Discovery, which might have all but ended Armstrong's hopes of a seventh consecutive Tour victory. Yet Klöden, Ullrich, and Vino seemed oblivious to that opportunity.

The Germans were waving their flags and cheering for Klöden with a nationalistic fervor so far unseen at the Tour. After cresting the summit, Klöden screamed down the back side of the mountain. Ten miles of steep S-turns lay between him and the finish. He would attack them like an Olympic skier barrelling through slalom gates, taking the shortest and fastest line possible.

Armstrong was in the chase pack, just under a minute behind. But once he made it over the top, the crisis had largely passed. Attacking on a downhill is risky business and doesn't often gain much time.

Though he got nipped at the line (the margin of victory was the slim width of a valve stem) by Rabobank's Pieter Weening,

Klöden scored an enormous moral victory. After failing utterly in the opening stage a week ago, finishing fifty-first, he now found himself among a group of ten riders within two minutes of snatching the yellow jersey.

But Armstrong, thanks to Ullrich's inability to seize the moment (or his simple desire to have the glory all to himself), was still the man wearing that coveted piece of fabric. Armstrong looked wan and red-eyed during the podium ceremony, his look a far cry from that of the man jauntily donning the SEAL Team Ten cap that morning.

A shower and a change of clothes can do wonders for a man, and as I watched Armstrong do a video interview an hour later, he was back to his old self. It was being shot for French TV, on the balcony of his hotel, overlooking Lake Gérardmer. Ski slopes and forest rose from the water on all sides. Vacation cottages lined the shore. It was all very lovely, with gravel walking paths and park benches that faced out to the water, inviting contemplation.

The guy next to me, a British writer sipping red wine from a large paper cup, openly feared for Armstrong's teammates. Armstrong is even-keeled in public appearances, but his impulsive temper behind closed doors is legendary. "What do you want to bet there'll be some very harsh words at that team dinner table tonight," he said.

As if on cue, Armstrong all but agreed. Discovery Channel, in Armstrong's estimation, had been overconfident. "It was definitely a crisis on our team. We need to evaluate it and not let it happen again. It's not a true indication of what we're going to see in the Alps and the Pyrenees, which are much steeper. But the boys on the team are getting too confident. This is the Tour de France. You'd better show up to play and have both feet on the ground. Nothing's guaranteed."

Lance Armstrong's summary of the day's stage was simple: "It was a bad day at the Tour." It was a remarkable statement for a man famous for saying "There are no bad days," thanks to the fresh perspective on life he'd gained after cancer.

Others had a bad day, too. The rugged course had been a severe test for all. Christophe Mengin, the almost-hero of Nancy, and Isaac Gálvez, who had gone down so hard at the finish in Pforzheim, both abandoned the race due to their injuries. Mengin was sporting a black eye that had swollen his left eye shut, and Gálvez's road rash had rendered his body a single oozing sore. There was no way they could continue. For them, the Tour de France was over.

But Dave Zabriskie had it the worst. One week to the day after experiencing the ultimate cycling high by winning the yellow jersey, he finished dead last. Zabriskie was so far behind that by the time he made his way down the Col de la Schlucht, Armstrong had already exchanged his cycling cleats for running shoes, answered preliminary interview questions, and completed the lengthy podium ceremony.

I felt sorry for Zabriskie. At the start that morning he had looked openly fearful. At the finish, his face was pale and he looked shell-shocked. It was as if he couldn't believe that his cycling abilities had just up and left. But that's what they had done, and it seemed only a matter of time before he was out of the race.

Stage Nine

July 10, 2005 — Gérardmer–Mulhouse
106.02 Miles

Overall Standings

1. Lance Armstrong (USA), Discovery Channel, 28:06:17
2. Jens Voigt (G), CSC, 01:00
3. Alexandre Vinokourov (Kaz), T-Mobile, 01:02
4. Bobby Julich (USA), CSC, 01:07
5. Ivan Basso (I), CSC, 01:26
6. Jan Ullrich (G), T-Mobile, 01:36
7. Carlos Sastre (Sp), CSC, 01:36
8. George Hincapie (USA), Discovery Channel, 01:47
9. Andréas Klöden (G), T-Mobile, 01:50
10. Floyd Landis (USA), Phonak, 01:50

IT WAS THE LAST STAGE before the first rest day. During the first Tour in 1903, the riders contested fifteen hundred miles of cycling in just six stages. There were between one and four rest days per stage. Over the years, the number of stages increased, the distance of each stage grew shorter, and the number of rest days was reduced. The two rest days for 2005 would bookend the riders' draining week in the mountains.

After the finish in Mulhouse, the riders would board chartered planes and fly two hundred miles south to Grenoble or drive in the team bus. Either way, the most important thing was to begin the rest process as soon as possible. Basel-Mulhouse Euro-Airport was located a convenient ten miles from the finish line, meaning the teams that flew might actually be wheels-up before finish-line spectators had located their cars in the parking lot.

Discovery's meltdown on the Col de la Schlucht guaranteed that there would be nothing anticlimactic about the hundred-plus-mile ride to Mulhouse. Not that the melodrama needed amplification. Stage Nine's six major climbs presented a monumental physical ordeal. One ascent, Ballon d'Alsace, was five miles of uphill at an average grade of 6.8 percent. The climb would be exhausting in the Citroën, let alone on a bicycle. It was a course made to break men. By the time they were done, the riders would kneel down and thank God for a day of repose.

But a day's rest would never be enough. Ballon d'Alsace was designated a first-category climb, the first such ascent of the 2005 Tour. As difficult as it would be, and as unique to the race thus far, first-category climbs would be considered somewhat common after the rest day, when the race entered the Alps.

The ninth stage would begin on the shores of Lake Gérardmer and travel uphill immediately. Then it would follow the mountainous contours of the Vosges region, up mountains and down into valleys, then back up again. On a map, the shape of the route resembled a jagged horse's head. Then, as if following the taper of the neck down to the fetlock, the roads straightened after descending Ballon d'Alsace. There the mountains ceased, replaced by thirty miles of flat farmland before the finish.

The geography was so harsh that until the mid-eighteenth century the area was cut off from the world by a lack of roads. The locals had taken advantage of that isolation to live as if they were an autonomous minirepublic.

Discovery's glaring failure on Saturday had confirmed that they were weaker than many had expected, and rival team directors were panting for a chance to attack the yellow jersey. Bjarne

Lance Armstrong about to pass Jan Ullrich during the opening time trial of the 2005 Tour de France.

Italy's Ivan Basso during the opening time trial from Fromentine to Noirmoutier-en-l'Île.

Floyd Landis, former teammate turned rival of Lance Armstrong, in full aerodynamic tuck.

Stuart O'Grady (left) and Robbie McEwen
tangle during the final sprint on the long
homestretch into Tours.

AP Photo/Christophe Ena

A disoriented Dave Zabriskie of Team CSC
just after his stunning crash.

Photo by Robert Laberge/Getty Images

Lance Armstrong pedals alongside the
Discovery Team car to chat with Johan
Bruyneel during the fifth stage of the
2005 Tour de France.

Javier Soriano/AFP/Getty Images

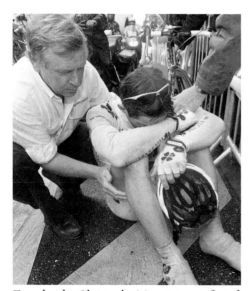

French rider Christophe Mengin is comforted by Tour de France chief doctor Gérard Porte, following his devastating crash into the barricades.   *AP Photo/Joel Saget/Pool*

Denmark's Mickael Rasmussen, showing the climbing strength that vaulted him into the polka-dotted jersey.

AP Photo/Franck Fife/Pool

A dazed and confused Manuel Beltran gets back on his bike after crashing on the road from Briançon to Digne-les-Bains.

Photo by Bryn Lennon/Getty Images

Germany's Jan Ullrich, Lance Armstrong's longtime foil, climbs just behind the yellow jersey.

AP Photo/Peter Dejong

Chasing Lance was taken to literal extremes during the first mountain stage of the 2005 Tour up the Courchevel. *AP Photo/Franck Fife/Pool*

Alexandre "Vino" Vinokourov being chased by the legendary El Diablo.

AP Photo/Alessandro Trovati

Surrounded by rivals Floyd Landis, Jan Ullrich, Ivan Basso, and others, Lance Armstrong paces a small group up the fearsome Col du Galibier. *AP Photo/Christophe Ena*

Tour rookie Chris Horner leads a daring breakaway on a hot, sunny stage between Miramas and Montpellier. *Joel Saget/AFP/Getty Images*

Big George Hincapie charges
up the Col de Peyresourde
during Stage Fifteen.

AP Photo/Peter Dejong

In a moment that stunned even the low-key Hincapie, he wins his first-ever Tour
stage by conquering the Pla-d'Adet.   *AP Photo/Christophe Ena*

Lance Armstrong fans came prepared to display the exact number of times he has won the Tour de France. *AP Photo/Franck Prevel*

The Tour de France peloton, pedaling in tight formation during the nineteenth stage of the 2005 Tour de France.

AP Photo/Alessandro Trovati

Lance Armstrong pedaling up the Champs-Élysées during the final stage of his seventh consecutive Tour de France championship. *AP Photo/Franck Prevel*

Lance Armstrong holds aloft the victor's chalice after winning his seventh and final Tour de France.

AP Photo/Bernard Papon/Pool

Austin Murphy and the author flank Neil "The Legend" Leifer at the base of the Col de la Madeleine.   *© Neil Leifer*

Riis was particularly eager, promising beforehand that his team had a definite plan for defeating Armstrong. Team CSC had a stable of riders capable of a powerful mountain breakaway. By sending one off the front at the appropriate time, they could wrest the jersey from Armstrong's back.

The question was, did Armstrong want it anymore?

The morning of the ninth stage began with a jolt. I had angled the Citroën onto the course at St. Maurice-sur-Moselle, at the base of Ballon d'Alsace, only to discover that the road was one-way; that I was going the wrong way; and that the course was not yet closed to non-Tour traffic. I swerved to avoid a collision and almost hit a family of four carrying their picnic lunch up the climb. I sat there a minute, overcome by adrenaline. But soon another car came along and I found the right way up the mountain. Families and cyclists and picnickers and outright partiers trudged up the road, hauling chairs, leading little yippy dogs, holding young children by the hand. Fathers carried coolers of beer on their shoulder, and children clutched homemade German flags. Amateur cyclists casually weaved downhill through the crowd. The climb passed through small towns, and fields of grass rioting with the purples, greens, blues, pinks, and yellows of wildflower high season. It felt like entire villages had emptied themselves, then formed again on the gravel shoulders of those mountain roads.

The camper shells were higher up, in the pines just below the summit. Above the pines, where Ballon d'Alsace was bald and rounded, sunbathers lolled in the mountain warmth. It was a peak with a great Tour history, having initially been contested during the 1905 Tour. Officials now considered it the first truly legendary climb in the race's history.

The summit was easily the most populated spot on the mountain. Colorful tents were spread out through the pastures.

Campers filled the parking lots. Vendors sold grilled sausage and ice-cold Heineken. The smell of suntan lotion and all that sizzling sausage filled the air.

And there was one more thing: polka dots.

A red-and-white polka-dotted banner is strung across the road at the apex of every Tour summit. Supermarché Champion, a chain of French grocery stores, pays for the banner. Just as points are awarded to sprinters for the final placing, points are awarded to cyclists for their position as they pass under each banner. There may be six or seven banners in a day. The man with the most cumulative points is awarded the polka-dotted jersey. This signifies that he is the Tour's top climber — officially, King of the Mountains. The jersey has garish red spots against a pure white background, but looks don't matter to the riders. Only the yellow jersey is more coveted.

As a result, it's common for a rider who has fallen far back in the standings to change his focus from the *maillot jaune* to King of the Mountains. France's Richard Virenque, who retired after the 2004 season, made a career of it, winning a record seven polka-dotted jerseys.

Dashing in a sort of renegade way, Virenque was an omnipresent figure in 2005, doing daily broadcasts for French television. The French fans had not had a Tour champion since Hinault twenty years before. As a result, they'd quickly become the Chicago Cubs fans of cycling, desperately craving a winner each year and never getting one. Virenque's polka-dotted victories and matinee idol looks were enough to make them clamor for his autograph — and to overlook a midcareer suspension for using performance-enhancing drugs.

When Nike obtained the rights to manufacture and sell yellow jerseys around the world Americans snapped them up, but the French wouldn't touch them. Surveys showed that the French people thought it "sacrosanct" to wear the yellow. It had to be earned. But they were just fine about buying polka dots.

In 2005 the Tour was even selling a polka-dotted wristband, in the style of Armstrong's yellow LiveStrong bracelets. The packaging stated the red-and-white band "symbolizes the amazing victory of the human body and the courage discovered in each of the winners," which was exactly the same thing the LiveStrong bracelet symbolized. The big difference was that proceeds from the LiveStrong band went to cancer research. Proceeds from the King of the Mountains wristband went to Jean-Marie Leblanc's bottom line.

From wrists to jerseys to banners, polka dots were everywhere.

But with Virenque retired, the French no longer even had the polka dots. At the start of Stage Nine it belonged to a skinny Dane named Mickael Rasmussen. Rasmussen was thirty-one, aging by Tour standards. He was also a former mountain biker who made the daunting leap to road riding. The results had been middling thus far, with just three victories in as many years. He had red hair, sharp cheekbones, and was exceptionally skinny.

Cyclists burn between 6,000 and 9,000 calories each day at the Tour. Some of that is replaced during the race at special "feed zones," where riders are handed a musette bag filled with energy bars, water, and carbohydrate drinks. But for all the calories they burn, cyclists have to constantly watch their food intake. Lance Armstrong, for instance, was once so obsessed with his daily caloric consumption that he actually weighed his food before each meal.

It's vital for Tour cyclists to stay lean. Even one or two extra pounds has a noticeable effect on their strength-to-weight ratio, particularly when gravity works against them while climbing the mountains. Before drug-testing, anabolic steroids were quietly popular among cyclists because they promoted lean body mass. Amphetamines accomplished the same thing. But with those now banned, proper diet is imperative. Many cyclists, such as Armstrong, maintain a slightly higher weight in the off-season, then trim down as they physically peak for the Tour. Some are better at it than others. Armstrong had quietly noted that Jan Ullrich came into 2005 about five pounds too heavy. One look at Ullrich's lean, striated musculature and it was hard to see where he might find five more pounds to lose, but that's the way it was at the Tour. However, Armstrong should know: A simple glance at his pre- and postcancer physiques shows the difference between being in very good shape and being chiseled. He looks like two different men.

Rasmussen took the concept of being lean to new extremes. He was painfully thin. Just looking at him made me want to buy him a burger.

But he was also a very determined bike rider. And what that fearsome Dane wanted, more than anything at the 2005 Tour, was to win the polka dots.

He broke from the peloton within minutes of pedaling away from the Lake Gérardmer starting line, and then never looked back — which is saying something for a man prone to nervousness. The Dane rode with the poise of a champion: Up the Col de Grosse Pierre, down to La Bresse, up the Col des Feignes, then up even farther to the Col de Bramont. There, strangely, a man naked from the waist down ran alongside him for a few yards, then Rasmussen was on his way down the mountain to Wildenstein. And then it was up all thirteen miles of Le Grand Ballon, and then fifteen miles back down into Malmerspach. The climbs were tortuous, but the descents required even greater courage, a series of byzantine hairpins overlooking long drop-offs. A single mistake when feathering his brakes, or the wrong angle coming into a turn, could be enough to launch a rider over the side. Things like that didn't happen often at the Tour, but gravity was gravity, and no one was immune. In 1951, for instance, Holland's Wim "Iron William" van Est lost the yellow jersey when he missed a turn and fell seventy feet down a cliff. Luckily, a tree broke his fall or the drop would have been much further.

Dangerous as they were, those perilous descents were also Rasmussen's best friend. The peloton was too big to navigate those tight turns at top speed, but a lone rider going for broke could fly down.

And fly he did. Three hours in, Rasmussen's solitary figure passed under the polka-dotted archway atop Ballon d'Alsace. The crowds came right into the center of the road to greet him, allowing just a narrow path the width of his bike. They screamed in his face, patted his butt, and cheered for him to go faster, as if he needed the reminder. A new electricity enveloped us all. The flags reflected it. No longer were they just German or American (not once had I seen anyone fly the French flag), but Dutch, Norwegian, Danish, Australian, British, and Irish — in spite of the fact that not a single Irishman was riding the Tour.

And then the fans and the screams and the insanity were behind him. The summit was Woodstock. The descent was unpopulated. All Rasmussen could hear was wind rushing past his ears as he churned the pedals, pushing top speed down the gut-wrenching plunge.

Making it all the more unnerving was the nature of the descent: half-mile straightaways followed by sharp right turns. Those downhill straightaways meant abruptly going from 50 or 60 mph down to half that in a switchback, then rolling out of the turn and pedaling hard to get back up to full speed. The good descenders kept their upper bodies loose — elbows unlocked, shoulders unhunched, neck unfrozen. Rasmussen was loose — so loose, in fact, that while racing down Ballon d'Alsace at 50 mph he actually took one hand off the bars to reach for something in a back pocket of his jersey.

After the mountains the course changed dramatically. The road to the finish was flat, lined with rows of poplar trees and cornfields, and so gusty that those poplars were leaning side-ways. Rasmussen churned his legs, willing his bicycle forward. He was in the zone, the friction of the world seemingly removed. He won the stage with ease, by more than four minutes.

Meanwhile, Bjarne Riis had made good on his word. Suspecting that Discovery wasn't likely to defend the jersey, he ordered Jens Voigt to chase down Rasmussen. Voigt had begun the day in second place, just a minute behind Armstrong. If his attack succeeded, he would likely claim yellow.

A Frenchman, Christophe Moreau, went with him.

Discovery left them alone.

As much as Lance wanted to wear yellow all the way into Paris, it was much better for the Disco Boys to let Team CSC defend, allowing Armstrong and Discovery to draft a few bicycles back. That way they rested their legs, rested their battered psyches, and would be mentally and emotionally poised to attack with gusto during next week's mountain stages. Jens Voigt was not a threat to win the Tour; he couldn't time-trial and he was going to spend the next week working for CSC team leader Ivan Basso.

So Lance eased up. Just like that, yellow slipped from his shoulders.

Now it was Voigt who had to spend the hours after the race being drug-tested and interviewed, going through the podium ceremony (though that was hardly a chore), and performing the other functional tasks expected of the man in yellow.

Armstrong did none of that. He entered the team bus as soon as the stage was over and rode to the airport. It was time to rest. Every single second of the Tour up until then was just a prelude to the real drama, soon to unfold in the mountains. He could afford to surrender the mellow Johnny if it meant just that little extra bit of time to prepare.

Almost unnoticed was the news that David Zabriskie had abandoned the Tour. He hadn't been the same since his crash during Tuesday's team trial. His injuries hadn't healed, either mentally or physically. It was yet another reminder of how cruel the Tour could be. A rider had to get up each day, sign in, get on his bike, and ride. No excuses. There was no special dispensation for crashing or mechanical failure. Ride or go home — and the shell-shocked Zabriskie was going home.

"He gave us the most perfect start we could have asked for," Voigt noted of Zabriskie's Tour-opening yellow. "He's a good rider and I hope he gets better soon." But how, I wondered, could a man ever possibly forget that crash in Blois, and letting that sacrosanct yellow jersey slip off his back so carelessly?

All went well as I drove away from Mulhouse under blustery skies. My time in northern France was through (with the exception of the final day in Paris). From now on, the Tour would take place in the sun-drenched south.

I could have made Grenoble that night if I'd been motivated, but because of the rest day, there was no rush. I cut through Switzerland, where it was raining but the terraced landscape was as vivid green as a Crayola. I got a room by the Geneva Airport, splurged on a filet mignon cooked in a marrow-and-seven-spice sauce, and found myself thinking back on the crowd cheering Rasmussen home with such enthusiasm. They were normal people, some of them cycling fans but most just average spectators out for a day at the Tour. Yet they were cheering for a skinny Danish cyclist they'd never heard of as if he were a blood relative.

It reminded me of the daily need for inspiration, and French aviator Antoine de Saint-Exupéry's rant against society's embrace of mediocrity. "You rolled yourselves into a ball in your genteel security, in routine, raising a modest rampart against the winds and tides and stars. Nobody grasped you by the shoulders while there was still time. Now the clay of which you were shaped has dried and hardened, and naught will you ever awaken the sleeping musician, the poet, the astronomer that possibly inhabited you in the beginning."

I have a feeling that people come to the Tour to experience that awakening. It can't be about just the bike race. It's as if, by watching others, those spectators may be inspired to push their limits. That awakening is the starting point of all personal journeys. Within some of us is a championship cyclist, within another a brilliant entrepreneur. In our lives we will be faced with great unknowns: the diagnosis of cancer; the call to help a troubled friend; the need to move forward after tragedy. As professionals we will attempt to chart paths that, however modest our lives may appear on the outside, involve deep moral decisions and complex tactical judgments. And though we may never ride the Tour de France, each of us, like the cyclists, faces a daily barrage of adversity, complication, and decision.

"By endurance, we conquer," was polar explorer Ernest Shackleton's family motto. It applied to more than just exploration.

I think those fans in Mulhouse were feeling something like that. For sure, Mickael Rasmussen was.

Part II

Mountains

Rest Day

July 11, 2005 — Grenoble

Overall Standings

1. Jens Voigt (G), CSC, 32:18:23
2. Christophe Moreau (F), Crédit Agricole, 01:50
3. Lance Armstrong (USA), Discovery Channel, 02:18
4. Mickael Rasmussen (Dk), Rabobank, 02:43
5. Alexandre Vinokourov (Kaz), T-Mobile, 03:20
6. Bobby Julich (USA), CSC, 03:25
7. Ivan Basso (I), CSC, 03:44
8. Jan Ullrich (G), T-Mobile, 03:54
9. Carlos Sastre (Sp), CSC, 03:54
10. George Hincapie (USA), Discovery Channel, 04:05

THEY CALLED IT a rest day, but for everyone involved with the Tour, the day in Grenoble bore no resemblance to a normal day of leisure.

For the riders, it was a short period of active recovery. After so many days of intense effort, their muscles were loaded with lactic acid and other waste products. Instead of lying about or playing Nintendo, the teams pedaled out on the roads surrounding Grenoble for an easy two-hour ride. They spun the cranks casually, bantering and enjoying the scenery. It was a time for taking a deep collective cleansing breath (Inhale peace. Exhale conflict. Repeat.) while steeling for rigors of the coming week. The following day would bring the first mountain stage, a 116-mile ride deep into the Alps, so even as they rested, the riders had to remain sharp.

For difficulty and popular appeal, nothing along the Tour de France route compares to the mountain stages. Indeed, the mountains *are* the Tour. There the race is won and lost. Any rider who ever dreamed of being a winner also dreamed of conquering the mountains. To win otherwise would be like triumphing on a bad call by a nearsighted referee — a win, to be sure, but not a truly satisfying one. Winning on technicalities was not what motivated the sort of person who rode in the Tour de France. Nor, if they were to be brutally honest, did they dream of winning the flat stages of northern France, nor the sprints, nor the time trials, and certainly not the team time trials (for every great cyclist is, at heart, an individual). No, they dreamed of the mountains; the Alps and Pyrenees, with their famous mountaintop passes like the Col du Galibier and L'Alpe d'Huez and Pla-d'Adet. If you want to be a god, you have to feel at home above the clouds.

Every cyclist knew that a misstep in the mountains — a weak attack; inability to answer an attack; or that special kind of failure brought on by sheer exhaustion, where a rider seemed to be pedaling backward — would haunt him the rest of his life. Blowing the chance to win a mountain stage would be like shanking the winning putt at the Masters. And one look at the Tour's official history book was enough to know that the Tour (and, by proxy, France) had a very long memory. The great riders received their due, but the failed riders were also mentioned, some — like Iron William van Est — more than a half century after their grand failure.

The week ahead shaped up like so: two stages in the Alps, two relatively flat stages through the warm southern region of France, then two stages in the Pyrenees. There would be a nice dramatic buildup to the action. Tuesday, the day after the rest day, would be the "easiest" day of climbing. Sunday, which concluded with an assault of the infamous Pla-d'Adet, would be the toughest.

So the riders took their rest day ride very seriously. Those ranked in the top twenty or so, the ones who'd been waiting for the Alps to show their stuff (or at least be in the hunt), mentally strategized their ascents and attacks. The team directors would have the final say about who made a bold move, and when. That information would be revealed each morning at the team breakfast, or as an abrupt command, as a reaction to the events unfolding out on the road.

Not everyone would be told to attack. Those domestiques who stood no chance whatsoever of winning a Tour de France, or placing in the top twenty, or even enjoying a professional cycling career beyond the end of the current season, would be ordered to sacrifice for their team leaders.

Regardless of role or ranking, every rider needed to be fresh. So that rest day ride meant avoiding strenuous climbs, high speeds, and the irrational impulse to perfect their sprinting technique. The combination of fresh oxygen and exercise flushed the garbage out of their muscles and into the bloodstream, where it would be eliminated before the first mountain stage. The rest day ride was a conversational ride. If the riders hadn't been so lean and so poised on the bike — head up, back flat instead of hunched, cadence crisp and effortless — they might easily have been mistaken for a local cycling club with incredibly spiffy uniforms.

For the rest of us, the day off meant getting to Grenoble and securing lodging so we could go about our business. Journalists, officials, riders, and caravan personnel poured into town. Thousands of Tour tourists were there, too. Many spectators had watched the first week at home, then flown to France from around the world to watch the second week in person. Grenoble being the gateway to the Alps, it was only natural they would spend the night in a city with comfortable lodging after their long travels.

In the abstract, the number of people in Grenoble for the

Tour wasn't daunting. But even after removing spectators from the equation, the specific figures were somewhat horrifying, as if we'd all enlisted in a rather determined paramilitary group. The Tour had 60 permanent staff and 200 temporary employees. They were all driving to Grenoble. Some 4,500 people had received accreditation to accompany the Tour or a team in some specific capacity (sponsors, team toadies, caravan, friends of friends), a figure that did not include 2,300 accredited journalists, 1,200 photographers and TV personnel, and 1,100 technicians and drivers. There were also 14 doctors and nurses, 180 technical service providers, and 45 members of the elite Republican Guard, a group of policemen with a permanent scowl and pre-disposition to maintaining order, who were to the average gendarme what the Navy SEAL was to a pimple-faced swabbie fresh out of boot camp.

Not included in those numbers, because they were the Tour equivalent of day laborers, were the 9,000 local police who would assist with stages near their towns, 13,000 additional gendarmes, and the more than 3,000 government officials from the Ministry of Sport (the French government licenses all sports and sporting events, even local clubs) who assisted in some way or other — though I can't say exactly what, because they always seemed to be sipping wine at the VIP area or trying to horn in on the media buffet.

The 189 riders, 11 team directors, and their 11 assistants were actually something of a minority.

It was quite a road show, and everyone needed a place to sleep. That reality had given my drive through Switzerland a greater imperative. But just before checking out of my hotel in Geneva, I got an e-mail message that solved the problem — while adding another.

"Got you and Austin a room at my hotel in Grenoble," Neil Leifer wrote. Leifer is a photographer, and something of a legend. He has shot more than two hundred covers for *Sports Illus-*

trated and *Time*. His subjects are some of the most known figures in sport, from Ali to Nicklaus to Gretzky, with a few presidents thrown in along the way. He was coming to the Tour to shoot yet another legend, Lance Armstrong. A month beforehand, he'd cold-called me to inquire about the best way to get around at the Tour. He was a nice man, in his mid-sixties, with Brooklyn in his voice. During those talks, Leifer let slip that he was so fearful of driving in Europe that he'd never once gotten behind the wheel on that continent in four decades of travel.

There was the rub. I was deeply grateful that Leifer had found me a room to share with my friend Austin Murphy, a writer for *Sports Illustrated*. But there were strings attached: Leifer wanted a spot in the car.

I crossed into France with all the pomp of crossing a state line. I honked the horn just for fun, but otherwise the Citroën was silent as I drove toward Grenoble. I hadn't had road tunes the entire trip because driving while wearing an iPod was a hazard at a hundred-plus. That hadn't really mattered until the Alps could be seen in the far distance. Their silhouettes were hulking and gray, and so high above the horizon that their summits punched up into the clouds. Something about them made me long for noise. I powered toward the Alps with those little white headphones buried in my ears, shifting up and down through that gearbox like it was a video game, finding power in the music and bliss in the feel of a steering wheel in my hands on a blustery, sun-drenched country road.

At Pont de la Caille, a medieval suspension bridge just outside Annecy, I parked and walked to the center. Limestone cliffs dropped deeply into a valley of pine on either side. A small creek burbled hundreds of feet below.

There was a touch of nostalgia on my final push into Grenoble. In eleven days of driving, I had put three thousand miles on the

Citroën — the rough equivalent of New York to Los Angeles. Empty water bottles littered the back; the passenger seat was a convenient map table, perfect for spreading the Michelin atlas, the Tour Roadbook, and a smaller Michelin map I'd recently picked up at a souvenir stand; my notebook and a pen were positioned next to the shifter, just in case something cool happened along the road; and my Asics European Duffle (a three-week bag, with special compartments for running shoes and a waterproof section for dirty and wet clothing) fit ever so snugly in the trunk. The Citroën drove fast, the suspension was tight, and the driver's seat was a molded fit for my backside.

But the time had come to turn it in. Austin and I were going to travel together for the last two weeks of the Tour, and we would need a bigger vehicle.

This would mark the third time we had chased Lance around France together. Austin, who would once again be covering the Tour for *SI,* is wry and witty and strolls through life with a certain swashbuckling panache. Like me, he is a husband and father. We were born just eight weeks apart, giving us a common generational frame of reference. As this was Lance's last stand, we also agreed it would be our last Tour road trip, too. We were going to meet in Grenoble, at the pressroom.

Leifer was the potential monkey wrench. Harmony on a road trip is vital. Putting a photographer into a car with two writers is asking for trouble. Photographers think differently — not just a little differently, but completely the other way around. Their jobs revolve around capturing the moment. A writer's job involves reflecting on the moment from a distance. There is a constant imperative to the photographer's life, a perpetual hustling to be in place to snap that next shot. Writers paint a picture, to be sure, but rarely do they snap one. We have an inevitable patience and parsing to do, a greater flexibility. Despite Leifer's art, and the fact that each photo involves many choices and exclusions, the truth was that we were the ones with the lenses; he was a mirror.

And photographers have *stuff*. So much stuff (cameras, lenses, and whatever else it is they carry in all those shoulder bags) that they often need an assistant. Leifer was fit for a man in his mid-sixties — sort of. But he wasn't going to be climbing Everest with a hundred-pound pack anytime soon. In other words, in addition to needing someone to drive him around, he'd need someone to carry his stuff.

Still, Neil Leifer was, first and foremost, The Legend. "Long after we're dead," Austin had reasoned, "people will still be looking at his pictures. It would be like riding along with history."

The Legend had already made it clear that he longed to perform his professional obligations in the most pristine location possible — no matter where in the name of God along the course that might be — in order to get the most exquisite Lance picture possible. Sometimes this would be tens of miles from the pressroom.

Twice I've taken road trips with photographers. Neither ended well. Room reservation or no, Legend or no, I wasn't sure it was a good idea for Leifer to be in the car.

I crossed the bridge into Grenoble under a blazing summer sun. The city was founded by a Gaulish tribe called the Allobrogi in 43 B.C. It was the scene of the French Revolution's first hostilities in 1788, preceding the uprising in Paris by almost a year. And Grenoble was where Eugène Christophe slipped on the Tour's first-ever yellow jersey, in 1919. Grenoble's history threaded its way through that of France, in a profound way that few other cities could claim.

In my mind, Grenoble had once evoked a mental image of a charming little ski town where everyone talked like Claudine Longet. But the place was boxy and sad. If the Berlin Wall were still up and somebody showed me a picture of Grenoble, I'd swear it was in East Germany. The 1968 Winter Olympics were held here, and the Olympic Village still stood, though nowadays "Olympic Village" meant "really old apartment buildings."

The press center was located inside the former Olympic figure skating venue where, in 1968, Peggy Fleming won her figure skating gold. Several tiers of seats rose to the top of the high ceiling. The banked pine walls of a velodrome now ringed the arena floor, but it wasn't hard to imagine Fleming skating around that room nearly four decades before.

"You going to the press conference?" an American journalist asked me.

"Who's speaking?"

"Jean-Marie Leblanc."

I'd shared an elevator with Jean-Marie back at Hôtel de l'Univers in Tours. He was running from one social engagement to another, and explained, apropos of nothing, that the secret was to have a drink at one party, a second drink at the next cocktail party, salad at the dinner party, and the main course at the final party. It was a politician's life, and it was clear that he reveled in it. When he got off I couldn't help but marvel at his polish and poise. I didn't want to like him, because I remembered the accusations about his pro-Gallic attempts to Lance-proof the course, and wondered if he would do the same to a French rider. But like him I did.

Still, short of canceling the Tour, there was absolutely nothing Jean-Marie had to say that afternoon in Grenoble of interest to me. It was, after all, a day of rest, and I was in no mood for the koans and veiled innuendo that attended his public speaking. The teams were all in seclusion and there was no racing, so there wasn't much for anyone — Leblanc on down — to say. There was a little talk about Jan Ullrich missing a turn and crashing hard the day before, but he had gotten back on the bike and seemed to be all right. Everyone took it in stride that Armstrong had given up yellow on purpose and that Armstrong, Ullrich, Ivan Basso, Floyd Landis, Alexandre Vinokourov, Levi Leipheimer, and perhaps Mickael Rasmussen were the only riders who would matter in the week to come. Jens Voigt, went the thinking, would be smart to sleep in his yellow jersey, because it was going to be snatched from his back in another day.

Because there was no race, the flat-screen monitors hadn't been erected, lending the pressroom a strange quiet. But Grenoble also marked the arrival of a new wave of journalists. They weren't there for the entire Tour, just the second week. With their new credentials and lack of familiarity with Tour routine, they milled around with a tentative air. All that would change once they got their bearings, but for now they looked very lost.

I walked back out into the bright afternoon sunshine, off to find the hotel. My plan was to check in, go for a run, and avoid Neil Leifer at all costs until I could sit down with Austin and figure out what to do with The Legend.

"I was thinking that maybe you and Austin would be interested in covering the Tour from my perspective," Leifer was telling me. We were eating at a sidewalk brasserie shortly after 11:00 p.m. Austin had been delayed in Lyon, so it was up to me to figure out the Leifer situation. The Legend was short, round, talkative, afraid of silence, and confirming my worst suspicions about needing someone to be his chauffeur, valet, photographic assistant, and all-around Man Friday. Yet he was utterly charming. His vignettes about Ali and Steve Prefontaine and Vince Lombardi were entrancing ("and then Muhammad said to me . . .") and his enthusiasm for sport infectious. By the time the salad course was done, I'd promised him a spot in the car. Halfway through the sautéed beef and pureed spinach main course, I was on the verge of tossing aside all my professional obligations and, Sherpa-like, humping his camera bags up and down the Alps — for free.

"It would only be for three days," he was saying. "I need to be at St. Andrews on Friday for Jack's last round at the British

Open. Of course, I need to be in Nice to catch my flight out Thursday evening. I was thinking that you and Austin might be willing to drive me into Nice instead of going to the stage that day."

The notion was appalling — or should have been. And yet it all sounded so logical.

But somewhere in my head, a still, small voice wouldn't give in. The Legend could have a spot in the car, but that was all. "I'll tell you what," I said, putting my fork down and leaning across the table. "I'll do my best to get you where you need to go. But that's all. I need to be at the finish every day. I'm sure that if I drop you off somewhere along the course there will be other photographers who would be glad to give a guy with your reputation a ride to the finish."

"But —"

"Trust me," I said. "It's all going to work out. You're going to get your shots, I'm going to get my stories, and we'll find a way to get you down to Nice on Thursday."

Suddenly, a familiar, grinning face loomed just over Leifer's shoulder. "Hello, everyone," said Austin. It was as if a gust of fresh air had swept across the table. I was so very glad to see my old friend.

Before The Legend could redirect his sales pitch to a more willing listener, Austin added: "I couldn't help overhearing your discussion as I walked up. Eloquently put, Marty."

Austin placed a calming hand on Leifer's shoulder. "Neil, that's exactly what we're going to do. You're in the car. The rest is just details. Welcome to the Tour."

Austin settled into a wicker chair and ordered more wine. The three of us toasted the adventure to come.

Stage Ten

July 12, 2005 — Grenoble–Courchevel
119.35 Miles

Overall Standings

1. Jens Voigt (G), CSC, 32:18:23
2. Christophe Moreau (F), Crédit Agricole, 01:50
3. Lance Armstrong (USA), Discovery Channel, 02:18
4. Mickael Rasmussen (Dk), Rabobank, 02:43
5. Alexandre Vinokourov (Kaz), T-Mobile, 03:20
6. Bobby Julich (USA), CSC, 03:25
7. Ivan Basso (I), CSC, 03:44
8. Jan Ullrich (G), T-Mobile, 03:54
9. Carlos Sastre (Sp), CSC, 03:54
10. George Hincapie (USA), Discovery Channel, 04:05

"TODAY," said Allen Lim, Floyd Landis's coach, "is a definitive day."

Lim was normally a calm man, but he looked nervous, licking his lips and avoiding eye contact. He was speaking of Courchevel, and the Alps, and the way the Tour standings could change dramatically when climbing entered the mix. It could be a change for the better. It could also be a change for the worse — and twelfth-place Landis couldn't afford any slippage. His coach's comments reflected this concern and were not exactly burning with optimism's flame. "I can help him get fit, but now it's out of my control," Lim sighed.

In fact, Landis had trained months for that first day of mountain racing. The twenty-nine-year-old redhead had come into the Tour with high expectations, but it had been an indifferent first week. A subpar opening time trial, a disastrous team trial, and a failure to go with Voigt's attack on the road into Mulhouse had left him 4:08 minutes out of yellow and 1:50 behind Armstrong. Landis had been loose the first few days of the Tour. He was eminently likable, and I rooted for him to do something special to prove his greatness. He had been quick with a joke in those first few days, always making sly comments about his three seasons of servitude on Armstrong's U.S. Postal Team. There had been confidence in his voice, an implied promise that he would somehow find a way to beat Armstrong — and maybe win the Tour. Very often Landis's attitude toward Armstrong was that of a son rebelling against his father. Which was fitting: Landis had been raised a Mennonite and became a professional cyclist against his father's wishes. Landis wanted many things, but perhaps most of all he wanted to be his own man. He had raced mountain bikes at first, becoming American junior national champion before moving to the roads in 1998. The leap couldn't have come at a better time. Mountain biking had soared in popularity during the 1990s, but Armstrong's Tour win in 1999 had once again brought road cycling to the forefront of public consciousness. Audiences — Americans in particular — began paying attention to the Tour as never before. A talented rider like Landis stood a good chance of becoming a star.

It was Armstrong who brought Landis over to U.S. Postal in 2002, lifting him from the bankrupt Mercury team. Landis rode his first Tour that year, serving as a domestique during Armstrong's fourth victory. Never one to buckle to authority, Landis earned a reputation as a dissenter at U.S. Postal. He chafed at the strict diet imposed on the team members during the Tour and the dictatorial manner in which Johan Bruyneel ran the team. Temporarily out of action after suffering a complete fracture of the right hip in a spring 2003 crash, Landis had showed his resilience by coming back stronger than ever. He rode the Tour in July and the Tour of Spain a month later.

That which does not kill a man makes him stronger, and Landis grew stronger each year he rode alongside Armstrong. The highlight of his career came during the seventeenth stage of the 2004 Tour, when Landis was handpicked to lead Armstrong through the pivotal Alpine stage from Bourg-d'Oisans to Le Grand-Bornand. It came the day after Bruyneel had ordered Landis to go easy during a time trial up L'Alpe d'Huez. Landis had pouted, thinking Bruyneel was trying to prevent him from displaying his wares to teams interested in luring him away from U.S. Postal at the end of the season. Landis rebelled. He had one of the faster time trials up L'Alpe d'Huez. Bruyneel angrily accused Landis of riding for himself — of not conserving his strength for the next stage. Bruyneel wanted Landis's legs fresh for the 125-mile stage to Le Grand-Bornand. Landis rode at the very front of the peloton, with Armstrong drafting right behind, calmly telling Landis the names of those riders who had faded away, one by one, thanks to Landis's punishing pace up and down three first-category climbs and one hors catégorie ascent. Landis, as a huge screw-you to Bruyneel, was riding the strongest stage of his life; on occasion he even had to slow down for Armstrong.

The final climb was called the Col de la Croix-Fry. As Landis churned to the summit, only Armstrong, Ullrich, Klöden, and Basso remained on his wheel. The finish line was at the bottom of the mountain, eight miles away.

"Floyd," Armstrong said conspiratorially, pulling alongside Landis as they crested the mountain. "How bad do you want to win a stage in the Tour de France?"

"Real bad," Landis said, his eyes growing wide.

"How fast can you go downhill?"

"Very fast."

Then, as the two Americans — one a maverick Texan, the other a maverick Pennsylvania Mennonite — crested the summit, Lance extended his arm and patted Landis softly on the small of his back. "Run like you stole something, Floyd."

Landis didn't need to be told twice. He sprinted down the mountain, eager to taste his first-ever stage win. Ullrich chased after him.

It is said that to understand the Tour, one must understand France's medieval history and its chivalric knights. Most famous of all was the great Chevalier Bayard, who, as he lay mortally wounded on the field of battle in 1524, asked to be tied to a tree facing the enemy so that he would not die in a pose of retreat.

This legacy of attacking even when the battle is lost is counterbalanced by the practice of rewarding a faithful rider for a job well done. This particular code of chivalry says that when a rider sacrifices himself to pull the race's top four riders up the mountain, and when that rider is so far back in the standings that he is no threat to the yellow jersey, the right thing to do is let him win the stage.

But Ullrich wanted Le Grand-Bornand for himself, violating another bit of Tour etiquette: He had done nothing to earn it. Neither he nor his T-Mobile teammates had spent a minute working at the front of the group all day. Instead, they had luxuriated in the American draft. So Armstrong made things right. He chased down Ullrich and the now-fading Landis, and made a few choice comments to the German about being a wanker and an ingrate. Lance refused to work with Ullrich, so the pace slowed. It became inevitable that Ivan Basso and Andréas Klöden would catch up again. Klöden, sensing Ullrich's mounting fatigue, was next to attack. Once again, Armstrong gave chase. As the two turned down the homestretch, it looked as if Klöden had it locked up. But Armstrong simply would not surrender.

His legs pumped relentlessly, brutally, scarily. He won right at the line, a giddy smile of surprise across his face and his arms thrown up to the heavens.

"Perfect," five-time Tour winner Bernard Hinault told Lance later. "No gifts."

But Le Grand-Bornand was one gift Armstrong had wanted to give. He hugged Landis once the teammate crossed the line. "Sorry, man," Armstrong said. "I wanted you to have that one."

"That's OK," Landis replied. "I'm just glad you got it. I had nothing left." It was one of the most powerful moments of the 2004 Tour, and it was made even more emotional when Armstrong dedicated the victory to Landis.

Now Landis and Armstrong were in the Alps again, only this time there would be no hugging. Landis's off-season leap to Phonak had infuriated Armstrong, who was privately referring to Landis, Tyler Hamilton, and everyone else who had jumped to other teams as "the pieces of shit we got rid of."

Armstrong had gotten the best of Landis during the first week, but this was the day Landis had trained for. He was a climber. To be a cyclist blessed with the ability to climb mountains was to own a singular gift. It was more than just physiology — the abundance of endurance-oriented slow-twitch muscle fibers in the quadriceps and glutes; the long femur for added leverage during the pedal stroke; the lightweight build; and, most of all, the strong heart and bellows-like lungs that powered it all like a great big engine. It was emotional, too. Climbers were mentally tough. They not only endured suffering, they reveled in it.

Some, however, were able to suffer more than others. Men like Armstrong, Greg LeMond, Miguel "Big Mig" Induráin, Eddy Merckx, Marco Pantini, and the other greats persevered when lesser riders cracked. Often, it was their perseverance (and their opponents' knowledge of it) that made the lesser riders crack, because it was a given that these greats would never throw in the towel. Stage Ten was Landis's chance to prove he belonged in a league with those who never surrendered.

The stage would take riders from the heart of Grenoble deep into the heart of the Alps. Jean-Marie Leblanc had done a superior design job. The course was scenic and flat leaving Grenoble, paralleling the autoroute and the tree-lined Isère River on the D523. The landscape was sunburned and the air was dry. The D523, a straight country road, forked to the right after thirty miles and began shimmying back and forth. At that point the riders commenced climbing, ever so slightly. The road led them to Albertville, site of the 1992 Winter Olympics, where the riders pedaled through a pass and into a mountain valley. One minute they were in farmland that smelled like dried grass and manure. The next they were in a deep valley of pine, with mountains jutting to the heavens on either side.

There were just two peaks to climb on Stage Ten. The first was the twelve-mile Cormet-de-Roselend, with an average grade of 6 percent. The other was the Courchevel, a thirteen-mile climb with a slightly steeper gradient. Their summits were fifty miles apart, separated by a long valley. Figuring that it would take the riders almost six hours to finish, the Tour sent them off from Grenoble at 11:40 in the morning, an unusually early start, but necessary if the stage was to finish in time for the French evening news.

The Citroën was gone, replaced by a Volkswagen Passat of the same gunmetal gray. The Passat was fully loaded as we drove to Courchevel: Austin driving, me navigating, and Leifer in back, sharing space with packs and camera equipment. The Legend passed the miles detailing the logistics, thumbs working furiously as he messaged on his BlackBerry.

* * *

By now many of the doubts about Armstrong's fitness had evaporated, so other teams would try to wear him and his teammates down via a series of long breakaways. The tactic worked like a bait and switch. A team such as CSC would send a secondary rider like Bobby Julich on a breakaway. It would probably take place in the twenty-five-mile-long valley between Cormet-de-Roselend and Courchevel. Because Julich was close to Lance Armstrong in the overall rankings (and a threat to win the entire Tour if he actually developed a three-to-four-minute lead), Discovery had to chase him down even though the extra effort would significantly weaken their legs. Meanwhile, CSC's top rider, Ivan Basso, would rest in Discovery's draft during the chase — as would all his teammates. The end result would see Discovery growing increasingly fatigued, Julich either winning or getting caught, and Basso's legs remaining fresh for an attack on the climb.

CSC wasn't the only team thinking like that. T-Mobile could send either Alexandre Vinokourov or Andréas Klöden (thereby protecting Jan Ullrich), and Phonak could send Santiago Botero (protecting Floyd Landis). Each and every one of those attacks would probably fail, but Discovery had to cover them all. Rather than riding at a steady tempo, the Disco Boys would be sprinting after the breaks in explosive bursts, then catching their breath just as the next team made them do it all again. The cumulative fatigue on their legs, if the theory held true, would prove overwhelming.

And Armstrong wasn't even wearing the yellow jersey. Still, all the riders remaining in the race knew that if they were to have a chance, they had to get him out of the way. Wherever he was in the pack, whatever color his jersey, they were all chasing Lance. It seemed as if they always had been.

"What's this word you guys keep calling each other, this 'dude'?" Leifer asked abruptly, pulling us out of the strategy session. "Is that like saying 'hey you'?"

Austin and I paused for a second, amazed that Leifer had never heard the expression before. "Yeah," I said. "Buddy. Hey you."

"Am I a dude?"

"Do you want to be a dude?"

"Yes, I do. I'm in the car with you two guys — you two dudes. I'd like it very much if I could be one, too."

"OK, dude."

We had taken a shortcut around Roselend and were now climbing Courchevel, a stark and hungry peak rising abruptly from that wide valley floor. The jagged mountains rimming the valley were gorgeous, in keeping with the Tour's harsh mentality. The juxtaposition between physical suffering and natural beauty was a Tour hallmark. "This is the thing that sustains me all year, during those trips to Norman or Tallahassee," said Austin, who covered the Tour in July and college football each fall. He was a former player himself, having been a wide receiver for Colgate. Lanky and quick with a free-spirited grin, he still looked the part. "The Rose Bowl is beautiful, with the San Bernardino Mountains — or whatever they call them — in the background, but it ain't no Courchevel."

Austin is fond of words. It is a charming trait. When speaking he selects each syllable for maximum effect. He modulates his pitch, inserts pauses for added drama, and pushes on his consonants for emphasis. His fortes are wry commentary and droll rhetoric. He is the only person I know who can use "alas" in a sentence without sounding pretentious. When he is "on" I find myself reaching for a notebook to record his humor. But as we drove through the French countryside on that sunny July morning, his delivery was too rushed. Adrenaline and the euphoria of returning to the Tour de France had made him uncharacteristically eager. His observations, nonetheless, were keen.

Spectator mania had increased with every passing day, but the leap was exponential as we headed up the steep mountain lane. A phenomenal number of national flags, cycling tour groups, and generally rabid individuals in all manner of dress had parked themselves along every inch of Courchevel's thirteen-mile ascent. There was the guy dressed as Superman, the guy wearing the Texas Longhorns cap, and, of course, Didi Senft, the German cycling fanatic who dressed as a devil. Senft, with his long beard and trident, had been donning the El Diablo getup for so many years that he had not only become a Tour fixture, but found a sponsor, whose logo now beamed from the devil costume and trident.

The glaring valley sun slowly dissipated as we climbed, replaced by low gray-black clouds. Courchevel was a hulking, sprawling eminence, the biggest ski mountain in the world. More than once on the slow and cautious drive (dodging bikes and spectators brandishing the flags of sovereign nations, whether or not that particular country was represented at the Tour), I thought we had reached the summit. But then we would round a curve and see that the actual peak was still miles higher, and on we would climb.

The finish line was atop the mountain, butting up against a high-altitude heliport. (The press center was three miles downhill from the finish.) The Legend, deciding the light at the top was too flat, walked down the mountain a few hundred yards to squeeze off a few shots.

The weather at the top felt like November: cold, threatening, and bleak. The air was frigid and chilled me to the bone. The Alps soared all around. There was an ominous, forbidding quality to them, as if they were capable of perpetrating some great evil.

The chaos in the finish area was total. Press and team functionaries huddled around video monitors to watch the race, keeping one eye on the weather, which was threatening rain. Fans leaned over the railing, many wearing cycling jerseys beneath their jackets. I found a spot in front of a monitor, zipped my fleece all the way up, then settled in to watch the "definitive" day play out.

What I witnessed was nothing less than a show of overwhelming force, the likes of which I had never witnessed before at the Tour. Early on, Johan Bruyneel thwarted any chance of a bait-and-switch tactic by CSC and T-Mobile by demanding that Pavel Padrnos, Benjamin Noval, and Manuel "Triki" Beltran set a rigorous pace up and over Cormet-de-Roselend. Instead of waiting to defend against a breakaway, Bruyneel had decided to launch a breakaway of sorts himself.

Quickly the peloton splintered. Jens Voigt, in the yellow jersey, dropped far off the pace. There had been talk before the stage of Bjarne Riis being such a traditionalist that he would defend yellow even if it weren't in CSC's long-term best interests, but no one from CSC lingered to pace Voigt up the climb. CSC was at the Tour to win, just like Discovery. Their contender was Ivan Basso, who was up front, riding in Armstrong's wake. Voigt was left to fend for himself. He would eventually finish thirty minutes behind the stage winner.

Padrnos, Noval, and Beltran rotated the lead as the Disco Boys powered through the long valley between Roselend and Courchevel. The tempo was apocalyptic, so fast that a Bobby Julich or an Alexandre Vinokourov would have looked like a complete rookie trying to attack. It was like a hustle: Give the challenger a false sense of confidence via a meaningless victory (allow him to break to the front), make the challenger double his bet (maintain an exhausting pace so he cannot break far enough away to relax), then pull the rug out from under him (reel him in and spit him out). It was bicycle strategy as devised by David Mamet and Ricky Jay.

The second shift took over as Courchevel neared. José Azevedo,

José Luis Rubiera, and Paolo Savoldelli had been drafting to the rear of the blue train, just a few feet but light-years in effort distant from Padrnos, Noval, and Beltran. Now these three took over pacing chores for Discovery. As if it were a matter of pride to match their compatriots, their pace was nothing less than sizzling. At the bottom of the long climb up Courchevel, the lead group numbered about fifty. Six miles later it was reduced by a third. The now-wasted Azevedo, Rubiera, and Savoldelli peeled off, their mission accomplished in most spectacular fashion.

The whole time this was going on, Armstrong had been drafting just behind his teammates, grooving on the jet stream of their superhuman tempo. Now he was down to two Disco allies: George Hincapie and the young Yaroslav Popovych. Hincapie, the sly veteran, took the lead next and began grinding upward. Originally, it was Azevedo who was supposed to drag Armstrong through that section of the climb, but he hadn't been feeling well that morning. Hincapie, naturally, had agreed to take his place. There was no flash about Big George, no trash talk, just a solid work ethic and a dependable nature. Hincapie was one of those guys who never made excuses, even if something was impossible. He always found a way to get the job done.

Popovych — "Popo" — hung back with Armstrong, waiting his turn. The Tour rookie rode as if he'd been boning up on Tour tactics his whole life. During the descent of Roselend he had crashed into a CSC team car, slashing his left elbow. Rather than use the debacle as an excuse to save himself for another day or quit the Tour altogether, Popo got right back into the fray. Discovery Team strategy mandated that he be ready to help Armstrong at a critical time in the race. Crash or no, he had to be there.

With seven miles left, Popo was there.

All Armstrong wanted was a slight acceleration of the pace. What Popo gave him was an all-out sprint. The Disco Boys, it seemed, were still embarrassed by their showing the previous

Saturday, and they wanted to make a statement. Popo's dash lasted just a half mile. On flat ground it wouldn't have been so fast — twenty miles an hour, maybe a little more. But climbing the world's largest ski mountain after five torrid hours in the saddle, sucking on the thin air of Courchevel's mile-high summit, Popo destroyed the field, making it possible for Lance Armstrong to sit up, ever so casually, stretch his back, and take a look at who was left. Then Popo peeled off, legs fried and lungs heaving, destined to labor up the rest of the mountain as best he could.

Armstrong didn't see Ullrich as he sat up to take inventory. The German had fallen back. Nor did he see Leipheimer or Klöden or his former domestique Floyd Landis. All that remained was a group of five: Armstrong, Basso, Mickael Rasmussen, and Spaniards Alejandro Valverde and Francisco Mancebo.

Basso couldn't hang. With five miles left, the group was down to four.

The pace kicked up, leaving just Armstrong and Valverde. It was reminiscent of La Mongie the year before, when Armstrong and Basso had dueled the final miles up the mountain. Now Basso was dropping farther and farther back, close to getting passed by Levi Leipheimer. It was Valverde's chance to make a run for it.

I stepped out of the small canopy containing the video screens as Armstrong and Valverde raced the last hundred yards. There was a sense that Armstrong would snatch the victory easily from the young Spanish rider. It was not to be. Valverde won in a sprint. Armstrong reached out to take Valverde's hand as they crossed the line. The Spanish press, which had been holding a vigil at the finish, went crazy. They jumped up and down for joy and then descended upon Valverde as he rolled to a stop. Armstrong was almost lost in the bedlam.

❊   ❊   ❊

Levi Leipheimer's sixth-place finish vaulted him into sixth place overall. Quietly, the Montanan who rode for Team Gerolsteiner was mounting a charge. As for Floyd Landis, he had ridden strongly, finishing 2:14 behind Armstrong. He tried to be casual about it all, making light of his inability to follow the attacks and keep pace with the leaders, saying everyone had had the same problem. But that was the thing: Winning the Tour meant doing things differently from everyone else.

Landis was now in tenth place, more than four minutes out of the yellow jersey — a yellow jersey that belonged once again to Lance Armstrong. There were still a lot of mountains to climb, but four minutes was a whole lot of time to make up on one of the best climbers in Tour history. Landis's hopes of winning the 2005 Tour de France title were all but gone. Realistically, the best he could dream of was finishing in the top three, in order to stand atop that podium in Paris.

It had been a decisive day indeed.

Stage Eleven

July 13, 2005 — Courchevel–Briançon
107.26 Miles

Overall Standings

1. Lance Armstrong (USA), Discovery Channel, 37:11:04
2. Mickael Rasmussen (Dk), Rabobank, 00:38
3. Ivan Basso (I), CSC, 02:40
4. Christophe Moreau (F), Crédit Agricole, 02:42
5. Alejandro Valverde (Sp), Illes Balears, 03:16
6. Levi Leipheimer (USA), Gerolsteiner, 03:58
7. Francisco Mancebo (Sp), Illes Balears, 04:00
8. Jan Ullrich (G), T-Mobile, 04:02
9. Andréas Klöden (G), T-Mobile, 04:16
10. Floyd Landis (USA), Phonak, 04:16

THERE HAD BEEN just one road leading down Courchevel the previous night. The traffic jam had been so atrocious it took us three hours to travel five miles. Austin, The Legend, and I hadn't arrived in Brides-les-Bains, a spa town known for its waters, until after 11:00 p.m. The town had been entirely dark, and our hotel's kitchen had just closed. A kindly waitress in a hurry to go home threw together salads and a cheese plate, then set bottles of red wine and mineral water on our table before disappearing into the night.

The day before, I'd asked Armstrong about the rivalry between Discovery and CSC, and he'd lashed out powerfully at Bjarne Riis's arrogance. It had been a week since Riis had called Armstrong "lucky" to be in yellow, and Lance was still fuming. He glared directly at me as he spoke, as if I were Riis himself. "To say that a six-time Tour de France champion is 'lucky to be wearing the yellow jersey' is not respect, it's not honest, it's not honest — it's not reality." He paused to gather his thoughts, but only for an instant. Sheryl Crow had come into the room and stood just behind his left shoulder. "The CSC riders are some of the classiest in the peloton. We race the riders, not the team director."

Coming hard on the heels of Armstrong's commanding ride up the mountain, this show of rage was a nice injection of color into the Tour. There had been too much circling the first week, too many diplomatic words. Now the gloves were off.

"Good morning, dudes!" Leifer yelled from across the lobby as the elevator doors slid open. He was bathed in morning sunshine. His voice was eager. "Are we ready to go?"

We still weren't sure what to do with Leifer. He was always in a hurry for us to drive him someplace, but he never seemed to do anything when we got there. I guess that was all part of being The Legend: being in the right place, wits about you, prepared for something to happen.

Today in particular, The Legend was in a hurry to get on the course. He'd gotten some shots of Armstrong coming around a switch back on Courcheval, but he wanted to do one better. Not only had the light been bad, but Lance had been wearing the blue-and-white Discovery jersey. Leifer hadn't covered a bike race since the early 1970s and, apparently, lived in some sort of cosmic bubble that made him oblivious to Armstrong's media omnipresence. He had a hard time figuring out exactly which of the riders he was supposed to be photographing. Now that Lance was in yellow, though, Leifer was excited: Armstrong would be impossible to miss. Eighty-six years after the brainstorm,

Henri Desgrange's canny decision to make the Tour leader more visible was still paying dividends.

During a normal stage it was possible to watch the start and the finish, but mountain stages meant picking one or the other. The roads were too few and too impossibly thin for an easy flow of traffic. Add in spectator congestion, and going from start to finish took far longer in a car than on a bicycle. Today we chose the finish.

A left turn took us out of Brides-les-Bains and onto the course. The Michelin atlas depicted the valley roads in red. The squiggles zigged and zagged like an electrocardiogram printout. These red threads were connected to one another by the thinnest, wispiest black lines imaginable — so small and faint that they looked like pencil sketches. Some of those thin black lines didn't even connect with a red line. They just stopped, as if the cartographer had taken a cigarette break and forgotten to pick up where he had left off.

But the black lines possessed a power and beauty belying their size. Those were the mountain roads, the ones leading either up through a mountain pass or up to a summit. Those were the roads that the riders would climb. Those were the lines where dreams were shattered and legends were born.

The Tour was bypassing L'Alpe d'Huez, the most notoriously strenuous mountaintop finish in Tour history, in 2005. But the route would go up and over Col du Galibier, a pass whose degree of difficulty and historical significance was just as great but whose notoriety was slightly less. The Tour rotates the usage of the various Alpine ascents, so despite all my previous trips, the Galibier was a climb I'd never witnessed in person. I was curious to see what all the fuss was about. The total route would be one hundred miles, and the Roadbook told me that it was twenty miles from the village of Saint-Michel-de-Maurienne up to the top of the Galibier — at 8,677 feet, the highest point in the 2005 Tour. An intermediate pass known as the Col du Télégraphe broke the climb into two sections. The two peaks were separated by a brief three-mile loss in elevation before being launched up the Galibier. Basically, it was two mountain summits in one climb.

A mountain summit induces a feral quality in cyclists. They are stripped to their essence: cold, not talking, gasping for breath in the thin air, focused only on surviving the climb. The average rate of incline for the Galibier was 6.9 percent. The top of the mountain would be either cold or in the clouds, or both, so once there, most riders would accept a jacket from the team car so their lungs wouldn't spasm from the frigid air (some preferred to forgo the jacket and adhere to the ancient Tour practice of stuffing a folded section of newspaper under the chest of their jersey) before the perilous twenty-five-mile descent to the finish line at Briançon, during which they would reach speeds of almost 70 mph.

But those were just factoids. Every mountain has a character all its own. Statistics about rate of ascent and length and time to the top couldn't tell me anything about the climb's character. Were the roads newly repaved or were they still buckled and cracked from the winter snows? Were there guardrails or would the cyclists be pedaling, protectionless, along a precipitous drop-off? The width: that of a single car or several broad lanes? And the view: green and lush, or stark? Those, and a thousand other subtle variables, defined a mountain's majesty and the climb's cruelty.

So seeing the Galibier in person was vital. The other climb that day, another hors catégorie monster known as the Col de la Madeleine, came first, however, and it was up her switchbacking slopes that Austin guided the Passat.

The road up the Madeleine was shaded, narrow, lined with sudden drop-offs. Jan Ullrich had attacked on that ascent in 1998, a ballsy move considering that the finish was still more than thirty miles away. He was soon caught by Marco "the Pirate" Pantani, a great Italian climber who would go on to win the Tour that year, then commit suicide shortly after his cycling career wound down six years later. Pantani rode like a mercenary that day, sucking Ullrich's draft and refusing to take a turn up front. Ullrich, unbowed, outsprinted Pantani to the finish by a wheel.

There was none of that drama during our drive. We passed a father dressed as Sylvester the cat, pedaling up the mountain with his two young sons, one dressed as Batman and the other as Anakin Skywalker. The crowds were thick, the sun was shining — even at the top — and everyone was in a festive mood.

Leifer surprised us by announcing he was going to catch a ride with two other photographers at Saint-Michel-de-Maurienne and then meet us at the finish. After dropping The Legend off, we had lunch at the Café L'Encas, a small eatery so close to the course that my chair butted up against the barricades. Every table around us was filled with tourists who had just cycled the Madeleine and were hoping to climb all, or parts, of the Galibier that day. There were two guys from Britain celebrating their fiftieth birthdays, a Tunisian woman with her arms and legs covered for religious purposes, Germans sporting the by-now-obligatory T-Mobile jersey, and, for the first time, Italians. The French-Italian border was just a few miles west, as the crow flies. The international assemblage of cyclists looked relaxed as they ate lunch, sipping sodas and asking their waitress to refill their water bottles, proud of how far they'd already ridden and prouder still of the uphill miles to come.

Later, as we ascended the Galibier, I saw the lot of them again. To a man — and a Tunisian woman — they were suffering mightily. Spit flecked the corners of their mouths, which hung slack-jawed. Many had abandoned the friends they'd been laughing with at the café, preferring to endure the mountain alone. Austin and I honked and waved at our new friends, trying to be polite and encouraging to all those people with whom we'd just broken bread. But each time, they gazed back with blank, unknowing stares, blinking now and then as sweat dripped down off their foreheads and stung their eyes.

I don't think many of them made it up before the riders. By the time Austin and I passed through the Col du Télégraphe, the Tour peloton was already ascending the Madeleine. Soon the amateur cyclists would hear the rumble of a gendarme's motorcycle as the course was swept. They would be asked to pull over to the side and wait for the peloton to pass before beginning again. I had the feeling many would do so gladly.

"Sommet 18 km," read a sign in the village of Valloire, just after the Télégraphe. It was a community where the homes were made of stone and painted dark brown. Once upon a time the pitiful little road snaking up the rocky and treeless mountainside was a smuggler's path. It looked like absolutely nothing I'd ever seen before in France. "A moonscape ringed by mountaintops, jagged like rows of shark's teeth," I wrote in my notebook as the Passat threaded through spectators bundled in fleece. There was no redeeming beauty to the Galibier. It was cold, sharp, and empty, a place for summer blizzards and scavenging crows. Campers lined the road now, parked nose to tail against the incline of the mountain. From far below, it was impossible to see the road itself, but campers and spectator throngs could be seen lining the long, steep switchbacks all the way to the top.

No other peak has been climbed more times at the Tour de France. "In the history of human affairs, does not this ascent of the Galibier on bicycles constitute the first triumph of mortal intelligence over the laws of gravity?" Henri Desgrange wrote in 1911. Shortly after the 1914 Tour, it became the front line for elite mountain troops from Italy and Austria during World War I. In 1939, Desgrange held a special three-part stage, which began at three o'clock in the morning and climbed the Galibier eighteen hours of riding later. Headlights were shined on the road so the racers could see where they were going, and the temperature was just twenty-five degrees. Desgrange waited for the riders at the summit and recorded their times as they went past.

The Galibier was tied to Tour legends like five-time champion Eddy Merckx, who had scaled those slopes in the relentless fashion of Chevalier Bayard. Perhaps he was best remembered not for winning on the Galibier but for finishing third in a 1975 stage despite breaking his jaw during a crash earlier the same day.

In 1993, the year Lance Armstrong raced his first Tour, the Galibier destroyed the young Texan. In his hotel that evening, he had to be talked out of quitting. He went on to race one more stage, then abandoned.

Nothing was easy about the Galibier. In 1998, the fog was so thick coming through the Télégraphe that the riders had had to find their way by following the stripes down the center of the road. Marco Pantani had attacked, despite the risk. He ascended the Galibier cloaked in fog and then raced down the back of the mountain. Pantani's breakaway undid Jan Ullrich, the defending champion. The Italian went on to win the Tour that year, and Ullrich has never been better than second since.

The weather got colder as we climbed. Two women dressed as clowns looked woefully inappropriate amid the bleak surroundings. A man had walked a hundred yards up through the scree in search of a private place to relieve himself, but there was absolutely no place to hide. Hundreds watched as he took a leak.

Thick crowds milled about the road, disregarding the line of Tour vehicles trying to get up and over the top. At some point, we, too, might hear the rumble of the gendarme's motorcycle and the command to stop until the peloton passed.

"Not to alarm you," Austin noted, "but that burning, acrid smell would be our clutch." Austin said. "Can you smell it?"

We pulled over to let it cool, not knowing if that would do any good. While Austin jotted some quick notes, I wandered over to a motor home where a large international crowd was gathered to

watch the race via satellite dish. The ever-unpredictable Alexandre Vinokourov, wearing his sea foam green jersey that indicated
he was Kazakhstan's national cycling champion, was leading a
small group toward the summit of the Madeleine. Vino was a
dangerous and explosive rider with so much talent that there
were rumors Discovery wanted him to take over as team leader
when Armstrong retired. A bad first week saw him in sixteenth
place going into the stage. Vino could move up very far in the
rankings with a strong performance, effectively attacking his way
back into the race. His Achilles' heel had been bad tactical
choices, but Vino was definitely a rider to be taken seriously.

Santiago Botero of Phonak was chasing him. Chris Horner, the
thirty-four-year-old American rookie, had made good on his plan
to attack in the mountains, but he couldn't hold Vino's wheel and
was dropping back. Meanwhile, Discovery Channel was once
again riding in tight formation, their blue train looking invincible.

Vinokourov had diverged from the peloton just eighteen
miles into the stage, trying to ride from one breakaway group to
another — "bridging up," as it was called — to an early breakaway. With his climbing skills, Vino definitely had the ability to
win the stage. Discovery's mission was to either catch him or
minimize his advantage.

As he crested the Madeleine, Vino had fifty seconds between
his small pack and Discovery, who were jerkily pulling the peloton up the mountain as if yanking themselves up a knotted rope.

Though enjoying the scene around the motor home immensely,
I raced back to the Passat. The final miles to the top grew more
and more congested, and the weather grew more inhospitable.
We entered the clouds. Fans sat on the edge of sheer drop-offs.
One of the Tour's rolling souvenir boutique vans died just below
the summit. Even as the line of cars grew longer and longer behind
the stalled vehicle, the gendarmes refused to allow anyone to
pass because they were afraid that a crash would block the road
entirely or a car would go over the edge.

Eventually Austin and I were up and over the historic Galibier, leaving the lunar landscape behind as we descended carefully into a long green valley. The road was officially known as the D902. A third of the way down the back side, it merged with the N91, which we followed clear through to the finish in Briançon. We parked the Passat on a muddy soccer field and ran straight for the pressroom to claim a spot in front of the monitors.

The question of the day wasn't whether Armstrong could win the stage — that wasn't important — but whether Vino's break-away would succeed. In fact, Vino grew stronger as the day went on. His lead as he passed through the Télégraphe was two min-utes over Discovery and the rest of the peloton, which was now being towed by George Hincapie. Vino soon dropped Botero. And then Vinokourov was climbing the storied switchbacks of the Galibier all alone.

The sight of the peloton charging in a broad phalanx up a mountainside can be stirring. But even more remarkable is the sight of a lone man charging upward unaccompanied. There is no one to help him. He must constantly quiet fears of his legs going dead halfway up the mountain and that gnawing anxiety that the ever-predatory peloton will gobble him up just a breath before the summit.

Vino's lead was 2:40 over Santiago Botero as he crested the Galibier. But Vino descended poorly, and Botero caught up. Together they raced down the N91 into Briançon, through Le Monêtier-les-Bains, with last year's Christmas lights still strung over the road, and Villeneuve and its commanding views of the Glacier Blanc. Vino and Botero, who knew each other well from their days as T-Mobile teammates, took turns pacing off of each other. Meanwhile, Discovery and the peloton were 2:30 behind. Mickael Rasmussen had continued his stranglehold on the polka-dotted jersey by sprinting away just before the summit to gain additional points. Rasmussen, much to everyone's surprise, had furtively scrambled to second place in the overall standings thanks to his big breakaway win of the ninth stage. He was just thirty-eight seconds behind Armstrong, close enough that the American had promised there would be no breakaways for Rasmussen.

The Dane was the Tour's new wild card. Everyone knew Rasmussen could climb. If he could time-trial just as well, the canny redhead stood a very good chance of making a run at yellow in Paris.

To be sure, Rasmussen wasn't going to try to make up those thirty-eight seconds before Briançon. The long and broad descents didn't favor him like the serpentine drop into Mulhouse. The Dane let the blue train swallow him up as it began chasing Vino down.

The finish-line crowds were expectant, tired. They'd been guarding their spots along the barricades since early morning. Close to the finish banner, they were Americans and Germans. Farther down they were French, and more plainspoken, wearing the polka-dotted caps passed out by the caravan. One and all, they peered down the finish corridor, waiting to see who would arrive first. Would it be Vino or would it be Botero? Or would the peloton have chased them down?

It was midnight. The stage was long over. Headlights came over the Galibier in a seemingly endless stream, cutting the darkness on the N91 like phosphorescence trailing the predawn wake of an aircraft carrier. The Tour's legion of trucks was just coming down the Galibier, having transported all the starting-line materials over that skinny former smugglers' trail where wars had been waged on and off the bike.

I couldn't imagine what it was like navigating a big rig around those switchbacks, with their long drop-offs, in the dark. And frankly, I was too tired to try. I stood beside the road as the trucks trundled past. The blacktop rumbled under the weight and vibration of the eighteen-wheelers. I could feel a whoosh of air as each one rolled by me. It had been a full day of driving and movement and crowds and processing information. I just wanted to stand there in the chill night air and decompress. The trucks were somehow calming.

Austin and I had arrived at the place where we would spend the night a half hour earlier. I had stepped into the chill Alpine air to clear my head after a long, exciting day. Now I walked back inside to eat, figuring I was on the verge of being missed. Leifer and Austin were upstairs in the restaurant, with a new addition to the group. Sportswriter Rick Reilly had joined us that evening. Like Leifer, the tall and ever-bantering Reilly was there for just a few days. He had his own car, however, a Mercedes sedan, meaning he didn't need a spot in the Passat. We had all driven back up the road from Briançon to where we'd found a place to stay near the Christmas lights in Le Monêtier-les-Bains. Instead of a hotel, we'd procured an entire ski condo for the price of a double room. It was rustic and charming, if a tad on the family-oriented side. Instead of a king or queen, or even a double, a pine bunk bed awaited in my loft.

"The motto of the Tour, as far as I'm concerned," Reilly was saying as I reentered the dining room, "is *'je suis fucked.'* This is the hardest event to cover in the world. Something's always going wrong." As the waitress, a plump girl in a peasant costume, brought a salad of wild greens garnished with a purple wild-flower, Reilly told the story of the journalist who showed up at the press center with two black eyes. "He got so frustrated from being lost that he started punching himself in the face. He just kept hitting himself, and then he shows up with these black eyes. Unbelievable.

"And one time," Reilly continued, "the parking lot for the press was actually inside a stadium. But when I came out, it was all locked. Can you believe that? A padlock! I tried to break it with a crowbar, but it wouldn't budge. Just when I didn't know what was going to happen next, this angel comes out of nowhere with a key. Amazing."

"Everyone has a bad Tour story," Austin agreed, before launching into one of his own. The Tour was like life, went the theme. It was hard for everyone, but in that struggle were moments of transcendent, often unnoticed, bliss.

The main course was roast duck with blueberry sauce. It was followed by peach and rose ice cream, served with a macaroon. We sat there for hours, swapping Tour stories, laughing about the dozens of times we'd gotten utterly, hopelessly lost. The room had wood floors and tables, with low-beamed ceilings. It looked like the country inn where Porthos fights for his dinner in *The Three Musketeers*. There was wine, of course, and tomorrow was another early day. We weren't bitching about the hardships. We were reveling in them. This was July and we were in France, at the Tour. There was no place on earth we'd rather have been.

"So," Austin said just before we called it a night. Leifer had told a behind-the-scenes story about Muhammad Ali and Mike Tyson. "How about Vino?" The Kazakh had won the stage, out-sprinting Botero to cap his heroic outing.

"I thought they were gonna catch him," I said.

"I'm glad he got the win."

"But you know what, don't ya?" Reilly interjected. "Vino's never catching Lance. There's no way."

"There's always the Pyrenees," said Austin.

"Nah," Reilly said. "There's no way. Lance'll crush them all."

We sat quietly for a few seconds.

"Shall we call it a night, dudes?" said Leifer.

"Yeah. Tomorrow's Bastille Day," I replied. It was a national holiday. The roads were sure to be choked with patriotic Frenchmen. "We need to get an early start."

Stage Twelve

July 14, 2005 — Briançon–Digne-les-Bains
115.94 Miles

Overall Standings

1. Lance Armstrong (USA), Discovery Channel, 41:59:57
2. Mickael Rasmussen (Dk), Rabobank, 00:38
3. Christophe Moreau (F), Crédit Agricole, 02:34
4. Ivan Basso (I), CSC, 02:40
5. Alejandro Valverde (Sp), Illes Balears, 03:16
6. Santiago Botero (Col), Phonak, 03:48
7. Levi Leipheimer (USA), Gerolsteiner, 03:58
8. Francisco Mancebo (Sp), Illes Balears, 04:00
9. Jan Ullrich (G), T-Mobile, 04:02
10. Andréas Klöden (G), T-Mobile, 04:16

BASTILLE DAY would be the Tour's last stage in the Alps. I was glad we were pushing on to Provence and the storied south of France, but it was hard saying good-bye to all that pristine, often terrifying, mountain beauty. A new city every day — that was the Tour. In a place like Grenoble, it was something of a blessing. But in Le Monêtier-les-Bains, with its twelfth-century church, smell of mountain pines, and nearby meadows full of brown-and-white cows, I felt the urge to linger.

Bastille Day marks the beginning of the French Revolution in

1789, when the people of France overthrew King Louis XVI and France became a government of the people for the first time. A mob of citizens stormed the Bastille, a fortress in Paris. Originally constructed in 1382 to defend the east side of the city, the Bastille had walls eighty feet high and was surrounded by a moat. It took its name from *bastide,* the French word for fortification.

The infamous Cardinal Richelieu, chief minister to Louis XIII, first began to use the imposing structure as a prison in the early seventeenth century. Richelieu, who once said, "If you give me six lines written by the most honest man, I will find something in them to hang him," made the Bastille a symbol of torture and religious and political repression. This reputation persisted throughout the eighteenth century, though by 1789 conditions had changed so much that wealthy prisoners were allowed to bring in their own furniture and members of their household staff to cook and care for them. It was actually somewhat cushy for an eighteenth-century jail, and on July 14, 1789, just seven prisoners were located inside those great walls.

But a symbol is a symbol, and the people of Paris had long since tired of the oppressive King Louis XVI and his wife, Marie Antoinette. French citizens took up arms and attacked the Bastille after hearing that troops were being sent out to crush their growing rebellion. Some three hundred sympathetic guards deserted their regiments in support of the cause, and the Bastille's short-staffed garrison surrendered after a long day of fighting. The seven prisoners were duly released. More than eighty attackers (and, curiously, just one defender) had died.

Subsequently, France became a republic, no longer ruled by a monarch. Four years later, the new government of the people made this official by forcing Louis XVI to his knees in the Place de la Concorde, built to honor his father, where they chopped off his head, thus making him the first person ever executed there. Many more would follow, including his queen, Marie Antoinette, who met the guillotine ten months later.

The monarchy was restored in 1814, after the fall of Napoleon. A lasting republic wasn't formed until 1871, and the first Bastille Day was celebrated nine years later, when it appeared that the concept of democracy just might take.

The French are a fiercely nationalistic people. Jean-Marie Leblanc's disdain for the Tour's six-time American champion was just one example. (The emotion wasn't anti-American: The French were similarly aghast when Belgian Eddy Merckx was so dominant in the late 1960s.) Strangely, however, I didn't see a single French flag being flown in the early hours of Bastille Day. From Briançon down to Digne-les-Bains, I saw farms, castles, orchards, vineyards, a house shaped like a witch's hat, and a man waterskiing without a wet suit in the glacial runoff of Lac de Serre-Ponçon, with its aquamarine coloring. I saw olive trees and purple fields of lavender sprouting under a hot summer sun. But I didn't see a single tricolor.

What made it all the more odd was that French cyclists treated Bastille Day with a powerful reverence. They went all out to grab the win, attacking early and often. Sixteen French riders had won the Bastille Day stage since World War II, most recently Richard Virenque in 2004. To win a Tour stage on Bastille Day was to earn lifetime glory in France. It was the sort of thing people remembered long after a man's cycling days were over, and would eventually be the lead sentences in his obituary. It was that important.

The 116-mile push from Briançon due south to Digne-les-Bains, which called itself the capital of lavender, seemed to offer the perfect opportunity for a Frenchman to win once again. It was a transitional stage, the first of two relatively easy days before the peloton confronted the Pyrenees. The definition of "easy" had changed somewhat, thanks to the Alps' severity. There were two second-category, two fourth-category, and a

third-category climb en route to Digne-les-Bains. The week
before, such a stage would have been considered downright
punishing. Not now.

Also in the French favor was the fact that the overall leaders
wouldn't be interested in winning on a day like this, preferring to
rest their legs after the Galibier. A rider like Vinokourov or Ullrich, seeking to move up in the rankings, would be unlikely to
attack. It would wreck his muscles for the Pyrenees. No, it was
far more entertaining to lie back and watch the French cyclists
expend their own legs with their kamikaze attacks.

Out of the 189 official starters, there were still 162 riders left
in the race. Only the top 21 were within ten minutes of Lance
Armstrong in the rankings. Only the top 75 were within an hour.
And 12 riders were more than two hours back. This was a day for
guys like that, a day for the meek to ride like hell.

There was a different mood in the air as the twelfth stage got
under way. The Tour was more than half over. The riders were
more relaxed and approachable, particularly the ones who were
far out of contention. Journalists began to talk about what they
would do and where they would stay in Paris. For the first time
all Tour, great numbers of riders began showing up in the prerace village, making free calls and checking their e-mails at the
France Telecom booth, or getting a haircut at the small salon by
the Crédit Lyonnais newspaper stand. Their bikes were always
with them, and I was reminded of something Greg LeMond
once told me, that "a cyclist without his bike is like a soldier
without a gun." Indeed, they didn't just walk their bikes through
the village but rode them, weaving through the crowds just as
nimbly as if on foot.

The rollout came a half hour before noon. Historic
Briançon — founded by the Greeks, inhabited by the Romans,
fortified by the Celts, destroyed and rebuilt by Louis XIV, and

defended from outside invasion during the Napoleonic wars —
was left behind. For eighty years, the Tour had made Briançon
such a regular stopover that the city's slogan was "Capital of
Cycling." The riders pedaled away, knowing they were bound to
return someday, in some future Tour — except, of course, Lance
Armstrong. For him, this was a final departure.

The drama between Team CSC and Discovery Channel was
simmering, but Disco had the upper hand. Jens Voigt had been
eliminated for not meeting the cutoff time the day before, making him the second CSC yellow jersey wearer to abandon the
race. This would damage Ivan Basso in the Pyrenees, as he
would have fewer riders to help him up the long climbs.

Voigt had never fully recovered from the long dash into Mulhouse that saw him don the yellow jersey. He was barely able to
walk after the stage from Grenoble to Courchevel, and it was a
testament to the German's will that he had been able to ride
something as daunting as the Galibier the following day. The
time cutoff was a maddeningly obtuse figure, dependent on the
stage winner's final time and overall speed, so a rider never knew
how close he might be to missing it while actually riding the
stage. But the simple math was that Voigt had finished more
than forty minutes behind Vino, so he was out.

The entire Discovery Team roster — the nine Tour riders and
the non-Tour developmental B team — consisted of twenty-
eight riders. Armstrong made millions of dollars per year, his
Tour team made salaries in the low to mid six figures, and the
rest earned mid-five-figure salaries. The team had been chosen
so well over the years that an Armstrong-led squad had not had a
rider abandon the Tour since 2001, when Christian Vande Velde
broke his arm.

But as soon as we walked into the media room in Digne-les-
Bains, word came that Manuel "Triki" Beltran had crashed during the day's first climb. Apparently, he had clipped wheels with
a Phonak rider and gone down hard on his face. Beltran got back

on his bike and rode for almost ten more miles, but he had little strength and was so disoriented that he thought himself to be the race leader. Bruyneel yanked him from the course and had Beltran taken to a nearby hospital. By the next morning, Triki would be on a plane for home.

On the surface, the loss of just one rider was a small thing, but Triki (the nickname came from a brand of cookies he had been fond of as a child) was a mainstay of the Spanish Armada. He had been relatively ineffective thus far in 2005, relegated to flat-land pulls instead of the major climbs that had been his forte, but with the entire Tour likely to be decided in the Pyrenees, it was vital that Armstrong have all the protection he could muster. Now Lance was down a man, and it was anyone's guess what might happen.

One thing was certain: Alexandre Vinokourov was the only rider who'd taken a serious shot at Lance so far. Time was running out. After the upcoming climb of the Pla-d'Adet, the mountains would be done, and with them, the chance to attack and take big chunks of time out of Lance Armstrong's lead.

Digne-les-Bains took its hospitality seriously. Every journalist received a bouquet of lavender upon entering the press center, as well as a gift bag with a jar of tapenade made from local olives. The town's population certainly contained the stereotypical Frenchman or two (cigarette in the corner of his mouth, baguette sticking from his bicycle pannier, a glass of Pernod and water in one hand), but also revealed a chic Italian and North African look. Napoleon had stopped in Digne-les-Bains on his return from exile, and the city's leaders appreciated that having a stage end in their *ville* on Bastille Day provided them yet another sliver of French history.

The stage was proceeding as projected, with French riders launching themselves off the front in waves of frantic, hopeful breakaways. Armstrong, Basso, Ullrich, and all the other major players were riding comfortably, getting their legs back and keeping a wary eye on one another. Rather than try to keep up with all the breakaways, which were so frequent that I couldn't make sense of who was in front and who was fading, I just determined that I would enjoy the afternoon in the sun. Then, when the winner approached, I would wander over to the finish area and be surprised at the identity of the first rider crossing the line. The French had had nothing to cheer about so far at the Tour. They deserved a hero to call their own.

They got one.

David Moncoutié, a Frenchman riding for Team Cofidis, broke away with just over twenty miles remaining and rode powerfully to victory. The elfin Moncoutié wore a look of disbelief as he crossed the finish line, a look that grew even more wide-eyed as he pedaled into the scrum of waiting French journalists. Moncoutié was frail and wobbly as he stepped off his bike, and more than a little dazed. But there was no denying the sheer joy emanating from his being.

"So what'd you do with Leifer?" Rick Reilly asked Austin and me. The great sportswriter mysteriously disappeared each morning, then rendezvoused with us at mealtimes and after hours. We were eating dinner just outside Aix-en-Provence, in a restaurant that had just lost its Michelin stars. This was the culinary equivalent of a general being demoted to captain. Our waiter, a prim and uptight man in an immaculate black suit, still seemed to be mourning the loss, distressed at the sort of people the restaurant now attracted — in particular, three unshowered Americans in shorts and T-shirts, with plastic Tour credentials around their necks. He watched us carefully.

"We got him a train," said Austin. "Dropped him at the station in Digne-les-Bains, gave him a big hug, and sent him on his way."

"He should be boarding his flight to Edinburgh right about now," I added.

The root of my frustration with Leifer, I had realized earlier, was more than just the broad chasm between writer and photographer. I secretly envied him his legendary status. Everyone, at one time in their life or another, takes a hard look in the mirror and asks if they are living life to its fullest. Watching the constant displays of human excellence at the Tour had made such thoughts a daily occurrence for me. The daily struggle to push myself to be my best often felt fruitless. I wondered sometimes where I was going and whether I would achieve all the goals I'd set for myself. There were times when those questions mocked me because I'd feel myself coming up so short. There's an old proverb that says that "a man is never old until regrets take the place of his dreams." Some days, try as I might to remember the biblical saying that perseverance produced hope, I felt very old.

And then there was The Legend, floating through life, all questions as to whether he had the right stuff long since decided in his favor. In the pressroom, there were photographers who would approach Leifer in the same way that fans would line up alongside the Discovery Team bus. They all wanted to be in proximity to greatness, perhaps as if they lacked the hope and perseverance to ever get there themselves. That arrival at his destiny — that self-fulfillment of becoming the man he'd always longed to be — was the same reason David Moncoutié was smiling so broadly after winning the stage. He'd done it, he'd really done it. The hope that had carried him through long days of training and given him the courage to launch a breakaway on Bastille Day after so many others had failed, had been justified. He'd pushed himself to the very limit, escaped the anonymity of midpeloton status, and achieved a moment of greatness.

But was it really greatness? Or was it that Shackletonian ideal of self-conquest through endurance? Something sublime lay on the other side of the conquest. I wanted to know what it was. I wanted to be *there*. Perhaps if I chased Lance to the end, I might get a peek at it.

Stage Thirteen

July 15, 2005 — Miramas–Montpellier
107.57 Miles

Overall Standings

1. Lance Armstrong (USA), Discovery Channel, 46:30:36
2. Mickael Rasmussen (Dk), Rabobank, 00:38
3. Christophe Moreau (F), Crédit Agricole, 02:34
4. Ivan Basso (I), CSC, 02:40
5. Alejandro Valverde (Sp), Illes Balears, 03:16
6. Santiago Botero (Col), Phonak, 03:48
7. Levi Leipheimer (USA), Gerolsteiner, 03:58
8. Francisco Mancebo (Sp), Illes Balears, 04:00
9. Jan Ullrich (G), T-Mobile, 04:02
10. Andréas Klöden (G), T-Mobile, 04:16

PROVENCE WAS SUBLIME at sunrise, baby blue sky limned by pale orange. The soil was the deep red of the African savannah, and the forests of pines contrasted sharply with the barren valley. It was a comfortable time, perfect for sipping coffee and writing lists. It was the day for one last transitional stage before the Pyrenees, and a sense of laziness should have endured from dawn to dusk. But it did not. That morning reverie dissolved as the sun inched higher into the sky, and the day soon became a frantic assemblage of images and experiences and miscues.

"I'm looking for Chris Horner," I said, poking my head inside a yellow team bus an hour before the start. Horner's was the lone bus without a crowd.

Horner's career had been spent in spots such as California's Redlands Bicycle Classic, the Tour of Georgia, and Italy's Tirreno-Adriatico, which he had raced in March 2005 after signing a one-year contract with Saunier Duval. Horner had crashed hard at that race, broken his hip, and gone back home to Bend, Oregon, to heal. His chances of making Saunier Duval's Tour roster had appeared slim. Yet he recovered quickly and was back on the bike soon enough to race June's Tour of Switzerland. Horner won a stage and soon found himself as a last-minute addition to the Saunier Duval Tour squad.

Twelve stages in, I wanted to know how Horner was hanging in there. Until now, the longest bike race of his life had been just twelve stages. He would almost double that at the Tour de France. But the bus driver wagged a finger in my face, reminding me that the riders were not to be bothered before the stage.

I moved on, figuring I'd come back. The Gerolsteiner bus was on the other side of the road. Levi Leipheimer's mother, Yvonne, stood outside wearing a Gerolsteiner blue T-shirt with "Levi" across the front. "It's very exciting," she said softly, then walked over and hugged her boy as he stepped out into the sunlight. Levi had the build of a jockey and a pained look on his face that said he'd rather be anywhere but in Miramas, answering questions. His replies were curt and standoffish, as befitting a man conserving his strength. The Swiss press, for reasons that weren't entirely clear, were deeply concerned that Leipheimer wasn't getting along with his teammates, and pointed to rumors that he ate alone and didn't have a roommate. "I came late for breakfast," Leipheimer said testily to the first rumor. "There are nine guys on the team," the plainspoken Montanan commented with a shrug about the second. "Someone has to have their own room. I'm not taking any chances. I don't want to get sick."

When one of the Swiss tried to shake his hand, Leipheimer recoiled. As with most of the riders, his lean body weight and the rigors of the Tour were wreaking havoc on his immune system. The germs spread through a simple handshake might be enough to give him a cough or a runny nose, which would compromise his ability to perform. Even a modest loss of fitness would mean seconds in the mountains.

"Levi," said a thin brunette with a microphone. She touched his arm as she spoke. "I'm Christi Anderson. I'm with Eurosport."

Leipheimer looked at her funny, then nodded his head without smiling. "I recognize your voice."

Christi did live commentary for the European television giant's English-language broadcasts. Her face was seen infrequently, but her voice-overs were a regular part of the broadcast. Somewhat out of character, Leipheimer spoke to her warmly before disappearing back inside the bus.

I knew Christi from previous Tours. She was married to a former professional cyclist and seemed to have a million insider contacts. She worked the Tour gossip like no one else. "Levi's a good guy," she told me as we walked away. "Very intense, but a good guy. They're saying his goal is to finish in the top five, not to win it all."

She nodded toward the small army around the Discovery bus. Some guy with a trumpet was playing "The Yellow Rose of Texas" from deep in their midst. I couldn't see him, but the bell of his instrument was angled upward and gleaming in the sun. He was very good; probably played in a marching band somewhere. The song had been funny and sort of cool the first time he had belted it out that morning. But after the tenth time I wanted to rip the trumpet from his lips and throw it under the wheels of a moving bus. I felt horrible for the person standing next to him.

"Lance is ready to be done," Christi told me as we walked

toward the Saunier Duval bus. "He's talking a lot about being through with the suffering. But he's a little nervous because this will be the first time since 2001 that he's got less than a full team going into the second set of mountains — and the second set of mountains is always toughest. It's like the Alps was just a warm-up for what we're going to see this weekend."

She switched from rider to rider without pausing for breath, as if reading off a checklist:

"Landis can't mention Discovery without dropping an F-bomb first.

"Julich is mentally scared of Lance. He won't attack him.

"Lance knows that Ullrich gets complacent when he's praised. Have you noticed how complimentary he's been toward him lately?"

My favorite was her appraisal of the need for mental strength. "It's all about having a big set," she said in closing. "The upper ten percent of the riders all have a big set of balls. Lance only has one, but it's a very big one."

Provence had gone from sublime to harsh. By midmorning the temperature was approaching a hundred. The loudspeaker was blaring Queen's "Don't Stop Me Now" in the prerace village, its reference to a character called "Mr. Fahrenheit" an homage to the heat. I didn't know what bothered me more: the fact that I was on the verge of sweating through my shirt or that the daily morning Camembert had been replaced by hard sausage.

Every rider in contention had a following of sorts around his bus, a group of stellar fans eager to use their enthusiasm as a motivational tool. The Lance fans were the most numerous, but every team had a group that followed it just as doggedly. Like a New York Yankees fan zealous about memorizing batting averages or a Manchester United fanatic who makes the strengths and weaknesses of midfielders his avocation, the fans were fervent and a tad more than loyal. Some adhered to the barricades, ignoring the metal ridge pressing into their bellies, just to see the riders in the flesh. Others wielded a quiver of programs, old posters, and Sharpie pens, anxious for the definitive encounter with their idols.

I walked back to the only bus without a crowd. Poking my head inside the yellow bus once again, I asked the driver for Horner. This time he shut the door in my face.

The rejection left me perversely emboldened. I vowed to come back, and continued my wanderings. The T-Mobile bus was also shut. Like Discovery, the Germans ran a tight ship. Over at CSC, Bjarne Riis was talking in somber tones to the Danish press. The Rabobank area was unusually crowded because Mickael Rasmussen was ranked second in the standings.

Rick Reilly was wandering between buses, too, a black sock hanging from each hand. He'd washed them that morning and didn't want to put them on until they were dry. Now and again Reilly flapped his arms to get a little air circulating, hoping that this would combine with the heat to wick away the moisture. To the crowd, he looked like yet another fanatic, and people struggled to understand the meaning of his obscure performance.

Austin was over at the Discovery bus soaking up atmosphere. "I got Lance," he said as casually as noting the time of day. Austin was on deadline, and his story needed a few Armstrong quotes. Mark Higgins, Lance's press liaison, had just sallied out to confirm the interview. Austin couldn't have looked more relieved if he had tried.

"Yellow Rose" drowned out my response, so we bumped knuckles in a wordless, fratenal act of congratulation.

"I would pay him to never play that again," Austin said.

Nearby, a woman with an American flag wrapped around her shoulders like a shawl was sharing her story about recovery from serious injury, thanks to Armstrong's inspiration. Next to her was a young woman barely confined inside a burnt orange Texas Longhorns tank top. As she leaned forward against the barricade, her breasts spilled almost entirely out of the top. The Disco bus was often like that: the person inspired by Lance and the person seeking to inspire Lance, side by side, longing to be noticed.

I walked over to give Horner one last try. The bus door was open again. The driver took one look at me and walked toward the back. I was about to head off again when he reappeared with a team official who spoke English. He was thin and wore an elegant Italian T-shirt. "Chris Horner is not on this team," the official said. "This is Cofidis. Chris Horner is over there, on Saunier Duval."

The mistake was, to say the least, embarrassing. The two buses looked nothing alike. But I laughed it off and thanked the Frenchmen for their time. The Tour never got out of control, but sometimes it got a little disorienting. Too much wine, too much distance, too many hotel rooms, too much. No one was immune — certainly not me.

Today would mark the end of the Tour's second week. The first seven days had had a certain pace to them, with an ongoing buildup. The second week had been a rocket-sled ride, one thrill after the other. Now the Tour was passing through the Gard region on its way from Miramas to Montpellier. The forested province had once been a Roman bastion, and evidence of that imperial age could still be found striding across the countryside. Outside Nîmes was the Pont du Gard, one of the most famous of all the Roman aqueducts, a three-tiered span built in 19 B.C. It was a ruin that had special meaning for me. In 1832, a distant forefather of mine had had a somewhat epic argument with his parents — so epic, in fact, that he ran away from his London home and stowed away on a ship bound from Liverpool to America. To escape detection, he assumed his stepmother's maiden name. As a result, I have a French surname that coincides with that of the great aqueduct, but not a drop of French blood in my body.

Miramas, once known for its explosives industry, and Montpellier were both on the Mediterranean. The day's course was a lazy parabola that wandered inland through pine forests and along limestone cliffs. The landscape was essentially flat, making it a perfect day for the sprinters and breakaway artists. The heat meant that Lance Armstrong and the other riders in the top ten would ride conservatively; striving too hard might dehydrate them for the long push into the Pyrenees the next day. The riders would be drinking a lot of water on the road between Miramas and Montpellier, seeking to ensure that they replaced all they were sweating out. That which didn't get sweated out would be eliminated through urination. The riders were quite adept at veering to the side of the road and pushing down their shorts to urinate as they pedaled. It was too costly, time-wise, to stop.

The finish in Montpellier was next to a huge sports stadium. As we waited, the video monitors showed that Chris Horner was attempting to break away. He'd assured me that morning that he was going to rest up for the mountains and that his legs were still aching from the Galibier, but he was doing anything but resting. He had sprinted away from the peloton with a five-man group just twelve miles into the stage. That group was Horner, Juan Antonio Flecha, Carlos da Cruz, Ludovic Turpin, and Thomas Voeckler. Horner, in twenty-eighth place, was the highest ranked of the five in the overall standings. At more than fifteen minutes behind Armstrong, he was no threat to yellow. The peloton had let them go.

But it wasn't that simple. Such a long break would mean riding for more than a hundred miles at lightning speed to keep the peloton at bay. Horner didn't seem to mind. He was just half-way through as I watched him cycling through the village of Garrigues-Sainte-Eulalie, which was named for a third-century virgin martyr, and Horner, the Tour virgin, looked fearless. He had come to France in search of a stage win, and I was rooting for him to get one. If only for his Bayardesque relentlessness, Horner was worthy.

I took a walk down to the finish area, on the Avenue d'Heidel-berg. It was lined with fans, of course. Montpellier was a cross-roads town, a favorite stopover for tourists traveling from Barcelona through the south of France to Italy. The high-speed TGV train made it possible for fans from Paris to travel to Mont-pellier in just four hours. The idea of combining a trip to the Mediterranean beaches with time at the Tour had drawn an enormous and varied crowd. A North African Muslim contin-gent gave the day just a hint of culture clash.

Veering into the Tour's backstage area, I halted at the gate leading into the podium amphitheater. Amazingly, the gate was unattended, so I walked in. I climbed the steps leading up through the back door of the inflatable gray shell. A wall divided the rear of the amphitheater from the podium area. At the base of the wall were small storage shelves. At the end of each stage, the various jerseys for the podium ceremony would be quickly silk-screened with the logos of the winning riders' teams, then stored on these shelves while awaiting the presentation.

Nobody was coming to drag me out of the amphitheater, so I ventured out from behind the wall and stood next to the podium itself. Now the fans along the course could see me. They looked up with curiosity, having little else to distract them while they waited for the riders.

I walked up the steps of the podium and stood on top, as if waiting for my yellow jersey to be presented. I resisted the urge to throw up my arms in mock triumph. The view was grand, if anticlimactic. Like all podiums, it was just an everyday platform unless you earned that spot on top. Then, of course, it was glorious.

Horner wanted to stand atop the podium as a stage winner, wanted that moment of glory. With under a mile to go, it was just him and Frenchman Sylvain Chavanel barreling toward the finish line. Chavanel had chased down the breakaway group earlier, and only Horner managed to hang on as Chavanel continued his charge away from the peloton. But the peloton was reeling them in, and it looked as if Horner and Chavanel would either win by a hair or get swallowed just before the line. The two had taken turns pulling each other along the course, but suddenly Chavanel was through sharing the load. His plan was to draft off Horner right up until just a few hundred yards before the finish and then sprint past for the win. It was a basic element of cycling strategy. Chavanel absolutely refused to continue taking turns up front.

Horner desperately craved that stage. Neither he nor Chavanel stood a chance unless they continued working together. On his own, neither man possessed the speed to stay out front of the peloton. But there was no way Horner was going to tow Chavanel to the line and then watch him stand atop the podium as two beautiful women slipped the stage winner's jersey over the French rider's shoulders. Chavanel was clearly unworthy.

So Horner sat up. If Chavanel was going to be an asshole, then Horner wasn't going to let him win. Chavanel's draft vanished, and his pace immediately staggered. Horner continued to sit up, the wind knocking into him. He let the peloton catch them, then coasted in as Robbie McEwen sprinted away for the win. "Second place was as good as last," he told me afterward. "I didn't come here to finish second, I came here to win a stage. And who knows? I just might get one before this whole thing is through. We got a long way to go until Paris." In fact, though, we didn't: There were only eight stages left, and the Tour seemed to be galloping toward the finish.

There were three key stages remaining: the next two days in the Pyrenees, then one last individual time trial, which would take place in Saint-Étienne. It would be the penultimate stage, one last chance for the top riders to make a go at yellow. For them, and for Lance Armstrong, it was now or never.

Stage Fourteen

July 16, 2005 — Agde–Ax-3 Domaines
136.71 Miles

Overall Standings

1. Lance Armstrong (USA), Discovery Channel, 50:13:50
2. Mickael Rasmussen (Dk), Rabobank, 00:38
3. Christophe Moreau (F), Crédit Agricole, 02:34
4. Ivan Basso (I), CSC, 02:40
5. Santiago Botero (Col), Phonak, 03:48
6. Levi Leipheimer (USA), Gerolsteiner, 03:58
7. Francisco Mancebo (Sp), Illes Balears, 04:00
8. Jan Ullrich (G), T-Mobile, 04:02
9. Andréas Klöden (G), T-Mobile, 04:16
10. Floyd Landis (USA), Phonak, 04:16

I HAD VISITED Montpellier with my wife a few years earlier. We were passing through on the train and had gotten off to sit outside in the sun and have lunch at a café near the station. It was all very idyllic, and throughout my time at the Tour, I had quietly looked forward to returning.

But Montpellier at noon and Montpellier at 1:00 a.m. were two different things. As Austin and I drove through the tangled medieval streets, I saw grizzled hookers whose hard faces were straight out of *Les Misérables*, late-night revelers, exhausted backpacking students fresh off the trains from Nice and Madrid, drifters, homeless people, and a whole lot of folks just walking around looking for action — for better or worse.

The hotel we eventually found was the sort where the night clerk's desk was behind bulletproof glass, and you had to be buzzed in because the front door was constantly locked. The room was large but smelled like an overflowing ashtray. We flipped for the lone bed and I lost, so I rolled out the sleeping bag and fell asleep watching highlights of Tiger Woods smoking the field at St. Andrews. The windows were flung open wide, and the night air was warm. I slept as if I were drugged.

Four hours later, we were up. The 136-mile stage from Agde to Ax-3 Domaines (so named because three French regions, or domains, converge near the mountaintop) would begin at 10:30 a.m. — an impossibly early hour by Tour standards. Most other endurance sporting events began near dawn, for reasons of traffic control (easier to obtain open roadways) and cooler temperatures. The fact that there were fewer spectators at daybreak, and fewer potential television viewers watching the broadcast, was beside the point.

The Tour, so dependent upon spectacle, would no more dream of starting at dawn than starting in Iraq. They owned the roads, so traffic wasn't an issue. Big crowds in person and on TV were expected. And the Tour wasn't really the Tour unless the riders had to suffer, so the heat was of no concern whatsoever.

The riders would spend almost six hours in the saddle that day, and we would spend almost as much time in the Passat. It was Saturday in the Pyrenees and the roads would be lined with orange-clad Spanish cycling fans who had driven the short distance into France to spend the weekend at the Tour. Once we left the Mediterranean coast and began climbing, the going would be slow and treacherous.

As we made our way into the prerace village, a loudspeaker was blaring a Sheryl Crow song about soaking up the sun. It was appropriate. Agde marked the first starting line near a beach since Fromentine, two weeks earlier. Fromentine had been gray and the Atlantic Ocean an angry green. The town had the feel of a fishing village gone reluctantly upscale to attract tourists — a deckhand wearing a bow tie. Agde, on the other hand, was sun drenched. The lighthouse at the end of the jetty was contained within an old citadel, but Agde's unabashed focus was tourism, not history. The beaches were covered by fine white sand the consistency of granulated sugar. The Mediterranean was blue and enticing.

The only clues that the Tour was about to abandon the ease of the coast — indeed, we would not see another sea, Mediterranean or otherwise, the rest of the trip — for the rigors of the mountains were the riders themselves. They lingered in the village until the last possible minute before the start, lounging in the shade as if in no hurry to get on their bikes and suffer for six hours.

I didn't blame them. There would be no escaping the heat. It was sunbathing weather, a time to slather on lotion and lie on the sand. Cycling all day in such temperatures felt punitive. After breakfasting on hard sausage, Grand-Mère coffee, and a local specialty listed as "Encornet à la Sétoise," Austin and I dipped our hands ceremoniously in the Mediterranean, then strolled past the steel-drum band wearing CSC jerseys to where we'd parked the Passat. It was time to drive.

The scenery had changed dramatically in the last three days. Driving through the sun-drenched south of France en route to the Pyrenees felt a whole lot like driving through central California — all farmland and sunburned hillsides. It was hard to believe that a week ago we were in rainy Germany, and that just three days earlier we had been shivering in fleece atop the frigid and forbidding Col du Galibier. By day's end, however, we'd be back in the mountains, hard along the Spanish frontier. We had sprinted from one side of France to the other.

I drove fast down the winding country roads. Austin typed on his laptop in the passenger seat. "Damn," he said, as we banged past fields of bright sunflowers, "you're making that gearbox your bitch." He closed his laptop and slid in a mix CD. Not for the first time on the journey I was thankful to be road-tripping with someone of similar musical taste. Our playlist ranged from Pearl Jam to the Mavericks to Bruce Springsteen — and so many others.

I turned the volume louder until there was no distinction between the drive and the rhythm, just a sonic fusion of noise and lyrics and road. "Taxing it and waxing it," we chanted along to Digital Underground, taking adolescent delight in cranking a song we could never play while out for a drive with our families.

Escapist as it may be, the road always refreshes and recharges me. The road is all about being in the moment while being outside my comfort zone and has a way of granting perspective. Each and every moment of the day is spent staring at a map, focused on finding one true path. That search continues long after the return to real life. I wondered, as we powered down the road with the music up so loud that I could not think, if there was an age when the road no longer has that effect.

"There's the course," yelled Austin, turning down the volume as we approached Ax-les-Thermes. "Turn right." With that, we entered a sea of orange: the Basques.

The Spaniards were extraordinarily exuberant. Some sort of spell came over them when they slipped on their orange T-shirts, draped bota bags over their shoulders, and watched a bike race. The year before, as we were climbing La Mongie, Basque fans had blocked the road and surrounded the car, then banged their palms against the roof. It wasn't scary so much as it was annoying, though the more annoyed we looked, the harder they banged. Eventually, the crowd had parted and we slipped through, only to enter another pocket of revelers and begin the process all over again. This continued for miles.

They were fiercely proud of their heritage, and hostile in a unique if benign fashion toward non-Spanish riders. One of my favorite photos from the 2004 Tour was of two Basques standing defiantly in the middle of the road, flipping off Lance Armstrong as he climbed toward them. They weren't flipping him off because he was Lance or because he was an American. They were flipping him off because he wasn't Spanish.

Jan Ullrich entered the fourteenth stage needing to make up some serious ground. He was more than four minutes behind Lance Armstrong in the overall standings, mired in eighth place. His chances of winning the Tour were virtually nil. The riders in front of him were formidable climbers, and there was a good chance Ullrich might not pass them. This meant he would not finish in the final three, and thus there would be no spot for him on the victory podium in Paris.

Ullrich was too good a rider for that. The thirty-one-year-old German was the only cyclist in the peloton besides Armstrong to have won a Tour, back in 1997. In doing so he had single-handedly launched a new mania for cycling in Germany. He was just twenty-three at the time, prompting *L'Équipe* to proclaim, "Voilà la Patron," effectively dubbing Ullrich the future of cycling.

But the *patrón* had turned out to be Armstrong. After sitting out the 1999 Tour with an injury, Ullrich finished second to the American in 2000 and in 2001. The unsmiling, stoic German was the perfect contrast to the cocky Texan. Critics liked to point out that while Armstrong trained throughout the winter, Ullrich packed on weight by partying and overeating. Many said it was a reaction to having been brought up in the rigid East German sports system, where Ullrich was forced to train and diet like a world-class athlete even before becoming a teenager. Cycling was all work for Ullrich, went the thinking; with Armstrong it was a passion.

The training layoff (or perhaps blowoff) was Ullrich's way of recharging his mental batteries between cycling seasons. But when he tested positive for ecstasy in 2002, his career appeared to have entered a tailspin. Deutsche Telekom, his longtime team, fired him. He served a six-month suspension from professional cycling and missed the Tour.

Ullrich refused to surrender. He rode the 2003 season with the financially troubled Bianchi Team, notching yet another second-place finish behind Armstrong. That year his daughter was born, bringing a greater buoyancy to his personality. When Ullrich failed to make the podium with a fourth-place finish in 2004, he seemed unfazed. Now and again he made allusions to retirement. The catastrophic opening time trial of 2005 seemed as if it might hasten that process. After the team time trial, he was mired all the way down in fourteenth place.

But Ullrich had battled back and seemed to be gaining strength and momentum in the mountains. He often rode directly behind and to the left of Armstrong, keeping the *patrón* right where he could see him. He entered the Pyrenees in eighth place, four minutes behind Armstrong. Ullrich wasn't a true threat to the American, but he rode as if he were. Anything could happen in the mountains, and when it did, Ullrich would be ready.

There were six major climbs between Agde and Ax-3 Domaines. The first four were relatively small: a trio of fourth-categories and a third-category ascent that ranged in length from one mile to nearly four. Essentially, those climbs bobbled among the foothills of the Pyrenees, the border between the coastal flatlands and the true mountains soon to come.

The fifth climb of the day was the longest and steepest. The hors catégorie Port de Pailhères was nine miles long, at an 8.1 percent average grade. Climbs like L'Alpe d'Huez and the

Col du Tourmalet were better known, but this one was actually steeper *and* longer. Afterward, the riders would descend into the town of Ax-les-Thermes and climb five miles uphill to the finish. In 2003, Ullrich had attacked on that final climb up the Tourmalet, passed a struggling Armstrong, and nearly moved from second place overall into yellow.

But in 2005, the German attacked one mountain earlier, taking the lead group by surprise. As decided at the T-Mobile Team meeting that morning, Vinokourov and Ullrich accelerated powerfully at the base of the climb. None of Armstrong's Discovery mates could match the pace. As the bunch containing Ullrich, Vino, Basso, Leipheimer, Rasmussen, and a handful of others powered up the mountain, Armstrong found himself without help.

He wasn't the only one in trouble. The attack was such a complete surprise that Levi Leipheimer — busting hard to stay with the front group — was out of range of his domestiques and without a water bottle. The sun was at the sort of harsh high-altitude angle that gives a man a sunburn and dehydration on just a short day hike. Riding the Tour de France without water under those conditions was like demanding a comeuppance.

Leipheimer was a man on the verge of blowing up. He had two simple choices: drop back or stay with the attack. The gutsy Montanan made the only decision he knew how to make. He clung to the attack with every optimistic fiber in his being.

Then a most amazing thing happened. Lance Armstrong pressed forward, drew even, and passed Leipheimer a water bottle. Floyd Landis did the same. Once upon a time they had been teammates; now these three men rarely spoke to one another. But foxholes make for believers and comrades. They needed one another, and in the most desperate way. Armstrong's weakened Discovery squad wasn't there to help him, and Landis's Phonak had been an iffy bunch at best. Now, unexpectedly, the T-Mobile riders were poised to destroy their Tour hopes. So the three Americans worked as a team once again. They helped one another because they needed one another. "I actually get along pretty well with Levi," Armstrong admitted later.

The alliance worked. Riding together, Armstrong, Landis, and Leipheimer hung with Ullrich. The German's attack failed. The lead riders descended the mountain into the village of Ax-les-Thermes, a varied pack. There they would begin the sixth and final climb of the day.

Austin and I parked the Passat in Ax-les-Thermes and took a gondola up the mountain. At the summit, I dropped my laptop in the pressroom and jogged down a forest trail that bisected the course. I was in search of Basques. Where they were, the party would be.

What I found, at first, were Americans: the couple from San Diego there because Lance had inspired the husband while he was battling Hodgkin's, and he had promised his wife they would go to the Tour when he got better; the two buddies who'd come straight to the Tour from Pamplona, still wearing the red scarves of those who had run with the bulls; and even Yvonne Leipheimer. "Did you see what they did?" she asked, visibly moved by the teamwork between Lance, Floyd, and Levi. "Wasn't that wonderful?" The whole Leipheimer clan was on the mountain, standing in front of a minivan with luggage jutting out the open rear cargo door. Affixed to the side of the van were a Montana flag, a "Go Levi" sign, a United States flag, a Gerolsteiner Team banner, and a sort of Leipheimer crest with the words "Levi" and "Butte" against a background of a bow and crossed arrows.

I walked farther down the course, whereupon I came around a tight bend into the sea of orange I'd been looking for.

In any throng of people, there is always someone who manages to stand out. That afternoon it was the heavyset man wearing a plastic matador's cap and sitting astride a stationary bicycle.

He went by the name of El Jefe — the boss. Between pulls on a beer and long streams of red wine from a bota bag, he rallied the faithful by yelling into a bullhorn. Now and again he blew an air horn. Rather than being annoyed, the hundreds of people around him looked to El Jefe as their *patrón*. They milled about, drinking and laughing, engaging in bota bag contests to see who could squeeze wine into his mouth from the farthest distance without spilling a drop. Now and again, someone would yell something very loud in Spanish and they would all cheer. Once upon a time, back in the days when Spain was ruled by Ferdinand and Isabella, this part of France belonged to Spain. El Jefe and his minions acted as if it still did.

El Jefe explained to me that this was his bachelor party; he'd never actually been to a cycling event before. The previous day had been a traditional day of premarriage, male-only feasting called the *txokoda*. Celebrating this feast on the slopes of the Pyrenees, at the Tour, was more impressive than doing it back home in Bilbao. Together, along with his groom's party and all those other Spaniards, we awaited the peloton.

As the helicopters approached, signaling the arrival of the riders, the mood on the mountain grew pensive, expectant. Those watching the race on TV in front of their motor homes or listening to the radio began moving away from the shoulder, out into the middle of the road. The closer the helicopters, the calmer the crowd became. When the helicopters were almost right over us, the Basques stood in the center of the road, so that the entire stretch of pavement was a wall of orange.

The Basques had a system to their mania that rivaled the Tour's precision. No matter who held the lead each day, the Tour's official lead vehicles roared first through the crowd. When they did, the Spanish throngs along the mountain moved to one side of the road. But as soon as the official cars passed, they all moved right back to the middle. They knew the riders would be coming through momentarily and that nobody from the Tour would come back to shoo them away. This was always one of the most incredible things about the Tour, that fans constantly ran onto the course, leaving only a sliver of room for the riders — if that. It was like allowing the drunks in the Fenway bleacher seats to sit in the outfield itself. Sometimes it made the race more fun. Sometimes it made it very scary.

The first rider was Austria's Georg Totschnig of Team Gerolsteiner. He was no threat to the leaders, so no one had followed when he broke away early in the day. It was obvious by his lead, and the fact that there were just two miles left to climb, that he would win the stage.

I didn't know Georg Totschnig from Adam. And I guarantee that El Jefe and the rest of the crowd didn't, either. But they came to life as they opened up the narrowest of corridors down the center of the road. He passed through with just inches to spare, the Basques shaking their fists and screaming Spanish exhortations so loud that I couldn't hear the helicopter thundering overhead.

I stood back as Totschnig passed through, and I didn't see a thing, but when a motorcycle carrying a TV cameraman churned up the road toward us, I moved to the center of the road. I turned my head to the left, and there came Armstrong, Basso, and Ullrich. Their eyes were forward, as if none of the madness existed. Armstrong's yellow jersey was unzipped to a spot just below his sternum, and his pale chest gleamed with sweat.

The next riders — in order, Landis, Rasmussen, Leipheimer — were also cheered loudly. But when Spain's Francisco Mancebo powered up the road right behind them, the Basques screamed with such ferocity that I wondered if the percussion from the sound waves alone might push Mancebo up the hill.

I stayed with the Basque fans until most of the peloton had gone through, long enough to witness something I'd never seen before: riders coming back down the mountain. The mountain-top finish couldn't accommodate the team buses, which were parked at the bottom. As slower riders were making their way up, those who had already finished were whizzing back down. I noticed Levi Leipheimer zipping past the Basques while making conversation with a teammate. He had one hand on the bars and a towel wrapped around his neck to ward off the chill. It was all so nonchalant.

Waving good-bye to El Jefe and the bedlam, I hiked back up the trail to the finish line. Armstrong, I soon learned, had left Ullrich behind shortly after passing me. He had then dropped Ivan Basso to take second in the stage. Rasmussen had failed so utterly on the final climb that he had lost a minute to Armstrong. The Dane was still in second place, but Ivan Basso and Jan Ullrich now ranked third and fourth. Levi Leipheimer was fifth. Floyd Landis was in sixth.

The stage was set for Sunday's ascent of the legendary Pla-d'Adet. It would be Lance Armstrong's final mountain stage, ever. If he rode it well, the Tour would be all but over. If he blew up, those other five would most surely take advantage.

Stage Fifteen

July 17, 2005
Lézat-sur-Lèze–Saint-Lary-Soulan (Pla-d'Adet)
127.41 Miles

Overall Standings

1. Lance Armstrong (USA), Discovery Channel, 55:58:17
2. Mickael Rasmussen (Dk), Rabobank, 01:41
3. Ivan Basso (I), CSC, 02:46
4. Jan Ullrich (G), T-Mobile, 04:34
5. Levi Leipheimer (USA), Gerolsteiner, 04:45
6. Floyd Landis (USA), Phonak, 05:03
7. Francisco Mancebo (Sp), Illes Balears, 05:03
8. Andréas Klöden (G), T-Mobile, 05:38
9. Alexandre Vinokourov (Kaz), T-Mobile, 07:09
10. Christophe Moreau (F), Crédit Agricole, 08:37

"ARE YOU AMERICANS?" asked the front-desk clerk. He was short, heavy, and wreathed in cigarette smoke. We were in Saint-Girons, checking out of the very old Hôtel Eychenne, which had long, creaking hallways and felt haunted. Austin and I had walked all the way back down the mountain after yesterday's stage, finally making it into Ax-les-Thermes well past dark. We'd eaten dinner across the street from a bridge where the Nazis used to hang members of the French Resistance.

"You're not gonna make some bad joke about our president, are you?" said Austin.

"I'm sorry?"

"Just kidding. Yes. We're Americans."

"And you are with the Tour de France?" the clerk added, nodding at our credentials.

"That's right."

The clerk inhaled deeply on an unfiltered Gauloise and smiled conspiratorially, as if he had something very special to share, but only with us. "Did you know that Lance Armstrong stays at this hotel when he practices for the Pla-d'Adet?"

We were a bit flabbergasted. Here? Armstrong? It was as if we'd stumbled into a secret lair. Those long hallways were a place where a famous man could check in and get lost for a night. The more I thought about it, I could see why Lance stayed here. And with each of these secrets and insights, perhaps the mystery would be closer to a solution: What was it about this man that made so many of us stumble along in his wake? Yes, he was a champion, but every sport had champions. What was it about Lance Armstrong that wasn't there with, say, Pete Sampras or Wayne Gretzky or even Michael Jordan?

We thanked the desk clerk for taking the time to share the tidbit. Despite their reputation for rude cynicism, the French displayed an eagerness to perform small kindnesses that never failed to amaze me. I had seen it countless times throughout the Tour: restaurants reopening the kitchen to serve us a hot meal; locals giving an impromptu, gentle French lesson as they imparted directions, so that we might not get lost again; and now this. The clerk's gesture was a good omen, a beguiling start to what would undoubtedly be the year's greatest day of cycling.

We threw our bags in the back of the Passat and headed out. "Frankly," Austin deadpanned, "I was rather inspired by the way you punished my rental car yesterday. Not that my masculinity was threatened in any way, but I now feel strangely compelled to do the same."

He found the D618 and we powered out of town. We were now on the course. The morning was gray. A clear stream tumbled alongside the two-lane valley road. Trees lined both banks. The fields along the road were a lush, overgrown green. I wrote a small reminder in my notebook that should I ever purchase land in France, the stretch outside of Saint-Girons would be the place. No wonder Armstrong stopped in during his training rides.

From Lézat-sur-Lèze, the riders would set out shortly after 11:00 a.m. on a 127.41-mile cycling showdown. The degree of difficulty was mind-boggling: four tightly spaced first-category climbs, during which the riders would nip into Spain for ten short miles. Then, after they popped back into France, there would be a mountaintop finish on the legendary Pla-d'Adet, a six-plus-mile ascent at an average gradient of 8.3 percent. It was so steep they should've been allowed to use ropes.

The top three cyclists were all just three minutes apart, and this would be a day when the strong, smart rider could make up that time. And with the Disco Boys again looking vulnerable, Armstrong's hold on first had become tenuous.

We passed through Saint-Beat, an ancient town first fortified by the Romans in 75 B.C. because it commanded the gorge leading into Spain. An eleventh-century church was still standing there, as were the ruins of a feudal castle from the same era. But Saint-Beat's most famous landmark was a simple balcony, jutting from the home of a dignitary. In 1897, Edmond Rostand had been inspired to use that balcony as the setting for the celebrated exchanges between Cyrano de Bergerac and his beloved Roxane.

We detoured off the course, taking a shortcut up the Vallée d'Aure to the Pla-d'Adet. A heavy morning mist hung over the road as we approached the mountain. Church bells rang as we passed through the village square in Camous, and we saw four residents talking to the priest after Mass. A Sunday market was under way, with awnings, fruit stands, and butcher shops set up in a gravel parking lot.

We had been blasting the music loudly, windows open, but turned it down as we slowed to drive through town. The whole world seemed suddenly quiet. Just then, the mist parted. A triangular peak, serrated like the tip of a very sharp knife, announced itself directly ahead. The moment had a dramatic feel, like that moment in a movie when the villain is introduced.

Enter the Pla-d'Adet.

Some mountains on the Tour looked gentle enough for the average amateur cyclist to tackle. It might take a while, but he or she would get to the top.

The Pla-d'Adet was not one of those peaks.

It was terrifying. Some massive glacier had once sluiced down the valley behind it, cleaving the Pla-d'Adet in two. The front of the mountain was steep and green, with long switchbacks zigzagging back and forth to the top and pine forest covering the lower elevations. The backside appeared to have been sawed off. The jagged cliff dropped miles down to the forested valley floor.

I stared up at the Pla-d'Adet and wondered how anyone could *race* a bike up such a monster. It was a peak so tough that in 1975, forty-three riders had finished outside the time cutoff.

"Should we park at the bottom and take the gondola up?" asked Austin.

"That's a long walk down if the gondola stops running before we leave the pressroom."

The riders would not be arriving for more than six hours, but the road going up the mountain had long been closed to all but official Tour traffic. Spectators were arriving early and leaving their cars at the bottom, then hoofing it up the switchbacks.

It was a sweltering, beer-soaked assemblage of cycling fans. They lined the steep road like so many movie buffs crowding the red carpet on premiere night. They had ridden up in campers, they had run, and they had walked. Many had pitched tents and slept on the shoulder or in the pine trees all weekend. Some were biking to the top as we drove, though that number diminished as we climbed higher, until there were none at all.

At the center of the congestion was a mile-long line of Spaniards poised just below the two-kilometer banner (meaning two kilometers to go until the finish). There was a different mood as we drove through: angrier than the day before, more hostile. I looked for El Jefe and his bachelor party but didn't see them. Like many Spaniards, they were probably positioned along the ascent of the Col du Portillon, twenty miles to the east, the only Spanish mountain in the 2005 Tour.

The Tour had anticipated problems with the Spaniards. Conspicuous for their dress and show of arms, just in case things got out of hand, were an elite group of the Republican Guard. They wore tight black T-shirts, black SWAT pants, combat boots, and 9 mm Sig Sauer pistols. We had never seen them before, not at this Tour or any other. "Seriously badass," Austin mumbled.

We parked sideways in some dry grass two hundred yards above the finish. There were exactly three wispy clouds in the sky.

The race had been going on for about an hour by the time we settled in to the pressroom, and still there was no video feed. French TV was showing a clay court tennis tournament. A crawl at the bottom of the screen mentioned that George Hincapie was off the front with a large breakaway group. "You see Big George is in the break?" asked Austin.

"Yeah."

"Odd, don't you think? There's nobody in that group that even remotely threatens the yellow jersey."

He was right. Hincapie had been in twenty-fifth place at the start of the day, and just as many minutes behind Armstrong.

The only rider in that fourteen-man break ranked higher than Hincapie was Óscar Pereiro, a Spaniard riding for Team Phonak, who was only twenty-fourth. Hincapie's job was normally to chase down threats to yellow, but he showed no signs of easing up and drifting back to the peloton. Twenty-five miles into the stage, and the breakaway group had an enormous 7:20 lead. An hour later, at the summit of Col du Portet d'Aspet (where a former teammate of Hincapie and Armstrong's, Fabio Casartelli, had been killed ten years earlier in a crash), the breakaway group's lead was almost twice that. Halfway through the stage, the lead was up to seventeen minutes.

All day long, Hincapie had been waiting for Bruyneel to order him back to help Lance. That selflessness had been the hallmark of his entire career. But now Johan Bruyneel spoke into Hincapie's ear via radio. "Do your own race, George," said the team director. Hincapie was being given free rein to go for his first-ever stage win.

The pace remained strong. Hincapie, made confident by the dominant way he'd powered up Col du Galibier just a few days earlier, began to look around at the breakaway group's other five riders: Óscar Pereiro, Michael Boogerd, Laurent Brochard, Oscar Sevilla, and Pietro Caucchioli. Hincapie figured he was the best climber in the bunch.

Steadily the gap between the peloton and the breakaway began to narrow. Lance Armstrong was pedaling strongly in a small pack with Ivan Basso, Jan Ullrich, Chris Horner, Mickael Rasmussen, and the other top climbers.

Hincapie's group was descending the day's penultimate climb, the Col de Val Louron-Azet, as Armstrong's group was still climbing. By the time Hincapie had raced through Saint-Lary-Soulan and begun the long climb up to the finish, it was obvious that someone in his breakaway was going to win the stage. There were four riders left, but as the ascent continued and began to brutally grind at their endurance, it was down to just two: Big

George Hincapie and Phonak's Óscar Pereiro. They took turns pulling each other up the mountain.

I've never subscribed to the rule that says there's no cheering in the press box. Sports are by their nature emotional, and life offers few other avenues so tailored to immediate expression. If an athlete does something superlative, I'm happy to let myself get swept up in that moment. Watching George Hincapie suddenly sprint away from Óscar Pereiro was one of those moments. To stand there and pretend to be impartial would have been absurd.

I stood just a hundred yards below the finish line. Hincapie's move came as they rounded the final corner and pedaled into view. "Go, George!" I screamed as Hincapie blasted toward the line. The mountaintop exploded in cheers as everyone else saw him, too. I have never heard so much noise. I was yelling as loudly as I possibly could. My voice was drowned out in the thousands of people roaring and cheering and clapping their hands and banging their open palms on the metal signage lining the finish corridor. "Go, George. GO. GO. GO!!!"

I was grinning from ear to ear and jumping up and down, punching my fist in the air. I doubt I would have cheered so hard for any other rider, even Armstrong. Lance was expected to win. Hincapie was not supposed to, not ever. He whooshed past me, so close that I could have reached out and slapped him on the back.

There are two time clocks at each Tour finish. One is the elapsed time for the entire stage. The other is the amount of time the other riders are behind the stage winner. It stays at zero and doesn't start ticking until the winner crosses the line. "The clock was at zero," Hincapie said later, stunned. "I've never seen it that way before."

Big George sat up when he realized victory was assured. He

took his hands from the bars and pressed them to the sides of his head in disbelief. It was done.

When Pereiro finished, he whined that Hincapie had screwed him over. With the exception of Spanish journalists and Disco critics, no one cared.

Armstrong was just a few minutes back, finishing seventh on the day. He'd ridden strongly and steadily, staying within himself, knowing that keeping the contenders close was more important than winning the stage. He'd passed and dropped Ullrich, gaining another 1:24 on his longtime rival. Mickael Rasmussen had also lost time to Armstrong, 1:28 in the case of the fair-skinned Dane. Basso had given up his attacks, later explaining that he didn't have any more challenge left in his legs. Nevertheless, his aggressive climbing had moved him into second place overall. Basso and Armstrong then crossed the finish line together, friends and rivals, giving new meaning to that old saying about keeping your friends close and your enemies even closer.

In that instant, the Tour was over.

Officially, there was still a week until Paris. But it was done, and everyone knew it. Ivan Basso was 2:46 behind in the overall standings. No amount of strategic manipulation by Bjarne Riis was going to help the CSC rider make up that much time. No one, in fact, was going to catch Armstrong.

But the story of the day was George Hincapie's victory. In the pressroom and in the bars and the shops atop Pla-d'Adet, you'd hear a friend find another and exclaim, "Did you see it? George won!"

Not Hincapie. Just George. Our George. Not the untouchable Armstrong, the man we were all chasing, who would forever be one step ahead. But George — the selfless blue-collar soul of Discovery's blue train. "Did you see it?" Austin said, when I found him after it was through. He was grinning widely, sunglasses pushed back up on his head.

"I was right there."

"George. . . . Can you believe it? Can you absolutely fucking believe it? How cool is that?"

Once we got past that giddy sense of disbelief, the subtext was equally astounding: Lance Armstrong was on the verge of winning one last time. Until Lance came along, the most Tour victories by any rider was five. Four men had won five times: Frenchmen Jacques Anquetil and Bernard Hinault, Belgium's Eddy Merckx, and Spain's Miguel Induráin. Lance had tied them in 2003. Then he had defied the odds to break that record in 2004. Now he was going to win seven. The figure was mind-boggling.

You could feel the tension whooshing out of the Tour. The rest day and the final six stages would be a coronation. The only question that remained was whether Lance would crash. All he had to do was stay upright and victory was assured.

There was a point in every journey where I stopped thinking of all I'd come to see and started thinking about going home. At the 2005 Tour, that moment came atop the Pla-d'Adet.

Others felt it, too. Farther down the mountain, the Basques had run amok, throwing beer bottles and rocks at cars, and just generally looking for trouble. The top of the mountain was rapidly becoming a ghost town. Those fans who'd driven up the day before were aiming their cars back toward the valley. Forklifts beeped and vroomed as workers began tearing apart the finish area. The sun disappeared, replaced by cold gray clouds that approached, then enveloped us. Wind began flapping the press tent so hard that I thought the white vinyl top might rip away.

There was a row of shops near the finish line. I was cold and needed a sweatshirt, but the Passat was parked a mile away, so I decided to just buy one. By chance, I wandered into an outdoor-apparel shop. The woman behind the counter was lively and pretty. "Cela vide la tête," she said cheerily.

"I'm sorry. My French isn't very good."

"It means your head is empty. That's what happens in the mountains."

"Is that a bad thing?"

"No. It means you look content."

I was.

If my head was happy, the rest of my body was in a state of upheaval. Since coming to France, I had eaten a number of interesting dishes. There had been cow stomach, pig stomach, sliced and dried pork sausage, apple tart, rare hamburger, Gruyère cheese, terrine de canard, and steak smothered in bleu cheese, to name just a few. None of those things had upset my ironclad digestive system.

The pressroom buffet atop Pla-d'Adet was relatively simple: small squares of salty cheese-and-olive pizza and equally small squares of quiche lorraine. But I began getting a queasy feeling shortly after I ate. I chalked it up to the altitude and drank cup after cup of water to fend off dehydration.

"How you doing?" asked an American writer. I must have looked pale.

"I feel a little funny."

I had a fever and was feeling nauseous, but I kept walking around and drinking water, hoping it would all pass. As I left the building, a mighty wind gusted up from the valley floor. The fresh air revived me, but only for ten minutes. By the time I had hiked back to the pressroom, all I wanted to do was lie down someplace and sleep.

"You know," the American whispered as I packed up my laptop, "I think I'm coming down with something, too."

"Hope you feel better."

But he didn't. Quite soon he was so sick he completely

shit himself and was reduced to throwing away his clothing. Naked except for a T-shirt wrapped around his waist, he was bundled into the back of an ambulance for the drive down the mountain.

I was relegated to the back of the Passat. Austin drove, Suzanne Halliburton rode in the passenger seat, and I tried to sleep off whatever it was that ailed me. My entire body was breaking down. I don't think it had anything to do with food. I think it had to do with finally letting up after two go-go weeks of nonstop driving and very little sleep.

The line of cars going down the mountain was bumper-to-bumper for fifty long miles. It looked as though our drive would last all night.

"Y'all should have taken the gondola up," said Suzanne, who had parked at the bottom then ridden up.

"You should have taken the gondola back down," Austin countered.

It was almost 1:00 a.m. when we dropped Suzanne at her car. I had slept fitfully, my legs curled up on the narrow seat, using Suzanne's hard laptop case as a pillow. I slid into the front seat and grabbed the Michelin atlas, trying to convince myself I was a hundred percent. Sick or not, I had to make myself useful. "I found a road," I said, staring at the map. The line of cars showed no sign of moving any faster. At the rate we were going, we wouldn't make Lourdes until dawn.

The road was just a squiggle on the map, what locals called a "goat trail." They clung to the sides of cliffs and were sometimes too narrow for anything but the smallest of vehicles. Once we got on it, there would be no place to turn around. Taking a goat trail was total-commitment driving, the supreme adventure of road-tripping through France.

"I'm game if you are," Austin said.

We took it. The road climbed the mountain on the other side

of the valley from the Pla-d'Adet. Looking across, we had a stunning view of the cars coming down. The line still reached all the way to the top of the mountain.

Our road was completely dark, unburdened by frivolous accoutrements like stripes, lights, or guardrails. Austin drove with a quiet confidence, never letting on that even a single misjudgment would launch us off the edge. Every few miles, we came upon very small villages, but otherwise our drive along the cliffs was uninterrupted by signs of life. If I looked off to my left, the valley floor was straight down. We could have rappelled from the goat trail to the line of cars. I was actually glad we were driving it at night — during the day it might have been terrifying.

But our gamble paid off. By the time we had descended thirty miles later, Austin and I had leapfrogged to the front of that line of cars. An hour later, we were in Lourdes, the city renowned for its healing waters.

The day had been extremely long, a mental and physical roller coaster. But there had been a sense of the outlandish that gave it a deep resonance: the grandeur of the mountain, Hincapie's stunning win, Armstrong's impending victory, the questionable quiche lorraine, the long line of cars, and our escape up the goat trail. Nothing, I thought, could top all that.

Then again, I'd never been to Lourdes.

Second Rest Day

Overall Standings

1. Lance Armstrong (USA), Discovery Channel, 62:09:59
2. Ivan Basso (I), CSC, 02:46
3. Mickael Rasmussen (Dk), Rabobank, 03:09
4. Jan Ullrich (G), T-Mobile, 05:58
5. Francisco Mancebo (Sp), Illes Balears, 06:31
6. Levi Leipheimer (USA), Gerolsteiner, 07:35
7. Floyd Landis (USA), Phonak, 09:33
8. Alexandre Vinokourov (Kaz), T-Mobile, 09:38
9. Christophe Moreau (F), Crédit Agricole, 11:47
10. Andréas Klöden (G), T-Mobile, 12:01

THE OFFICIAL SITE of the rest day was sunny Pau, which was so popular among Victorian Britons that they claimed it was actually part of England. But Austin and I stayed twenty miles southeast in Lourdes. Lourdes was famous the world over for its healing waters, and its economy was built around catering to the pilgrims who flocked from near and far to be cured. Another type of pilgrim was there on the rest day: Lance fans. We stayed at the Hôtel Christina, on the banks of the Gave de Pau River. Just a simple look around the breakfast room showed a clean split between those clutching rosary beads and those with a yellow band on their wrist. It was startling to witness, the divide was so clean.

More than forty million of the LiveStrong bracelets had been sold in the first year alone, and Leblanc's polka-dotted knockoff seemed about as much a threat to Lance's charitable efforts as I might have been in a bicycle race against Armstrong — that is, not a threat at all. Forty million was a massive number, and it pointed to something rather amazing: The band was about a specific cause, to be sure, but it had also turned out to be about something universal. It wasn't just about rallying behind Lance Armstrong the cyclist but about supporting the Lance who'd survived cancer and found a way each and every day of his life to challenge his mental, physical, and emotional limits. The yellow band became, in essence, a symbol of hope and faith that was just as powerful to its wearer as the rosary beads were to the pilgrims who'd made their way to Lourdes. It was as if by wearing the bracelet, the average person could be inspired to live a more courageous life. The yellow coloring, so obviously a symbol of Tour greatness, reinforced that notion.

I had purchased a LiveStrong band on the Champs-Élysées on the last day of the 2004 Tour. Nike had an army of local college kids selling them there, as they had throughout many earlier stages. (One great awkward moment of that Tour was watching that eager French sales staff trying to sell yellow bands to the peloton before a stage. Some riders accepted a bracelet, but most demurred. Cancer was cancer, and hope was hope, but wearing a competitor's talisman on one's wrist was tantamount to heresy.) The sales staff carried the LiveStrong bands in a musette bag very much like the ones the riders snatched from their team car at the feed zone of a stage. During a race the riders would pedal past the outstretched hands of a team functionary, grasp the musette bag, and sling its long cotton straps around their shoulders until the food could either be eaten or slipped into the back pockets of a cycling jersey for later consumption.

Cycling through the feed zone was as simple as extending a hand to grab the team bag, and as complex as doing so while pedaling at twenty-five miles per hour in a crowd of nearly two hundred bicycles, all the while keeping just one hand on the bars — not so simple at all really, but just another example of the remarkable acrobatics Tour riders performed daily on their bikes.

Buying a yellow bracelet on the Champs-Élysées, by contrast, had been as simple as sliding a euro through the slit in a small coffee can that the sales staff carried, then reaching into the musette bag to pluck out the yellow band. I had torn off the frail wrapper and slipped the LiveStrong bracelet around my wrist right there on the Champs, then held out my left arm to study this new look. The LiveStrong band made a fine companion to the silver bracelet my sister left me. I had originally worn the narrow metal loop while competing in a two-week adventure race in the mountains of South Africa. She had just been diagnosed with pancreatic cancer, and whenever I got tired or felt like quitting, I would tap the silver band, reminding myself that my struggle was Lilliputian by comparison, and then press on. I gave her the bracelet as a sign of solidarity after I got home. She wore it until she died, and then I got it back.

I still wore the silver bracelet, but my LiveStrong band had snapped soon after I bought it. I was hoping to buy another at the 2005 Tour, because purchasing a LiveStrong band at the Tour de France seemed to carry a greater emotional significance than buying it online. But those cheerful college kids with their musette bags were nowhere to be seen in 2005. Jean-Marie Leblanc — who had added a gaudy yellow-and-black-striped arrangement to the polka-dotted bracelet — didn't want the competition, especially from Lance.

The very fact that LiveStrong bands were not for sale at the Tour added a certain poignance to the sight of all those pilgrims in Lourdes with one around their wrist. The band wasn't just a souvenir to them, purchased on their French vacation to flash to all their friends back home. It was a vibrant acknowledgment that Lance Armstrong's accomplishments had helped them live with greater purpose.

When Lance Armstrong speaks about being diagnosed with cancer, he talks about the great fear that coursed through his body, and how suddenly he was no longer an athlete but just another patient, fighting to stay alive — from competitor to victim. But Armstrong also refers to October 2, 1996, as the greatest day of his life. The cancer changed him. It also allowed him to change the world, something the brash young Texan had no right to expect before his doctors sat him down that day and told him that the testicular cancer had spread so far they would have to open up his skull to slice some of the malignancy from his brain. That was the day he had a choice to make: Would he accept his victim status or would he fight back?

We are all victims at one time or another. Whether or not we choose to stay that way is up to us. Most times it's not even something as big as cancer that knocks someone down so hard they never ever want to get back up again. The rest of their life becomes a quiet settling, a constant excuse rather than a striving.

Armstrong rejected his victim status. With heart and with science he beat cancer, which was achievement enough. He could've, as he often joked, passed his days drinking Miller Lite and managing a Mexican restaurant. As a cancer survivor, not much more could be expected of him. But Armstrong rededicated himself to cycling, because he felt deeply alive and joyful and complete when balanced on two narrow wheels. What good was winning the fight to stay alive if you didn't do any actual *living* when the battle was won?

Armstrong wore a gold cross around his neck, even when he rode the mountains, where the slightest bit of weight could become burdensome. However, he openly disavowed any religious affiliation. Yet the fact that he not only came back to compete but had actually won six straight Tour de France crowns was a miracle, plain and simple. Nobody in the history of cycling had ever won more than five Tours, let alone six in a row. And yet here was this guy, who by all accounts should have been six feet under, wearing the yellow jersey with such frequency that some joked the color might as well have been tattooed on him.

Before the cancer, Lance had been just another bike racer. His fan base consisted of Texans and endurance-sports junkies, but he was unknown to the world at large. Thanks to 10/2/96 — or just 10/2, as it was known in the Armstrong camp — he inspired millions of people who could otherwise have cared less about bike racing. I'd seen them on the roads throughout France, their numbers growing larger and larger with every passing stage, until they had become an omnipresent force. There was nowhere you could go at the Tour and not see a Lance fan. And now a small cross section of them sat all around me in that crowded breakfast room at the Hôtel Christina, many of them wearing cycling shorts as they dissected the Pla-d'Adet, George Hincapie, the Tour in general, and, of course, Lance. The glow on their faces was that of the true believer.

For Bernadette Soubirous, the greatest day of her life was February 11, 1858. The fourteen-year-old peasant girl was hunting for firewood on a cold winter's afternoon when the Virgin Mary appeared to her in an apparition. Bernadette returned to that spot in a meadow along the Gave de Pau the next day, and a few weeks afterward. Each time, the figure in white appeared to her.

This was not necessarily a good thing for the tubercular Bernadette, or France. Her family was so poor that they lived in a twelve-by-twelve room that had once been a prison cell. Her father had been blinded in one eye during an accident at the mill where he worked, and eventually the mill's closure left him unemployed. Desperate to feed his family, François Soubirous had once been arrested for stealing two bags of flour and as a result spent eight days in Lourdes's jail.

And even after he was released, the label "thief" followed him and his family. At the time Mary appeared to her, Bernadette was attending a special school for the children of paupers. The teenager was so simple that she was placed in a class with seven-year-olds. So when word about the apparitions got out, it was easy to see why she was not initially believed — particularly because the vision appeared only to Bernadette.

But before long, the citizens of Lourdes began flocking to the grotto where Bernadette went to visit with the Virgin Mary. At one point, Bernadette later wrote, the apparition instructed her to drink from a muddy spring and eat grass for sustenance. Bernadette had been praying until then, her face glowing with such reverence that even the most cynical eyewitnesses were moved to comment on her deep faith. But when the peasant stranger began eating the grass, then turned to the crowd, her face all but unrecognizable thanks to a patina of smeared mud, there were serious questions about her mental health.

However, Bernadette continued returning to the grotto. The crowds around her went from just tens, to hundreds, to more than a thousand. On March 25, 1858, Bernadette asked a very simple question of her invisible friend: "Would you tell me who you are?"

"I am the Immaculate Conception," came the reply.

Bernadette couldn't read or write, and she had never received formal religious education. She didn't know what the words meant. So when she asked the local priest to explain, he was so shaken that he sent Bernadette away. It had been just four years since the Vatican officially conferred the title "Immaculate Conception" onto Mary. There was no way an illiterate, uneducated child could know such a thing. The priest declared that Bernadette's apparitions had been real.

An Augustinian priory was soon built on the site, and then a great cathedral. Nowadays, there are a series of chapels stacked on top of one another inside that magnificent structure, big to small, much like a Russian doll. Christians flock to the grotto, the act of pilgrimage seen as a way of temporarily stepping away from one's daily cares and into the presence of God. Some come for healing, some come just to pray or ask forgiveness for their sins, and some come for the sense of well-being that washes over them when they feel as if they are nestled in the palm of God's hand.

Me? I was still feeling a little queasy from the day before. I didn't actually go to the grotto to be healed, but it was silly to be in Lourdes and not see the famous place. Austin, who, after completing the goat-trail drive, had written until dawn to beat his *SI* deadline, was rightfully exhausted. But he still had to find some sort of Internet café from which to send his piece. Somewhere along the way he also hoped to find a Laundromat. I set out alone to find the site. The grotto trolley lumbered past as I stepped out of the Christina and followed the Gave de Pau, but instead of hopping on I decided to walk. White-tailed swallows flitted above the slowly moving water. Local teenagers, pants rolled up to their knees, fished in the shallows.

However pure the intentions of the pilgrims, commercialism at its cheesiest reigned on every street, and street corner, in Lourdes. It was like a Catholic Dollywood. There was the Vatican Parking Garage, the Hôtel Madonna, the Joan of Arc and Bernadette restaurants, and countless curio shops selling everything from postcards of the cathedral to special plastic jugs for transporting holy water. (Apparently, one had the water blessed in Lourdes and then hauled it back home.)

The roads soon became crowded with people in wheelchairs, many of them very old. They were Italian, Spanish, French, English, American, and more. I knew I was on the right path. It rained very hard, a cold summer downpour that drenched me to the skin. But the pilgrims remained out in the rain and so did I. Less than two minutes after it suddenly commenced, the rain stopped.

The Tour had pervaded my thoughts for more than two weeks. How could it not? So I began to think of the pilgrims as a peloton, and the peloton as a metaphor for life. Only those with — to use Christi Anderson's flavorful term — big balls chose their own path. Life was full of ruts, including some perfectly decent ones, and it took great confidence and faith to forge anew and ahead. Close behind were those with the right physical requirements but not the right mental makeup to lead. Then came the guys who were just happy to be there but who had a touch of the victim in them, blaming others for their calamities.

Of such thoughts are pilgrimages on an unsettled stomach made. Soon I was in the grotto line, the Gave de Pau off to my right. There were two lines of the faithful: those who had exchanged their personal wheelchairs for the official blue grotto wheelchairs, and those on foot. The air smelled like Mass: candle wax, old people, must. Local Boy Scouts in uniforms and red neckerchiefs pushed the blue wheelchairs.

It was stone silent. The lines moved forward, weaving into each other as we walked through the grotto. No speaking or stopping to linger was permitted. At the rear of the grotto, the muddy spring from which Bernadette once drank was visible beneath a thick sheet of Plexiglas. I touched the smooth rock of the grotto wall, and then it was done.

I felt strangely uplifted as I followed the official evacuation route down along the Gave de Pau. There was a great peace to the moment, and a connection to something greater than myself.

Once, years before, I had been out cycling. It was late in the afternoon and I wasn't wearing my helmet. There was a place where the inside lane branched sharply right to a freeway on-ramp. I had to cross the on-ramp to get over to where the bike lane resumed. A truck, its driver realizing too late that he was about to miss the freeway, had swerved sharply over from the far lane. He was going about fifty-five miles per hour when he hit me. I flew off the bike — literally flew, like a missile. My helmetless head was aimed straight for the curb. Time slowed, and as I soared I noticed the world with remarkable clarity. A man was sitting where my body was headed, looking at me with great curiosity, and I wondered if he was going to attempt to catch me. I knew that I was soon to be dead, that my head was going to bash into the curb and my skull would be crushed. I thought, *This is what it feels like to die.* And in that instant, I was filled with the most incredible peace. It was what it was. Everything was going to be OK.

I hit the ground so hard my bike jersey and shorts were shredded. I lay there all but naked. But that stranger had in fact received me. He had prevented my head from hitting the curb. I was bloody and I was battered, and the languid pace and granularity that had accompanied me while airborne was instantly displaced by the quiet, wobbly calm of shock. I dragged myself off the road and turned to him to ask if he could call an ambulance.

But there was no one there. In fact, there was no one within a hundred yards of me. I'd had my moment of peace, and my apparition, just like Bernadette.

Lance had his 10/2, and had developed a focus and purpose to his life as a result. Bernadette had her February 11, changing Lourdes forever and soon finding her purpose in life as a nun.

I'd had a pivotal moment, too. I'd come away more aware than ever that life is too short, and I had a mandate to live life to its fullest. And to be sure, I'd done plenty in the years since. But rather than develop some greater focus or purpose, I felt like I still didn't know what I wanted out of life. The tricky part about feeling as if you can do anything is remembering that you can't do *everything*. As a child, for instance, I'd had the fervent dream of running in the Olympics. I got so busy chasing my other dreams that I let that one slip. I focused on becoming a husband, father, provider, and writer. Running was last on the list. Rather than accepting that my Olympic dream was never meant to be, I let it haunt me as almost a sort of failure. Again that old proverb: "A man is never old until regrets take the place of his dreams." Each of us has a longing to discover our most heartfelt desires and seize our destiny. But what if it was necessary to sacrifice those dreams in order to fulfill that destiny?

Looking around at my fellow pilgrims that afternoon in Lourdes, I wondered how many were here seeking an answer to that sort of question. That was certainly the case for much of the LiveStrong contingent. They had all sacrificed in one area of their lives to excel in another. They should have been fulfilled. Instead, there was a quiet longing for more. I heard it in their conversations and in the furious way that those who had brought bikes attacked their group rides. There was a restlessness about them, a restlessness I knew well because I felt it, too. Not in some heavy burdensome way, involving rumination and anguish. But in the way of a searcher, trying to find his or her path through life. Talking to the LiveStrong bracelet brigade, I found there was a sense that their time in the presence of Lance was a means of figuring some of that out. We all wanted his focus and sense of mission.

In 1841 Scottish historian Thomas Carlyle wrote that "no sadder proof can be given by a man of his own littleness than disbelief in great men." Carlyle's great-man theory argued that history was molded by heroes. Whether artists, clergy, generals, or political leaders, such men effect change. Of course, Armstrong was not a general or a politician, and, born a commoner, he would never be a king. He was "just" a bike racer. But at a time in history when America is divided along religious, ethnic, and political lines, between red states and blue, evangelical and secular, black and white, Christian and Muslim and Jew, there is an almost universal support for this man. The LiveStrong bracelet was proof: worn by people of all ages, genders, and political beliefs, unifying a nation torn apart by hanging chads and 9/11 and the bitter November 2004 elections. The silicon loop stood for courage and the notion that we are in this together. In a world that often seems without heroes or hope, Armstrong was both.

With just one week left in the Tour, the reason we were all chasing Lance was becoming clear. We were drawn to his perseverance, courage, and focus, and the greatness that came as a result. We all wanted those things in our own lives. The question was, how did we get them? He was the example. I decided it was time to get the answer from him, personally.

Stage Sixteen

July 19, 2005 — Mourenx–Pau
111.91 Miles

Overall Standings

1. Lance Armstrong (USA), Discovery Channel, 62:09:59
2. Ivan Basso (I), CSC, 02:46
3. Mickael Rasmussen (Dk), Rabobank, 03:09
4. Jan Ullrich (G), T-Mobile, 05:58
5. Francisco Mancebo (Sp), Illes Balears, 06:31
6. Levi Leipheimer (USA), Gerolsteiner, 07:35
7. Floyd Landis (USA), Phonak, 09:33
8. Alexandre Vinokourov (Kaz), T-Mobile, 09:38
9. Christophe Moreau (F), Crédit Agricole, 11:47
10. Andréas Klöden (G), T-Mobile, 12:01

THE DASH TO PARIS was on. There were just six stages left in the 2005 Tour de France. Only two really mattered to the top ten riders. The first was the time trial on Saturday in Saint-Étienne. The other was the final stage into the City of Light. Barring calamity, there would be no radical changes in the overall standings between Tuesday and Sunday. Jan Ullrich's fourth-place status was almost three minutes behind the time of Mickael Rasmussen. It would take a time trial of disastrous dimensions on

Rasmussen's part for Ullrich to move into third place overall and thus secure a spot on the podium in Paris.

As for Lance Armstrong, he was entering the push to Paris with nearly three minutes' advantage on second-place Ivan Basso. His Disco Boys were rested and eager to protect yellow. And though Armstrong was jittery about thinking too far ahead, and though he tried to deny it, that gaping lead of his lent the week an air of coronation. The fans and the press and the riders knew it: Lance Armstrong was going to win his seventh consecutive Tour de France. Some men strive their whole lifetime to win a single Tour. To win two is icing on the cake. But to have two Tour victories be the difference between yourself and legends such as five-timers Eddy Merckx, Jacques Anquetil, Bernard Hinault, and Miguel Induráin was unthinkable. You could sense the special nature of Armstrong's achievement by the third wave of journalists to enter the pressroom. No longer were they sportswriters. Now it was network news guys from the London and Paris bureaus, dropping in to put Armstrong's victory in context. Trouble was, that victory was so incredible that there was no context for it.

So the only question of the final week was whether or not Lance Armstrong would win an individual stage, something he'd actually failed to do thus far. But those who knew the Tour well realized that this was not the time for careless risk. The focus of Armstrong's week would be staying out of trouble and honing himself mentally for the time trial. A crash could have disastrous effects.

As a result, the stages between Tuesday and Saturday had a certain nerve-racking quality to them, albeit in an entirely different manner than that of the previous two weeks. Then, it was all about the hunt. Now, it was all about not screwing up.

For Austin and me, returning to Pau was something of a homecoming. That city in the southwest corner of France was the first stage Austin and I ever covered together. That was back in 2001. We had arrived by train from Toulouse on the morning of the second rest day. Armstrong was giving a press conference in the Palais Beaumont, a cavernous convention facility housing the pressroom that afternoon. A few days earlier, Armstrong and Ullrich had had one of their signature duels during the ascent of L'Alpe d'Huez. Before the attack that would drop Ullrich for good, Armstrong stood up in the pedals, turned around, and stared the German down. I had literally yelled at my television in disbelief as I watched back home: It was a singular act of gamesmanship, a school-yard taunt, one badass to the other. Almost immediately it was nicknamed "The Look." I was eager to ask Armstrong about it.

Lance was duly ushered in and took his seat at the small table, around which a crowd of journalists and photographers gathered. A minute went by, maybe two. Nobody seemed in any hurry to ask Armstrong a question, so I jumped right in. "Lance," I said loudly. All eyes turned to me, as if I were committing some enormous gaffe. Armstrong looked at me and smiled, then sat there as if I'd said nothing at all. "Lance," I said again. "About 'The Look.'" He glanced at me and smiled again, but his eyes warned me this time. So I sat back in my chair, somewhat humiliated and confused. The photographers and other journalists offered me indulgent looks that noted my status as a Tour rookie.

"I think you're supposed to wait until they call on you," Austin leaned over to whisper. At this point a Tour official came out and introduced Lance Armstrong in French and then in English.

Public embarrassment is always better left forgotten. But as I pulled into Pau to catch the finish of Stage Sixteen, a picture in the official yellow Tour Roadbook caught my eye. It showed Armstrong at that press conference, looking off to his right as if about to respond to a rather bizarre request. In the background, the rest of the press corps is either smirking or engaging in a hearty laugh. My face is just out of the shot, but clearly that had been my moment. (For the record, Armstrong had denied that it was an intentional attempt to humiliate Ullrich. He claimed he was just looking around to see who was tired and who wasn't.)

"You see this?" I asked Austin.

He looked over at the Roadbook and laughed. "Yeah, I remember that day. I was going to tell you to shut your mouth, but you were so determined."

I told him of my new quest: I was going to ask Lance about the personal fulfillment issue before we had left France.

"You'll never get him alone this week," he replied. "Too many network guys. And you can't ask that in a press conference because everyone in the room is on deadline. All they want to hear is how Lance felt that morning and what he said to Johan when there was an attack."

"I'm missing your point."

"My point is . . ." He stopped. "The hell with it. You know this race as well as anyone. If you want to stand up at a press conference and ask Lance about all those people out there who want to touch the hem of his cloak, then just do it. You're going to anyway. You're in that mode. I can see it."

We never set out to be these two great road-trip buddies. The first time we drove the Tour together had been in 2001. I was going to be there at the same time as Austin, and it made sense to share a car. We'd known each other as colleagues for several years, but beyond a shared passion for adventure, there was no reason to think we'd get along so famously. We rented a BMW that year. It was blue and I don't remember the model, except that the clutch was shaky. We both knew French well enough to order coffee, but the nuances escaped us.

Austin filled the tank with unleaded instead of diesel that first time out. The car sputtered to a halt on the shoulder of the autoroute just a few miles later. The U.S. Postal Service Cycling Team's bus driver gave us a big friendly wave when we tried to flag him for help. By the time we were towed to a garage and the car's fuel system was flushed, we had missed an entire stage. The only upside had been the tow-truck ride. Apparently, when one is towed in France, one does not ride in the cab with the driver. We sat atop the flatbed, inside our car, hovering ten feet above the road on our way to the garage. It was like a magic carpet ride. The view of the countryside was magnificent.

All the way to Paris, the journey was a series of adventures and misadventures. I scored interviews with Hinault, Merckx, LeMond, and Armstrong. Austin didn't get the first two but got a one-on-one with Lance. When we said good-bye in Paris we didn't know quite how to say good-bye. It's one thing to spend ten days riding in a car with a guy, talking about your wife and kids and the quality of the morning run. It's entirely different to make the decision to either shake hands or do the buddy hug. We did neither. He filed his story, I filed mine, and then we walked down to the Left Bank at midnight and pretended, like all the other post-Tour tourists, that we were Hemingway.

But it was 2004 that marked my favorite Tour road-trip moment. At the La Mongie stage Armstrong was poised to take the yellow jersey from Thomas Voeckler. The peloton rolled out of Castelsarrasin just before noon, bound for a long day in the Pyrenees before a mountaintop finish. We took the *hors* course, turning off in Lannemezan and following the route markers south. Ten miles later we saw the first signs for La Mongie. The road began to climb ever so slightly. So far that day we had traveled through mostly small towns and farmland, but now that changed, too. Gone were the sunflowers and lavender, replaced by green pastures, sheep, and cows. The farmhouses looked more rustic, constructed of stone and dark woods. The roads were slender, lined with poplars and elms, and from another time. Once they had been cow paths, connecting pastures. Now they were paved, but in that buckling, crumbling manner of a road subjected to extremes of heat and cold.

"I think it's gonna rain," I had said, noting dark clouds forming over the Pyrenees.

"That's good for Lance. He hates the heat," Austin answered distractedly. His focus was on driving as quickly as possible. We were following another car with media stickers on its windows, but the driver seemed oblivious to the spectators parking their cars along the roadside and beginning the trek toward the course. Passing, honking, and speeding, he drove as if the lane were his own personal test track. "Must be a TV guy," I said. In the journalism world, television sorts are known for their proprietary sense of arrogance.

"Too crazy for me," Austin replied. "I'm gonna let him go."

We were silent as Austin eased off the gas, tense. It was as if that other car had been our conduit to the summit, guaranteeing that we wouldn't get lost and that we'd make it to the course before the road closures. "We'll get there," Austin said, reassuring neither of us.

"I know." My answer was hopeful but not certain. I studied my Michelin atlas, one finger placed atop our exact location.

And then we saw the barricades. The gendarme waved us onto the course, and we happily began chugging up La Mongie. Towering forests of pine lined the road. Spectators were everywhere, ignoring the rain that was suddenly drenching the mountains. A sort of benevolent nationalism reigned. Spaniards, Aussies, Americans, Frenchmen, and Canadians flew their flags. They stood in multinational clusters, drinking beer by the flagon.

At first the climb didn't seem like it would be that difficult on a bike. The first few kilometers were a gradual incline. But there came a point when it would be possible for the riders to see the finish line as they climbed, and know that it was five very steep kilometers above them. That 6.8 percent gradient advertised by Tour officials was an average, it turned out. The grade of those final five kilometers was closer to 13 percent.

The blue Beemer's clutch began to smell like it was on fire. The closer we got to the summit, the more spectators we saw lining the road, meaning Austin was constantly shifting and braking to avoid hitting some drunken Spaniard. My map reading done for the day, I closed the atlas to take it all in. I made jokes and observations, but Austin was too afraid of hitting someone to let his focus slip from the road for even an instant.

"Fuck," he whispered, shifting gears. "Fuck."

Soon the corridor was a sea of Basque orange, barely wide enough for us to pass. The fans sang Spanish songs as we slipped through, and they slapped the Beemer's hood and windows. Their flame-colored shirts contrasted sharply with the deep green of the pines. Now and again the switchbacks took the road to the edge of a cliff and we could see into the distance. The valleys far below were Yosemite-esque in their grandeur. Castles sprouted like dandelions from the elm forests.

Then we were back in the gauntlet. The whooping and slaps on the car and Austin's quiet whispers of "fuck" continued as we drove above the tree line. No longer were we surrounded by forest, but by stark granite. On top of every flat surface was a tent or camper and a dozen Basques. Now and again the flag of some other nation made an appearance, but with Spain on just the other side of the mountain, there was no mistaking whom that mountain belonged to.

Finally, we reached the summit. Parking the blue Beemer in a gravel lot that smelled not of grass or rain but of smoking automobile transmissions, we raced down to the finish line. All told, we had been in the car for nearly six hours. The riders were almost right behind us.

I positioned myself just beyond the finish line, with a crowd of photographers. The rain had stopped. A pair of enormous video screens were displaying the race for the throng of spectators, but they faced in the other direction, so I couldn't see the action.

"Can you see what's happening?" Austin asked.

"I haven't got a clue."

"He and Basso just attacked. Hamilton and Ullrich are off the back," said a British writer who was able to speak French, and thus translated the public-address announcer's play-by-play.

Armstrong and Basso were less than five minutes from the finish, dueling it out through that corridor of orange and pandemonium. The cheers would all be for Basso, the young Italian whose mother, it was well known, was very sick with stomach and liver cancer. The public-address announcer screamed their names, putting the accent hard on the second syllables. Four kilometers left. Three. The photographers strained for position, all trying to get that vital shot of the winner raising his arms as he crossed the line. I was squeezed in the crush, standing on my tiptoes but seeing nothing except the hairy nape of a photographer's neck. I forced my way deeper into the scrum until I could see the blue banner denoting the finish line stretched above the road.

Two kilometers. "Arm-STRONG! Bas-SO" came the announcer's cry. Without even seeing the video screens, I knew that, this close to the finish line, both riders would be in a tactical mode. One of them would eventually attack and sprint for the line, but neither rider knew who would go first. Pedaling at a level above their anaerobic threshold, knowing that the fire in their legs and lungs would cease in less than two minutes, they watched each other and waited. When to light the final fuse was a tactical decision, and there were less than 120 seconds to make it.

One kilometer. The crowd's roar was deafening. I could barely hear the PA announcer. "Can you see them?" Austin screamed in my ear. He was on his tiptoes, too.

An instant passed. Suddenly the crowd shifted slightly and I could see the finish line and the hundred clear yards of roadway behind it, where the spectators had been forced to stand on the shoulder behind the protective barricades.

"There they are," said Austin.

As Armstrong and Basso rounded the final switchback, Basso attacked, standing up in the pedals and pouring it on. Armstrong was right behind him. Basso's move, however, had been so sudden that even the quick-witted Armstrong could not recover. Basso won by the width of a bicycle tire.

Armstrong and Basso were good friends. Some said that Basso was the Texan's only friend in the peloton outside his own team. But in an act of gamesmanship, Armstrong would say he let Basso have the win. Whether he did or not didn't really matter. The euphoria of what I'd just witnessed would inspire me for hours to come.

But the next day, as the stage finished atop the Plateau de Beille, it was Armstrong who was victorious. Austin and I, unable to get back down the mountain for all the traffic, decided to camp atop the Pyrenees. Long after the sun went down, I was serenaded by patriotic French music from a nearby tavern. I don't know what time they finally shut it down, but when I woke up at 2:30 a.m. and gazed at the Milky Way, the DJ had toddled off to his camper shell. The next time I woke, it was six-thirty in the morning. The sun was rising orange and blue behind me, a light rain was sprinkling my head, and before me a rainbow arched across the jagged mountain peaks marking the border between France and Spain. On the other side of the pasture, Austin was stepping out of his tent and stretching to greet the day. He punctuated the moment with a burst of flatulence.

"Can you believe this?" he'd asked, waving an arm grandly in the direction of Spain. There was inspiration in his words, as if he were a crazed maestro conducting an unseen orchestra. It was yet another of those Tour moments reminding me that we were part of something bigger than ourselves — part of history. Then, without missing a beat, the great maestro had added, "On your feet. Let's get on the road."

Stage Sixteen into Pau was won by Óscar Pereiro, the same man who had been outsprinted by George Hincapie on the Pla-d'Adet. Chris Horner had attacked during the stage and looked like he might be able to challenge once again for a win, but had to fall back when stricken by diarrhea. As always, those concerns were handled on the side of the road, as quickly and discreetly as possible.

I went to the interview room that day, hoping Armstrong might show up for an impromptu press conference. It was just me and a bunch of Spanish writers who were eager for a few words from Pereiro. But Armstrong didn't make an appearance. He had finished in a chase pack at the front of the peloton and lost no time off his lead. Now he would quietly rest after a hot day in the sun. I sat through the press conference, not wanting to disrespect Pereiro's accomplishment by getting up and walking out.

For the seventeenth stage, instead of pushing due north, to Paris, we headed northeast up the gut of France, into a hilly region known as the Massif Central. For the first few miles the course had a familiar feel: small farms, pockets of forest, towns consisting of just a dozen stone buildings. The riders were able to see the Pyrenees off to their right, in silhouette. The peaks soon became just a memory (*"Au Revoir, Les Sommets"* read the banner headline in that morning's *L'Équipe*) and the land became sun drenched and dry. Sunflower fields outnumbered cornfields. The last thirty miles marched up and down winding lanes, many of them framed by tall sycamores on either side. They shaded the road and resembled cathedrals.

Paolo Savoldelli of Discovery got the win, outsprinting Kurt-Asle Arvesen of Team CSC down a long straightaway. Once again I camped out in the interview trailer, chasing Lance. My questions were ready, but Armstrong didn't show. This time all my fellow pressroom inhabitants were Italian. I didn't understand a word of what was being said and passed the time writing up a list of questions I wanted to ask Armstrong.

"You really think you'll get him?" Austin asked as we powered out of Revel. His next deadline was Sunday. And though it was still four days off, he was starting to turn inward and get quiet. Indeed, he hadn't said much all day.

"I'll get him," I said.

"He's not gonna show until the time trial."

"That's OK. I'll wait."

The landscape was painted with cornfields, rows of trees along the road and between farms, and rolls of hay resting in golden, freshly mowed fields. We had made arrangements to stay at a former convent school in Sevage that had been converted into a hotel. Checking in, we discovered the T-Mobile Team was staying there. German voices echoed in laughter up and down the tiled hallways. That morning, Alexandre Vinokourov had announced he was leaving the team at the end of the season. If Jan Ullrich's squad was sorrowful about losing the Kazakh and his crazy green uniform, they had a funny way of showing it.

Or perhaps T-Mobile was chuckling because they had been given our rooms by accident. Displaced, we drove another ten kilometers down the road to Dourgne. Using the atlas, we found our new hotel without getting lost — the first time Austin and I had ever done so in all our Tours together. The room was small, but with two full beds. We left our luggage and made it to the restaurant just in time for dinner. We ate outdoors, under a grove of sycamores. I noticed a monument off to one side of the trees and got up to investigate. It was an obelisk dedicated to those local men who had died in World War I, the war to end all wars. Of course, another war had come along, and the World War II dead were etched at the very bottom of the obelisk, like an afterthought.

Marcos Serrano of Liberty Seguros won Stage Eighteen. I didn't care. Anticipating that Armstrong might not show, I had stood in the back of the interview trailer rather than taking my customary seat front row center. After a while I slipped out the back door.

Serrano was exactly one hour, sixteen minutes, and thirty-three seconds behind Lance Armstrong in the overall standings. He was the tenth-ranked Spaniard in the race and third on his team. The Tour had entered the equivalent of the NBA's garbage time. A guy like Serrano, with nothing to lose, was supposed to win that sort of nothing stage.

But within all that, there was a nice moment of fortitude: Ivan Basso attacked on the final climb, a three-mile uphill at more than 10 percent gradient. Basso was 2:46 back, in second place, and the attack was his way of taking one last stab at winning yellow. The climb was just two miles long but preposterously steep and packed with fans. Nevertheless Armstrong, Jan Ullrich, and Australian Cadel Evans quickly caught Basso's wheel. The four of them charged hard up the mountain, leaving behind the race's other top contenders. At the end of the day, Armstrong and Basso were still 2:46 apart, but Ullrich had picked up thirty seconds in the overall standings. He might not have been riding to win the Tour anymore, but a strong showing in Saturday's time trial could vault Ullrich into third place overall.

During Stage Nineteen, Austin and I had holed up in a hotel thirty miles north of the course to write. On TV we watched as T-Mobile's thirty-five-year-old Giuseppe Guerini broke away to victory. It was the second win of his career, the first having come in 1999 atop L'Alpe d'Huez. During that race, a photographer had leaped out to take Guerini's picture as he approached the line. The crash had become part of Tour lore and had helped begin a more stringent policy for keeping fans and photographers behind the barricades during the final two kilometers of the race.

But now Guerini had a clean win, and the glee on his face was reminiscent of David Moncoutié's dazed look after winning on Bastille Day. It was a pleasure to witness, even if the smells and food of the pressroom were an hour's drive away.

Lance Armstrong, of course, finished comfortably within the pack. He had made it through the week without crashing. All that lay between him and his seventh Tour victory was Saturday's time trial and the cruise into Paris.

"This is it," Austin said. "Let's get an early start."

Stage Twenty

July 23, 2005 — Saint-Étienne–Saint-Étienne
34.41 Miles

Overall Standings

1. Lance Armstrong (USA), Discovery Channel, 81:22:19
2. Ivan Basso (I), CSC, 02:46
3. Mickael Rasmussen (Dk), Rabobank, 03:46
4. Jan Ullrich (G), T-Mobile, 05:58
5. Francisco Mancebo (Sp), Illes Balears, 07:08
6. Levi Leipheimer (USA), Gerolsteiner, 08:12
7. Cadel Evans (Aus), Davitamon-Lotto, 09:49
8. Alexandre Vinokourov (Kaz), T-Mobile, 10:11
9. Floyd Landis (USA), Phonak, 10:42
10. Óscar Pereiro Sio (Sp), Phonak, 12:39

IT WAS IMPOSSIBLE for me to approach the final time trial in Saint-Étienne without thinking back to that first stage in Fromentine, exactly three weeks before. The peloton had raced 2,112 miles. I had driven — through the circuitous process of getting to and from starts and finishes, getting lost and then found, and connecting between stages — more than 5,500.

A time trial early in the Tour and a time trial late in the Tour are two vastly different races of truth. One is an introduction, the other a finale. The 155 cyclists still in the race had ridden through near-impossible conditions in the last three weeks: thunder, rain, high altitude, searing heat, and damp cold. Many had crashed or barely avoided a crash. Their legs were shot, their bodies were in a perpetual state of exhaustion, and their moods ranged from relief that it would all soon be over to insecurity and nervousness about the two stages still to ride. Back in Fromentine, they had been rested and eager, and that was oh so long ago.

Bob Roll, the offbeat American cycling commentator and former rider, has said that by the last week of the Tour all the riders "want to do is go home to their mommies." But it is that last week which separates the elite riders from the rest of the peloton. It's then that the elite riders find a way to set aside their pain and fatigue, remembering that the race will soon be over but the haunt of failure arising from a mental letdown can last a lifetime.

The sky was overcast and warm at half past ten, just fifteen minutes before the first racer would be away. The time trial would mark the twenty-fourth time the Tour had visited Saint-Étienne, a commercial hub in the heart of the Rhone Alps whose origins dated back to the fifteenth century. Two riders had an emotional connection to the course that could provide them with a significant mental advantage. The first was Alexandre Vinokourov. Not only did he make his home outside the city, but his good friend and fellow Kazakh Andrei Kivilev had been killed in a high-speed bike crash outside Saint-Étienne in 2003. This place meant a great deal to Vino, and he raced to claim it for himself and to reclaim it for Kivilev.

The other rider with an advantage was Jan Ullrich. The cyclists would be racing the exact same time-trial course they had contested in 1997, back when the German had won both the Saint-Étienne time trial and his only Tour.

The course had a unique arrangement, with the start to the left side of the media center and the finish to the right. It was possible to walk a few hundred yards out one door to watch a rider roll down the start ramp, then jog back past the media center and team bus area to watch the riders charging up the long finish corridor. I resolved to spend the day doing just that.

The first man to start was Iker Flores. Unlike in Fromentine, when being the first man down the ramp was a function of a racer's number, Flores started first because he was dead last in the standings. It would go that way all day, a reverse countdown to the top rider. Gaps of two minutes would separate the riders (the top twenty riders, however, would be separated by three minutes). As always at the Tour, there was a dramatic purpose to the order. If the yellow jersey rode first, barring something like a crash that required the cyclist to quit the Tour right then and there, the fans along the barricades and viewing at home would have little reason to watch the rest of the stage. It would be like giving away the identity of the killer in the first chapter of a murder mystery.

As Iker Flores rolled down the ramp and immediately lowered into a tuck at one-thirty in the afternoon, he was struggling with the ambivalence of being the "lantern rouge." A reference to the red lantern that once hung from the caboose of a train, the title had been accorded the last-place rider since Arsène Millocheau finished sixty-four hours, forty-seven minutes behind winner Maurice Garin in 1903. Until the last decade or so, it was actually such a backward honor that riders well out of the race would sometimes hide in bushes along the course or pedal very slowly to intentionally drop to the bottom of the rankings. The lantern rouge was often paid handsomely to make post-Tour personal appearances at small-town races throughout France and Northern Europe. Fans would come out to see the man who had persevered even when there was no hope of victory.

But Jean-Marie Leblanc had never been a fan of the lantern rouge and had formally gone on record to declare that the title no longer belonged at the Tour. There would be, he said, no bonus earnings for Iker Flores when he finished the Tour, no sudden burst of notoriety. Flores was to be last.

Flores was a very small man with jet-black hair. The Spaniard rode for Euskaltel-Euskadi and was already looking beyond the Tour de France to late August's Vuelta a España — the Tour of Spain. "I'm going to go home when this is all done, and take two days at the beach, with no riding the bicycle. Then I'm going to start training for the Vuelta."

There was such acceptance in Flores's voice that I had to marvel. He was a domestique, resigned to working hard for no obvious reward. Life was one bike race after the other. Sooner or later he would either rise up and become strong enough to win or slowly fade out of cycling. "It's hard being in last place," Flores told me. "We all want to go home, but we don't want to go home yet."

I liked Flores and cheered for him to move up out of last with a powerful time trial. It was a long shot — Flores was more than eight minutes behind 154th-place Wim Vansevenant of Belgium — but there was always hope. Flores, however, lost three more minutes to Vansevenant and was certain of becoming the final lantern rouge.

At least he was finishing. Thirty-four other riders had either dropped out between stages or suffered the indignity of being packed into the *voiture-balai*. The "broom wagon" — so called because it was used to sweep up riders who quit the race — trolled along at the rear of the peloton each day, looking for those riders who had pulled over to the side of the road to abandon the Tour. Before a cyclist was allowed inside, his race numbers were summarily stripped from the back of his jersey.

Iker Flores may have been the lantern rouge, but he wouldn't know the indignity of having those numbers peeled from his back.

❊   ❊   ❊

The crowd was filled with children, some sitting on their fathers' shoulders, watching the man in yellow. Among them were Armstrong's three kids, who had flown in with his mother for the time trial. The little Armstrongs ran around inside the Discovery Team area as their father warmed up on his wind trainer. He seemed unperturbed about the time trial he would soon ride, lost somewhere between the tunes he was listening to on his iPod and the sight of his children frolicking at his feet. When Senator John Kerry paid Armstrong a visit, the cyclist sat up and chatted, headphones still in place, then went back to the bike once Kerry wandered off to the village.

It was a little after 4:00 p.m. when Austin and I headed back into the media center to watch Jan Ullrich's ride. The big guns were on the course. Floyd Landis was already away, as was Levi Leipheimer. Both men had quietly cobbled together very respectable Tours. Neither one would make the podium, but each had shown poise and grit, particularly during the hard mountain stages. Both were solid on the time trial.

The same, however, could not be said of Mickael Rasmussen. Though a good climber, Rasmussen had finished 174th — fourteenth from last — in the opening time trial. Fourteenth from last! As he rolled out of the starting house three minutes behind Jan Ullrich, Rasmussen had a terrified look on his face. He wasn't one for concealing his moods well, and it showed in this case.

With Rasmussen set to be on the course for a little more than an hour, I figured it was safe to wander over to the buffet for a snack before making myself comfortable in front of a monitor. But no sooner had I left the room than I heard a stunned roar from within. I ran back inside to peer at a monitor. Rasmussen had crashed. As time-trial courses went, the Saint-Étienne was one of the more physically demanding. The route went upward from the city, past the village of Saint-Héand on up into the Lyonnais hills. The highest point on the course was more than a thousand feet above the starting elevation, and the roads throughout were narrow and twisting. After a harrowing descent into Saint-Romain-en-Jarez, there was a three-mile climb, then another dangerous descent back into Saint-Étienne. Such a course should have favored Rasmussen. It complemented his climbing skills, and the serpentine roads would make it difficult for a more powerful rider to get up a full head of steam, then carry it for miles, as had been the case in Fromentine. All Rasmussen had to do was climb the way he was capable of, descend fearlessly, and maintain tempo, and he should have been able to hold off Jan Ullrich and his 2:26 deficit.

But as the split screen showed Ullrich fairly destroying the course, Rasmussen was melting down. His first crash came while he was pedaling through a roundabout. He stopped to fix a flat, then stopped to change bikes, misjudged turns, and crashed once again late in the stage. The stunned roar was soon replaced by gasps of laughter, as Rasmussen's ride turned from drama into unlikely comedy. Not only were Rasmussen's slapstick mishaps unprecedented, but he had a sidekick, too. Each time Rasmussen slammed into the pavement, a team mechanic wearing an orange T-shirt came out of the trailing Rabobank car to help him get going again. The nervous Dane would mount his bike, and then the mechanic would give him a running push. On a normal time trial, the mechanic would never leave the car, but today he was getting a real workout. "I hope for his sake that he took the time to stretch," Austin mumbled. "That guy's gonna have to ice his hamstrings after today."

Rasmussen finished the stage with the seventy-seventh-fastest time, losing more than six minutes to the yellow jersey, which was almost as much time as he'd gained during his breakaway victory into Mulhouse two weeks earlier. He dropped from third to seventh in the overall standings.

Meanwhile, Ullrich raced into third place. He rode like the

terrorizing German of old: dominant, powerful, and unafraid. It was a far different Jan Ullrich than the rider who'd been gapped by Lance Armstrong in Fromentine.

As for Armstrong, he was good enough to beat Ullrich by just twenty-three seconds. He flashed through the Rhone Alps like a yellow blur, his legs turning a powerfully high cadence for mile after mile. He knew where he was going, and so did we.

It was time for one last ride. It was time for Paris.

Paris

July 24, 2005

WE POWERED NORTH through France, determined to spend the night in the shadow of the Eiffel Tower. Austin and I had cleaned the Passat out that morning, but now we littered it anew with energy-drink cans and sandwich wrappers. The line of motor homes, as always, showed the way.

Paris was still very much awake when Austin and I arrived a little after one. The area around the Place de la Concorde was teeming with pedestrians, and a carnival was under way, complete with Ferris wheel. Gendarmes were tending to a young woman who was lying on her back in the middle of the Rue de Rivoli, crying after being hit by a car. Pedestrians flowed freely across the road, treading the same cobbles on which the Tour cyclists would race in the morning.

Austin and I were staying at different hotels, so he dropped me at the Hyatt Regency Paris-Madeleine, with a promise that we'd hook up in the morning.

I wheeled my three-week Asics European Duffle to the front desk and inquired about my reservation. "And what is your name?" asked the clerk.

"Martin Dugard."

He grinned like I was putting him on. "You are kidding, right?"

"No. I'm serious."

"Really?"

I learned that by a quirk of fate, I shared my name with a French writer who won the Nobel Prize in Literature for 1937. My parents' accidentally naming me after Martin du Gard was like a French family naming their son William Faulkner.

The clerk looked up my name on his computer. "Well, Monsieur Dugard, I have a very nice surprise: You have been upgraded."

I was tired. It was great news. It's always nice to have a little room to stretch out. "Super." After all that time in France, I accented the second syllable and made the *e* into a long *a* without thinking twice. Soo-PAIR.

He handed me the key with a flourish. "Welcome to the Presidential Suite."

What is life like in the Presidential Suite of a fine Paris hotel? The space is massive and designed for comfort. I had a full stereo system, a private patio and garden, a rain shower, a giant TV, and a soundproofed wood-paneled bedroom with a fluffy down duvet. But best of all, there was the wraparound balcony overlooking the rooftops of Paris. I opened the door and stood outside, gazing directly at the Eiffel Tower. Lit up top to bottom, it shone like a beacon. A spotlight on top twirled around and around, just in case a low-flying plane accidentally strayed into its airspace.

I stood out there for an hour, gazing at the Eiffel Tower and reveling in the sights and smells of Paris. Only when they turned off the lights did I traipse inside to my fluffy down-covered bed and drift, reluctantly, to sleep.

And then my tour of France was done. Lance won. It was a majestic time to be in Paris, at the Tour. The day had dawned drizzling and damp, but a bright sun burst through in the afternoon. Vino outsprinted the peloton to win in a breakaway, thus snatching fifth place from Levi Leipheimer. After the podium ceremony, in which Lance hugged not just his friend Ivan Basso but also Jan Ullrich, he was granted the privilege of speaking to the crowd. "The Tour de France," he told them, "will live in my heart forever."

The fans along the Champs-Élysées roared their enthusiasm. Many of them were tourists who knew nothing of the Tour. They had stumbled into it accidentally, as if lucking onto a parade. But once they were there, they stayed.

The day before, I'd finally tracked Lance down for that one last question. It was at a press conference, and I knew I wouldn't be able to monopolize the discussion, so I asked him a single question: What did he think of all these people chasing him around France, looking to touch the hem of his cloak? "The people who come to see me or see a phenomenon," Armstrong replied, "need to know that the person who can help them best is themselves."

Each life is full of successes and regrets and challenges and fears. Not all dreams will be realized — nor should they be. It's the dreams we sacrifice that give our other choices meaning. As long as you press forward, always forward, the power to live a rich and rewarding life, the life we've dreamed of, exists inside us all. That life may not be as long as we hoped. But it can overflow. This is our race, these are our mountains, this is our great and beautiful loop. Tears are OK. Fear is OK. But so, too, is courage.

Muscle is a curious thing. For the cyclists finishing the Tour, their legs were rubbery and exhausted. But now, with some rest, they would recover. Physiologists and physicians who study muscle growth will tell you that the way to build muscle is actually to exert enough stress upon it to tear the muscle fibers, then to rest so those fibers can regrow, and to repeat this process. If it is done correctly, the fibers become stronger with each tear and recovery. The damage done becomes a slingshot to something greater. One thing Lance Armstrong reminds us is that the biggest muscle in all of us is the heart. In a sense, I'd known it all along. We all know it. But sometimes you've got to see a person who has been through the battle already — someone who has struggled, faltered, and risen victorious — to fully absorb the notion, then use it as inspiration to launch forth into life's next series of adventures. Thus, Chasing Lance.

The stars above are too far for us to reach, but we can use them to guide us home on a dark night. A yellow wristband. A silver bracelet. The smell of freshly plucked lavender. The warmth of the sun. A man gliding forward on a bicycle. The things we chase, the things we follow, the fight within us. That's what Chasing Lance was all about. And even if he were never to ride again, I'd know where to find him.

It is what it is.

Tour de France 2005 — Final Overall Standings

1. Lance Armstrong (USA), Discovery Channel, 86:15:02
2. Ivan Basso (I), CSC, 4:40
3. Jan Ullrich (G), T-Mobile, 6:21
4. Francisco Mancebo (Sp), Illes Balears, 9:59
5. Alexandre Vinokourov (Kaz), T-Mobile, 11:01
6. Levi Leipheimer (USA), Gerolsteiner, 11:21
7. Mickael Rasmussen (Dk), Rabobank, 11:33
8. Cadel Evans (Aus), Davitamon-Lotto, 11:55
9. Floyd Landis (USA), Phonak, 12:44
10. Óscar Pereiro Sio (Sp), Phonak, 16:04

Epilogue

The world of professional cycling, of course, did not come to a standstill just because the Tour was done. Levi Leipheimer won the Tour of Germany in August, beating runner-up Jan Ullrich on Ullrich's home turf. At the same time, Floyd Landis was dropping out of the Tour of Spain after just six stages, despite beginning the contest as a prerace favorite.

Suzanne Halliburton e-mailed on a somewhat regular basis. As always, her reporting skills were kicking up dust. Back on the college football beat, she managed to write a revealing story about the University of Texas program that temporarily led to their football practices being closed to the press. In late August Suzanne went one better. She and Lance Armstrong had a conversation in which he mentioned he was thinking about making a comeback. She broke the story, then stood by it when the Associated Press reported that Lance had just been joking. In the end, she was vindicated. Mark Higgins, Lance's press liaison, issued a statement acknowledging that Lance was indeed thinking about riding again. "That's what my story said," she e-mailed me in triumph, "*thinking* about it."

Austin and I spoke by phone three or four times a week. We had once again parted awkwardly in Paris, doing that buddy hug in front of the Hotel Grand Intercontinental, as a somewhat bemused bellman looked on. The phone calls were our subtle way of debriefing.

As August rolled toward September, Austin and I began admitting things like "This was the best Tour yet" and waxing nostalgic about our time with The Legend. Leifer, for whom we had developed a deep fondness, was pushing for the three of us to return for one more Tour road trip together.

A lot had gone on since the Tour ended. On August 23, the French sports newspaper *L'Equipe* accused Armstrong of testing positive for the blood-oxygen booster EPO during his 1999 victory. Shortly after that, Lance and Sheryl Crow got engaged. Then came Suzanne's disclosure that he might unretire because he was so furious with the Tour officials. *L'Equipe* and the Tour being owned by the same parent company, he suspected collusion between the two led to the leak of sensitive information about laboratory discoveries. "For the first time —and these are no longer rumors or insinuations, these are proven scientific facts — someone has shown me that in 1999, Armstrong had a banned substance called EPO in his body," Leblanc said in *L'Equipe*. "The ball is now in his camp. Why, how, by whom? He owes an explanation to us and to everyone who follows the Tour. What *L'Equipe* revealed shows me that I was fooled. We were all fooled."

Armstrong immediately fired back that he was the subject of a "witch hunt." He added that he was considering legal action against the Tour and Leblanc.

The allegations revolved around six urine samples Armstrong submitted during his 1999 Tour victory. They were frozen and assigned a tracking number that was supposed to have been kept anonymous. *L'Equipe* claimed that they had been tested for EPO. However, it was equally clear that the samples were handed over to a French laboratory for research purposes instead of for drug testing. It is common practice among researchers to use urine samples to hone testing procedures. There was speculation about whether the sample could have been spiked to besmirch

Lance's reputation. Dr. James Stray-Gundersen, who collaborated with French scientists François Lasne and Jacques de Ceaurriz to develop the urine test for EPO just before the 2000 Olympics, went on record as saying this was possible in Armstrong's situation. "It's not necessarily the case that funny stuff happened, but there's that possibility, and motive," Stray-Gundersen told the *San Francisco Chronicle* on August 25.

The issue of whether or not Lance Armstong used performance-enhancing substances will probably never die, but since the accusations were made, both the International Olympic Committee and the UCI, cycling's governing body, have come down in favor of his innocence.

There was so much to talk to Armstrong about, yet he's impossible to reach. Then, while driving down the freeway on the last day of summer, my phone rang. "Hey, Marty," said a familiar voice, "it's Lance."

I pulled off the road and grabbed my notebook.

Armstrong had just finished a bike ride. Even with the Tour finished, he told me, he found himself returning to the bike — though just not with the same competitive intensity. "My thermometer's reading ninety-nine degrees," he laughed. "I was out for an hour and a half, and it felt like I was dragging a manhole cover the whole way."

I began at the very beginning of the chasing Lance saga: Le Grand-Bornand in 1999, and LeMond's appearance in Armstrong's trailer just before the pivotal stage. "We were flattered," he told me. "I mean, here's a three-time Tour de France winner coming into our chitty-chitty bang-bang — that's what we called those little tiny trailers we used back then — to talk with us before the biggest stage of the Tour so far. At the time, I didn't see it as the past and future of American cycling coming together, because that would have been presumptuous on my part. I hadn't won a Tour yet."

Armstrong paused. "Am I happy with the things that Greg LeMond has said about me since then? Absolutely not. I think the comments are beneath him. Do I care? Yeah, but not that much."

Life since the Tour finished had been busy for Armstrong. He'd been traveling four to five days a week, finding it hard to come to a standstill after the whirlwind summer. "I don't like to lie still and I don't like to be bored," Armstrong explained. "A body at rest," he reminded me, "stays at rest."

He was unsure about his future, and whether it would involve a nonprofit or a for-profit line of work. There was no way, he added, that he was coming out of retirement. "I don't miss it," he said of cycling and its politics, "and in the light of all that's gone on in the last month there's no way I could go over and ride the Tour de France again. There are people over there who are playing by a different set of rules. And besides, I've got everything I need: I'm healthy, my kids are healthy, I'm with a woman I love very much, and I've got a few zeroes in my bank account. I just want to take some time and figure out what I want to do next." But not too much time.

What my pursuit of Lance had shown me was that life was to be lived to its fullest; that daily process of pushing forward, always forward, constantly exploring and expanding one's capabilities, was the great mandate. Even seven Tour de France championships was no excuse for resting on one's laurels.

Armstrong and I talked for a long while, until all my questions had been answered and our conversation had veered from the Tour. "Thanks," I said finally.

"Great talking to you," Armstrong said as we hung up. "So long."

Acknowledgments

This book wouldn't have been possible without the patience and vision of Eric Simonoff, and the insightful genius of Geoff Shandler. Both worked extremely hard to make it a reality, and I am forever in their debt.

A special thanks to Lance Armstrong, Bill Strickland, and Mark Higgins.

Thanks also to Junie Dahn, Peggy Freudenthal, Gordon Wright, Amanda Erickson, Liz Terry, Katy Shobe, Ric La Civita, Brian Rodgers, Chris Noonan, Jim Woodman, and Dr. Steven Brady.

In France, thanks to Bob Babbitt, Suzanne Halliburton, Rick Reilly, Jeremy Schaap, and Neil Leifer.

Thanks to Monique and Marc, always in my heart.

The Tour wouldn't be the Tour without Austin Murphy.

All my love and thanks to Calene, Devin, Connor, and Liam.